Farewell to the Peasantry?

Farewell to the Peasantry?

Political Class Formation in Rural Mexico

Gerardo Otero

SIMON FRASER UNIVERSITY

Westview Press

A Member of the Perseus Books Group

Copyright © 1999 by Westview Press, A Member of the Perseus Books Group

Published in 1999 in the United States of America by Westview Press, 5500 Central Avenue, Boulder, Colorado 80301-2877, and in the United Kingdom by Westview Press, 12 Hid's Copse Road, Cumnor Hill, Oxford OX2 9JJ.

Library of Congress Cataloging-in-Publication Data

Otero, Gerardo.
    Farewell to the peasantry? : political class formation in rural
Mexico / Gerardo Otero.
        p.   cm.
    Includes bibliographical references and index.
    ISBN 0-8133-3645-7
    1. Peasantry—Mexico—Political activity.   2. Political
leadership—Mexico.   3. Social classes—Mexico.   I. Title.
HD1339.M4089   1999
322.4´4´08863—dc21
                                                                99-10741
                                                                CIP

The paper used in this publication meets the requirements of the American National Standard for Permanence of Paper for Printed Library Materials Z39.48-1984.

10   9   8   7   6   5   4   3   2   1

This book is lovingly dedicated to the memory of my son and great friend Rodrigo Otero-Ordóñez (1979–1997). His company during and after his seventeen years of life has been warm and inspiring. Even now, with the deep pain of his loss, I feel his presence as a strong, invigorating force that has been essential to my completion of this project, which I dedicate to his life and surviving spirit.

Contents

Tables and Illustrations

viii

Preface

This book is about the agrarian question in Mexico, the social class structure, agrarian struggles, and agricultural state policy. In different ways—as a student, as a teacher, as a researcher, as a person—I have been concerned with this topic for over two decades. Curiously, however, what originally sparked my interest in this topic was the urban question.

As an undergraduate student in Monterrey, Mexico, during the early 1970s, I was very impressed with the squatter settlers' movement, then at its peak. Not only did I think of it as a highly explosive social movement, but I was also appalled by the unimaginable conditions of misery under which people in the slums lived. I had never seen such poverty, not even in the countryside of La Laguna in north-central Mexico, the region in which I grew up. I wondered why large numbers of people would migrate to the second-largest industrial city in Mexico when employment opportunities there were scarce. Soon I realized that the vast majority of these migrants actually came from central and southern Mexico, where the agrarian crisis was taking its toll much more severely than in the north. I finally began to understand that both the urban and the agrarian questions were, in fact, two sides of the process of capitalist development in my country.

Research for this book has been supported by many institutions since the early 1980s. In particular, I received grants for field work from the University of Guadalajara and Simon Fraser University (the President's Research Grant). The Center for U.S.-Mexican studies gave me a grant to pursue research as part of the Ejido Reform Research Project, coordinated by Wayne Cornelius and David Myhre. Finally, I have received two generous grants from the Social Sciences and Humanities Research Council of Canada, one for 1994–97 and another for 1997–2000. The first was critical in allowing me to finish the necessary updates for this book. I gratefully acknowledge all of these funding sources.

Because the field work that undergirds the theoretical framework of this study took place in the state of Puebla, I would first of all like to thank my students and colleagues in the Department of Social Anthropology at the Autonomous University of Puebla in the early 1980s. It was in discussion with them that I began to incorporate the concept of culture into my analysis of agrarian problems. I also became indebted to the people of Xochimilco, in the municipality of Tecamachalco, Puebla, for opening their hearts and minds to me and for providing a place to stay while I was doing field work.

Before my Ph.D. studies at the University of Wisconsin (from which this book originated), I took an M.A. at the University of Texas at Austin. There, four visiting professors had a strong theoretical influence on my work: Bernardo Berdichewsky, Juarez Rubens Brandão Lopes, Norman Long, and Bryan Roberts. As my thesis supervisor, Norman was warm, inspiring, and quite generous with his time.

While I was in Madison, the Department of Rural Sociology provided me with a very pleasant working environment and abundant material support. The Department chair, Gene Summers, was always kind and ready to help.

Of the many intellectually exciting experiences in Madison, one stands out: the Andean Seminar organized by Gene Havens in the fall of 1978. I will always be grateful for the stimulating exchanges I had with Gene, Manuel Chiriboga, Jaime Crispi, Jorge Dandler, Fernando Rojas, Carlos Samaniego, and Bernardo Sorj.

There were many people who read and commented on parts of this manuscript as it became a dissertation. I wish explicitly to acknowledge the help of Brett Brown, Tomás Duplá, Jonathan Fox, Jess Gilbert, Robert Jenkins, Cassio Luisseli, Pat Mooney, Keith Moore, Max Pfeffer, Joey Sprague, William Thiesenhusen, Norberto Valdéz, and Gene Wilkening. Bill Canak and Mike Rogers are friends whose incisive and detailed critiques helped me reorganize and develop many of my ideas. David Kaimowitz was a virtual fourth member of my reading committee.

I am indebted to Jack Kloppenburg and Florencia Mallon for reading the entire manuscript and providing me with valuable comments. Special thanks go to Jack, who gave me time off from my duties as a research assistant to complete my writing. For timely support and encouragement, Marta Tienda merits particular recognition. Also, in discussing with me parts of this book, Marta was helpful in reorganizing the arguments, clarifying a number of points and, generally, in making them more compelling.

Erik Wright provided me with reliable and responsible support from the very beginning of my doctoral studies. As one of my three reading advisors, Erik's incisive and radical class-reductionist critiques saved me from my own culturalist excesses. Roger Bartra was also a reader in my committee. Despite the fact that much of my project represents a critique of his early work, he has always been open to and supportive of my point of view. In any case, I must acknowledge that Roger's work has had a profound influence on my thinking. In fact, Roger's now-classic *Estructura Agraria y Clases Sociales en México* (1974a) (*Agrarian Structure and Political Power in Mexico, 1993*) laid the very foundations for future research and discussion on the agrarian question in Mexico.

I can hardly find words to describe how highly I value my academic and personal relationship with my major professor, Ivan Szelényi, and how fortunate I am to have worked with him. I can only hope that Ivan's example and influence has been reflected in my own development as a person and a scholar.

The ideas and materials now in Chapters 3 and 4 were first presented at the Center for U.S.-Mexican Studies at the University of California, San Diego, where I enjoyed a postdoctoral visiting fellowship in 1986-87. Its challenging public was highly stimulating and inspiring, and then-director Wayne Cornelius always supportive. Several colleagues at the center provided helpful input. In particular, I remember very fondly my conversations with Pablo Arredondo, Vivianne Bennet, Wayne Cornelius, Ann Craig, Joe Foweraker, the late Daniel Nugent, Victoria Rodríguez, Jeff Rubins, and León Zamosc in the Sociology Department. Marilyn Gates, my colleague at Simon Fraser University, read parts of this book and gave me thoughtful and useful comments on short notice. As external reviewers for Westview Press, Michael Kearney and Peter Singelmann read the entire manuscript and made useful suggestions for revision of Chapters 1 and 8.

Westview's editorial team, lead by Karl Yambert, was kind and efficient in keeping this project on schedule. The copy editor, William Kaufman, went beyond the call of duty: not only did he correct grammar and style, but he also raised intelligent and knowledgeable queries that forced me to clarify some important points and concepts.

Kurt Oosterhuis provided able technical assistance for the data analysis for Chapters 4 and 6. Francisco Javier Gómez Carpinteiro's help in coordinating the application of a survey questionnaire for sugarcane growers in the region of Atencingo, Puebla, was crucial for Chapter 6. He kindly opened his house in Atlixco, where I stayed for several weeks while testing, refining, and applying the questionnaire in 1995. A fine anthropologist, he was a most helpful interlocutor during this process. Daniel García, a sugarcane grower in Izúcar de Matamoros, has been a keen supporter of my research in the region since 1988. I fully credit all this help, but responsibility for any remaining limitations is mine alone.

My parents, in Torreón, were always interested in the progress of my work and encouraged me to carry on. In occasional discussions my father provided me with perceptive insights into the rural scene in La Laguna, and his connections of a lifetime in the region enabled me to arrange important interviews on short notice. He was a field geologist with the sensitivity of a good anthropologist. I owe much of my understanding of rural Mexico to the long conversations and field trips with my father. He left us in 1989 and now rests in peace.

If any factor has been indispensable to my completion of this book, it has been the joy and fulfillment of having had the company of my immediate family: Paty, Alex, and until recently, Rodrigo. My younger boy Rodrigo left us at age seventeen, after a tragic car accident that took his physical life. In his own way, Rodrigo too was greatly concerned about the effects of Mexico's agrarian crisis, particularly its urban expressions. When we returned to Mexico after my postgraduate work, he was very saddened to see the many kids at traffic light intersections in Guadalajara, juggling or acting like clowns in order to make a few pesos. At one point he earned his first pay ever by imitating those kids and using his considerable gymnastic abilities. The most heartening thing was that, rather than spending his first pay, he approached an elderly poor woman and gave it to her. He had great compassion. I know that my son touched all of us who knew him in beautiful ways and that the love he inspired in all of us will make him live in our hearts and actions forever. This book is lovingly dedicated to his memory.

1

Political Class Formation in Rural Mexico

The struggle for democracy must have as one of its primary goals the establishment of a viable and democratic political society [or state] . . . but democracy also requires the construction of a vibrant, vigorous and pluralistic civil society (Diamond 1992, 7).

Mexico's countryside has been one of its most explosive political sectors in the twentieth century. In 1910 Mexico was convulsed by the century's first major revolution, and then, in the century's waning years, the uprising of the *Ejército Zapatista de Liberación Nacional* (Zapatista National Liberation Army, or EZLN) on New Year's eve of 1994 reaffirmed the volatility of rural Mexico. These two critical junctures in Mexican history attest to the peasantry's tenacity as a social actor.

The central issue in both political conflicts was land (Wolf 1969; Otero 1989a; Collier 1994; Harvey 1996, 1998; Gilly 1998). During the Porfirio Díaz dictatorship (1876–1910) peasant communities were deprived of most of their lands by a small class of land proprietors. This action eventually helped to trigger the 1910 revolution (Katz 1982). At the end of the twentieth century, the Chiapas revolt was in large part a response to the changes made in 1992 to Article 27 of the Constitution, according to which the state is no longer responsible for carrying out land redistribution (Cornelius 1992; Cornelius and Myhre 1998; DeWalt, Rees, and Murphy 1994; Otero, Singelmann, and Preibisch 1995). I will show, however, that in the past two decades the demand for land has been augmented by new dimensions of struggle that center on issues of production, self-management, autonomy, and democracy (Baitenmann 1998; Harvey 1998; Gordillo 1988; Otero 1989b; Moguel, Botey, and Hernández 1992; Rubin 1997).

The peasantry has been the subject of major debates among the forces of the political left in most developing countries. At issue has been its role in a transition from capitalism to socialism, a dynamic that first arose in Russia at the turn of the century (Edelman 1987). As in Russia, two main camps have developed an interpretation of this problem. Populists, on one hand, have regarded the peasants as having a progressive role within socialism and have held that peasant communities would have no special difficulties in such a transition. This was also the view of most observers inspired by the Chinese revolution and the writings of Mao Zedong. On the other side of the polemic are those who have stressed the "petit bourgeois" side of the peasants based on their role as owners of their means of production. Presumably, this fact renders peasants more likely to ally with the bourgeoisie. Lenin himself thought that the peasantry was undergoing a rapid social differentiation that was impelling its members toward either of the two main classes of capitalism: On the one hand the majority was becoming a rural proletariat, and on the other a small minority was becoming part of the agrarian bourgeoisie. In his view, then, poor peasants would do best to ally with the rural and industrial proletariat in the struggle for socialism (Lenin 1967).

With Mexico's 1910 revolution having prolonged the existence of the peasantry for several decades, a heated polemic has arisen since the 1970s concerning agrarian structure, peasant differentiation, and the character of struggles in the countryside. This polemic has been the cutting edge of discussions of the agrarian question in Latin America (de Janvry 1981; Harris 1978; Hewitt de Alcántara 1984; Foley 1989; Barry 1995; Veltmeyer 1997). Scholars from other countries have generally turned to the Mexican debate for theoretical inspiration in analyzing the agrarian classes and political processes in their own homelands.

The empirical puzzle that ignited the Mexican polemic consists of the following: In some regions rural workers seem to behave like peasants, while in others peasants seem to behave like workers.[1] According to Leninist theory, workers were supposed to be struggling for wages, better working conditions, unionization, and, ultimately, socialism. Authors in this tradition have insisted on the need for a "vanguard party" to correct the "false consciousness" of workers, thus enabling them to act on their true class interests in the relations of production. Others, inspired by the Russian economist Alexander Chayanov (1974), emphasize the rural workers' access to land and thus their status as peasants rather than proletarians.

Starting from this polemic, but also seeking to transcend it, I will present and contrast the history of three Mexican agricultural regions, highlighting my own interpretation of the process of political class formation. Unlike the two dominant positions in the Mexican polemic, which stress either access to wages or access to land as the main determinants of the character of struggles—proletarian or peasant—I argue that the process of political class formation is mediated not only by the position of class agents in production relations, but also by state intervention, the prevailing forms of regional cultures, and the varieties of leadership. Moreover, the structural position of most of these social agents is that of an agricultural semiproletariat rather than that of a proletariat or a peasantry. For it is the semiproletariat that finds itself in the most unstable condition in relation to its material basis of reproduction, torn as it is between occasional wage labor and access to land that is an insufficient basis for subsistence farming. This semiproletariat makes up the largest proportion of the rural population in Mexico (Bartra and Otero 1987). I contend that the account of class structural determinants has been misconstrued and incorrectly specified. Furthermore, even when correctly specified, class positions do not directly determine political class formation (Laclau, 1976; Laclau and Mouffe 1985).

In contrast to the Mexican polemic, which assumes that peasant and proletarian struggles take place in the context of a struggle for the transition to socialism, I view things more modestly, particularly in the aftermath of the Cold War. At this point, the socialist alternative is hardly on the political agendas of any significant political forces in Latin America (Castañeda 1993; Carr and Ellner 1993; Harris 1992). In my view, political struggles in the countryside take place within the confines of capitalism. If anything, they help define what kind of capitalism and what kind of democracy Mexico will have in the coming decades.

It is not surprising, then, that some of the key terms in the current political debate are *transparency, community participation, autonomy, independence, accountability, self-management, appropriation of the production process,* and *control of territory.* It may well be argued that the EZLN is the organization that has pushed most radically and decisively for reforms that include such demands, which lead toward a societal democracy rooted in civil society rather than limited to the state. This shift has been implicitly suggested by the political practice of the EZLN: Rather than focus on a "revolutionary" political party whose goal is to take over the state, the EZLN proposes to concentrate on the theme of several key social movements in Mexico since the 1980s, namely, the construction of civil society (Cook 1996; Foweraker and Craig 1990; Fox 1996a).

While capitalism may be quite compatible with liberal democracy insofar as it is confined to the electoral dimension of politics and completely separated from the market and the economy (Meiksins Wood 1996), a societal democracy centered on civil society may pose some problems for capitalism. At the very least, a societal democracy may lead capitalism in an economically more equitable direction (Semo 1996; Otero 1996a).

My analysis of agricultural direct producers and their political class formation, then, is related to the construction of civil society within an authoritarian context. Civil society can be defined broadly or narrowly. Broadly defined, it is the sphere of interaction between the economy and the state, and includes social movements and the intimate sphere of the family. Narrowly defined, civil society consists of

> voluntary political association oriented by its relation to the state, but self-limiting in not seeking a share of state power . . . a realm of freedom in which individuals are not forced to act in strategic pursuit of material reward (as required in the economy) or constrained by the power relationships embodied in the bureaucratic state (Dryzek 1996, 47).

Three scholars of democratic theory coincide in observing that the political realm per se cannot offer the citizenry substantial power (Dryzek 1996; Meiskins, Wood 1995; Touraine 1997). John Dryzek also sees globalized capitalism as a major obstacle to deepening democracy. In his view the prospects for democracy "in capitalist times are better . . . in civil society than in the formal institutions of government, across rather than within national boundaries, and in realms of life not always recognized as political. Thus, democratization is more readily sought against the state, apart from the state, and across states, rather than by or in the state" (Dryzek 1996, 3–4). In these terms, the focus of my analysis in this book is the construction of civil society as a condition for democratization against the state and apart from the state.

The purpose of this book is thus to question class-reductionist assumptions in certain variants of Marxism and populism about political struggles and movements. The main boundaries of the Mexican debate and my own conceptual approach are presented in Chapter 2. Chapters 3 and 4 show that the agrarian structure in Mexico has been largely misconstrued and that the bulk of agricultural direct producers are semiproletarians, neither fully peasants nor proletarians. Then, on the basis of the three regional case studies in Chapters 5 through 7, I show that in regions in which peasant social relations prevail, semiproletarians are mainly involved in peasant-style struggles. Where the process of depeasantization is recent (up to one generation), even proletarians have largely struggled to regain a peasant condition. When a peasant culture has been severely undermined by capitalist development and the commodification of social relations, however, semiproletarians might still engage in struggles for land, but with a new, postcapitalist thrust: The demand for land is accompanied with the demand for other means of production and the democratic control of the production process. I call this a "postcapitalist" demand because it involves a "bottom-up" approach in decision-making within the labor process, and the fruits of production are to be distributed equitably among direct producers.

The term *postcapitalist* describes a situation in which semiproletarians successfully resist proletarianization by organizing a cooperative production purposefully, aiming at gaining substantial degrees of independence from both the state and private capital. Such an undertaking must deal with the capitalist market, but its organization contains the seed of a postcapitalist organization of all economic activities: bottom-up self-management and democratic control of production.[2]

I also intend to show that, independently of whether conflicts center on peasant, proletarian, or postcapitalist demands, they do not have a predefined character as either bourgeois-hegemonic, oppositional, or popular-democratic. Instead, the character of state intervention affects people's capacity to defend their interests and influences the character of their class organizations established for such struggles. When interventions are favorable to the direct producers (peasants, semiproletarians, or proletarians) but the initiative lies with the state itself, the people's organizations are usually coopted and integrated into bourgeois-hegemonic discourse and politics; when the state threatens the basis of the reproduction of the direct producers, their organizations assume an overtly oppositional character. Furthermore, when the state intervenes on behalf of the direct producers because of their pressure, strength, and mobilization, their class organizations might assume both an oppositional and popular-democratic character.

Finally, a third critical variable is leadership type. Leadership influences the kinds of alliances that are established once class organizations are already formed and whether such organizations retain their independence from the state and/or the ruling class and their autonomy from other political organizations. Three basic types of agrarian leadership are explored: charismatic-authoritarian, corrupt-opportunistic, and democratic. In the Mexican case, charismatic-authoritarian and corrupt-opportunistic leaders are clearly associated with bourgeois-hegemonic political outcomes where organizations lose their independence and/or autonomy. With a democratic leadership, in contrast, class organizations have the best chance of constructing popular-democratic alliances with other organizations at the regional and/or national level and retaining their independence and autonomy.

The three regions under study in Chapters 5 through 7 share a number of characteristics that warrant comparison. Their contrasts, of course, also help to demonstrate the pertinence of my hypotheses. The most important commonality is that a capitalist organization of agriculture was installed in the production units, which were the original focus of agrarian struggles in the 1930s. All were modern agricultural enterprises hiring wage labor and producing profitable cash crops. Also, the three regions are in the most fertile valleys of their respective states, and agriculture is based on irrigation systems. Typically, commercial crops are produced in all three regions: sugarcane in Atencingo, cotton in La Laguna, and wheat in El Yaqui Valley.

Another common element is that each region is part of states marked by the regional inequalities common to Mexico as a whole, particularly with regard to types and quality of land. All three states have fertile valleys as well as marginal and depressed areas. The latter are referred to as *la sierra* (highlands). One significant difference is demographic density and the relative importance of valleys and *sierras* in each state. The state of Puebla, where Atencingo is located, has one of the highest demographic densities in Mexico; while Sonora, the state that houses El Yaqui Valley, has one of the lowest. Coahuila and Durango, the states that share part of their territory to make up La Laguna, are somewhere in the middle in population density, but closer to Sonora's.

Furthermore, most of the rural population in Puebla lives in the *sierra* regions rather than in the fertile valleys, while in Coahuila, Durango, and Sonora it is the other way around. Consequently, Puebla has a larger proportion of pauperized peasants and semiproletarians who are immersed in a less commodified economy. In contrast, partly because the northern *sierras* are too desertlike and infertile to provide even a meager subsistence for a peasant family, northern semiproletarians are immersed in a much more commodified economy and are dependent on wage incomes. These intrastate differences apply, of course, for the peasantry in all three regions.

The histories of El Yaqui and La Laguna show important parallels in the extent of capitalist development by the time of agrarian reform. One crucial difference, however, is the presence of Yaqui and Mayo Indians in Sonora as opposed to the predominantly *mestizo* labor force in La Laguna. The cultural impact of this contrast was manifested mostly in the periods right after the revolution (the 1920s) and during the *Cardenista* agrarian reform (1934–38), when the Yaqui demanded land primarily to restore the territorial basis of their independent culture (Hu-DeHart 1984; Spicer 1980). In La Laguna, *mestizo* hacienda peons were waging typically proletarian struggles around unions and collective bargaining against capitalist cultivators.

The contrast between the Yaqui region and Atencingo is also quite important. Although an Indian population was likewise present in Atencingo's surroundings, their culture and history was very different from that of El Yaqui Valley. They had already endured centuries of subjection, first under colonial rule and later under the dominant forms of development in independent Mexico (Carrasco 1969). Furthermore, the precolonial history of ethnic groups in central Mexico is linked to the domination of the Aztec state, a "despotic-tributary" form of exploitation and domination of Indian communities (R. Bartra 1974b). The Yaquis and Mayos, in contrast, were agricultural peoples with a tribal form of social organization that featured decentralized authority structures based on villages, like most of the North American tribes (Spicer 1969a, 1969b, 1980; Hu-DeHart 1981, 1984).

Such commonalities and differences are crucial to understanding the significance of yet another common element: Collective *ejidos* were created through agrarian reform during the administration of Lázaro Cárdenas (1934–40).

The *ejido* was the preferred postreform tenure for beneficiaries of land distribution after the revolution. The *ejidatario*, the holder of such land title, is not a fee simple proprietor as in English Common Law; this "owner" reaps the usufruct of the land and has the right to work the land individually. The *ejidatario*, however, was not legally enabled to transfer those rights to nonheirs until 1992. During the administration of Lázaro Cárdenas, collective *ejidos* were promoted more than individual ones, but both forms of organization were contemplated in the law. A modification of the Mexican Agrarian Code in 1971, though, provided for the renting of *ejidal* land by more capitalized farmers from those who lacked the necessary capital (R. Bartra 1974a, 142 fn.). Renting of *ejido* plots had become fairly generalized by 1992, especially in irrigated agricultural areas. The new Agrarian Law of that year thus further legalizes rental to non-*ejidatarios* and even allows for the sale of *ejido* plots, provided that two-thirds of the *ejido* assembly approves (Cornelius 1992; DeWalt, Murphy, and Rees 1994).

The avowed purpose of promoting a collective organization was to preserve the economies of scale of large capitalist haciendas after expropriation. Given the diverse cultural backgrounds of direct producers in each region, however, their struggles eventually displayed marked differences in the process of political class formation, despite the fact that they all occupied a similar position in production relations: that of agricultural wage workers. Political class trajectories and destinations were thus determined not so much by economic class position as by the predominant regional cultures, state intervention, and the prevailing types of leadership.

Methodological Note

My exploration of the construction of civil society in rural Mexico, then, focuses on the effects of state intervention, regional cultures, leadership, and production relations at the community and regional levels. These levels, along with the family, are considered as different units of analysis, and I intend to move back and forth among them, depending on the issues to be dealt with. The focus will be the family when I am dealing with the structural class variables in the relations of production; but it will be the village or region when I am dealing with the agrarian movements.

The national level is of course preserved, for it is the level at which state policies are intended to have an impact. Depending on the relative strengths of contending groups and classes at the regional level, though, the state might practice exceptions from its general, national policies. Mexico's relations with the world economy are important but not explicitly discussed here because they are internalized for the social formation as a whole. Therefore, the impact that Mexico's dependent insertion into the world capitalist economy has on political class formation will be expressed in the country's internal dynamics of class struggle.

The reasons for moving about several units of analysis are straightforward. First, most of the literature on agrarian classes takes the family as the unit of analysis for establishing class boundaries in production relations. Furthermore, I choose the family over the individual because I believe that this is a more adequate unit for understanding structural class processes in a country where kinship has a heavy specific weight in social relations. Second, agrarian struggles are thought of fundamentally as collective actions. Therefore, the village or region is a more pertinent unit of analysis for the study of collective actions and social movements. Finally, this is predominantly a qualitative study, based on comparing the histories of agrarian struggles and the ethnography of three regions of Mexico.

Even though the following analysis is limited to one country, it is framed in the tradition of "comparative historical macroanalysis" (Moore 1966; Skocpol 1979, 1984; Katznelsen and Zolberg 1986). Rather than contrasting the social histories of various countries in terms of certain variables, my contrasts are among regions within a vastly heterogeneous country. As Aristede Zolberg has written about this method, it bears a family resemblance to quantitative multivariate analysis, but it is hardly identical with it: "The process of abstracting configurations from historical reality and their treatment as variables entails a certain degree of intellectual make-believe, which is justified only to the extent that we remain aware that it is make-believe." (1986, 401) It is also important to keep in mind that such a perspective does not achieve generalizations in the statistical sense, but it does attempt to enhance our general understanding of the process of political class formation by systematizing the observation of cross-regional commonalities and variations. Only with systematization can we eliminate interpretations founded on a mistaken attribution of uniqueness to certain aspects of regional configurations and identify the combination of factors that best accounts for the variation that is found. (The last sentence is a paraphrase of Zolberg [1986, 401] in which I basically substituted the word "region" for "nation.")

Organization of This Book

The next three chapters of this book are dedicated to theoretical, historical, and structural issues of agrarian development in Mexico. Chapter 2 delineates the main contours of the Mexican polemic and presents the alternative theoretical approach proposed in this book. It offers an exposition of the book's research agenda and a definition of its hypotheses and concepts.

Chapter 3 presents a critical history of agrarian reform in Mexico. The official view of government ideologues often portrays this process as the product of a peasant revolution that brought justice to the rural masses. In contrast to this view, I argue that land redistribution in Mexico was the way chosen to develop and entrench capitalism in Mexico while building a basis of support for the modern Mexican state. Changes made to Article 27 of the Mexican Constitution in 1992, however, along with new agricultural policies, represent a major overhaul of the original agrarian reform program, and they are also discussed in this chapter.

Chapter 4 evaluates the main socioeconomic result of the Mexican agrarian reform from the 1930s to the 1990s: the pauperization of rural people, which has brought both peasant and capitalist agriculture to a crisis. It provides an account of the global agrarian transitions and the social differentiation process in the Mexican countryside. The double crisis of Mexican agriculture, one referring to the capitalist sector, the other to the peasant economy, is explored. Looking at the roots of this double crisis, an analysis of cash crops in contrast with subsistence crops is provided using data on production and prices from 1940 through 1995. Then, based on the 1970 census, I present a spectrum of social differentiation of agrarian producers in Mexico that reflects the extent to which the peasant economy had been eroded by that year. Next, by contrasting these data with those of 1960, I show that the middle peasantry tends to disappear in the midst of a polarizing agrarian structure. Data from surveys conducted in 1990 and 1994 on the *ejido* sector alone tend to confirm these results, although some land reconcentration is beginning to take place among middle peasants, at least within this sector (De Janvry, Gordillo, and Sadoulet 1997).

The main conclusions of Chapter 4 are as follows: (1) There has been a profound process of social differentiation among the peasantry because of the double crisis of capitalist agriculture and the peasant economy; (2) the vast majority of agricultural direct producers were already in a semiproletarian class position by 1970; and (3) the uneven development of capitalism in Mexican agriculture has created a vast regional heterogeneity in class structures.

Thus, the central feature of the process of dissolution of peasant economy is depeasantization without full proletarianization. The result is that the vast majority of agricultural direct producers are in semiproletarian positions, torn between wage-labor and peasant production. Nevertheless, the cultural and socioeconomic contents of semiproletarian positions vary regionally. The question then becomes, In which direction do semiproletarians struggle in agrarian class conflict?

Chapters 5 through 7 address this question by focusing on each of the three regions specified above in order to study in detail how direct producers entered the process of political class formation. Even though the Mexican agrarian structure is highly heterogeneous, I chose to focus on direct producers who shared a very similar structural position in production relations in each of the three regions by the time of the agrarian reform in the 1930s: They were all agricultural workers selling their labor power to capitalist *haciendas*. Despite this similarity in positions within production relations, the struggles and class organizations pursued in each region were different from one another; the political class trajectories were diverse. The result is that agricultural workers ended up in different political class destinations in each case. Thus, because the initial structural class position by itself may not explain differences in political class formation, I provide an explanation based on regional cultures, state intervention, and leadership styles.

Chapter 5, which discusses La Laguna (in Coahuila and Durango), tells the story of an agricultural proletariat whose political class history followed a complex trajectory. The agricultural workers of the 1930s, dubbed "peasants" by contemporary observers, posed typically proletarian demands: higher wages, unionization rights, and collective bargaining. Rather than satisfying these demands, the state responded with a massive land redistribution in the region, where agrarian capitalism was most developed in Mexico. After obtaining land, for over a decade the new *ejidatarios* went through a phase of successful postcapitalist production based on self-management and democratic production in the newly created collective *ejidos*. But the state and the agrarian bourgeoisie could not tolerate such economic and political strength in a subordinate class. Through years of official boycott the *ejidatarios* became an impoverished and divided semiproletariat that now produces mostly for the state-controlled bank. Although the class destinations in La Laguna are more diverse than those in the other two regions, most direct producers are clearly subordinate to the economic and political apparatuses of the state, having evolved into semiproletarian state workers with quite fragmented class organizations.

In contrast, chapter 6 deals with the region of Atencingo, Puebla, where the agrarian struggles throughout the period considered (1930s to 1990s) have had a peasant character. After bitter struggles against the owner of a capitalist sugar mill, which the new *ejidatarios* had to supply with sugarcane by law, they finally succeeded in dismantling the collective *ejido*. The resulting form of productive organization relied on individual *ejido* members. An internal process of social differentiation set in by which a minority of *ejidatarios* hired significant amounts of labor power. These new, relatively prosperous peasants diversified production to include nonsugarcane crops. Thus, the class destination of a sizable minority was what I have called "peasant-entrepreneurs." At the other end of the spectrum, the majority of Atencingo peasants evolved further into a semiproletarian condition, with increasing numbers of household members having to migrate to become proletarians in Mexican cities or in the United States. The proletarianization of such family members, though, has been external to the regional rural economy.

The Yaqui valley region of southern Sonora is the topic of Chapter 7. The Yaqui Indians were the original inhabitants of its fertile lands. Although these direct producers also occupied salaried positions in production relations long before the 1930s, their struggles centered on regaining the territorial basis for their nation and culture. But the aggressiveness and violence of capitalist penetration converted their national struggles and those of the large *mestizo* population that eventually migrated to the region—a semiproletarianized labor force—into a form of postcapitalist struggle: The new demands involved not only land but also the rest of the means of production and the democratic self-management of the productive process.

Finally, the concluding chapter summarizes the central arguments and draws systematic comparisons and contrasts among the three regions. It establishes how state intervention, regional culture, and leadership types are the mediating determinations that best explain political class formation in each region, even when the starting economic class position was the same in all theses regions. Drawing on recent literature on rural Mexico, this chapter then addresses the political implications of changes brought about by the neoliberal reform that has swept Mexico since the mid–1980s.

Notes

1. Juan Martínez-Alier (1977) noted this seeming paradox for the Peruvian peasants and agricultural laborers. The former struggled for unions and the latter for land.

2. I use the term *postcapitalism* as an ideal type. In some concrete cases we might find collective *ejidos* that tend to hire significant amounts of wage labor, beyond the labor power of their members. In these cases the *ejido* might be closer to a capitalist cooperative than to a postcapitalist one.

2

The Mexican Debate and Beyond:
Class, State, and Culture

The "agrarian question" in Mexico was the focus of a protracted debate in the 1970s and was reenacted in the 1980s. In this chapter I discuss each side's characterization of the agrarian social structure and the resulting political conclusions. I then propose alternative questions and hypotheses that reframe the agrarian question. I present the empirical evidence for my hypotheses in the subsequent chapters. Here I challenge class-reductionist assumptions in the two main stances of the debate, arguing that regional cultures, state intervention, and leadership types are also crucial in determining political class formation.

Structural Differentiation and Political Class Formation in
Rural Mexico: Profiles of the Debate

Two of the central issues in debate have been (1) the character of Mexico's agrarian structure and (2) the nature of class actors and their political strategies. In other words, what is the character of the political class formation of agricultural direct producers (peasants, semiproletarians, and proletarians)?

The central question that seems to have guided this controversy is as follows: Are peasants on a unilinear trajectory towards a proletarian status, dependent on wage labor, or can they remain peasant producers as capitalism develops? This question clearly refers to the structural dimension of agrarian class dynamics, i.e., to the position of class agents in the process of production and circulation. A key characteristic of the debate is that, regardless of the stance taken, *campesinista* or *proletarista,* most authors have assumed that there is a necessary correspondence between the position occupied in production relations and political class formation. Indeed, the problematic of both *campesinistas* and *proletaristas* is implicitly the same: "Tell me what is the class position of direct producers (defined by the relations of production), and I'll tell you how they *are supposed* to behave politically." This theoretical phenomenon can be labeled "class reductionism" as defined by Ernesto Laclau (1977). According to this view, given a certain position of class agents in production relations, they are supposed to have a set of material interests that are clearly identifiable by Marxist social scientists and for which the agents will "logically" struggle.

Both the *proletarista* and *campesinista* stances acknowledge that, through the agrarian reform process, a peasantry was created or expanded following the 1910 revolution. *Proletaristas,* however, see a very advanced process of dissolution of peasant production, resulting in depeasantization, proletarianization, and pauperization. In contrast, *campesinistas* stress that peasants have managed to resist capitalist penetration and continue to produce on the basis of family labor; while acknowledging that capitalist penetration can be profoundly damaging to peasant production, the *campesinistas* believe that the peasantry as a whole does not necessarily face extinction.

This disagreement has led to a lack of consensus as to how to define Mexico's agrarian classes in general and the peasantry in particular. In any case, both perspectives have emphasized either access to wages or to land as determining the character of struggles as proletarian or peasant.

I will now turn to how each position in the Mexican debate characterizes the social differentiation process historically and what political implications have ensued; I will then go back to theory and point out the problems of such characterizations in this realm. I will conclude the chapter by proposing a shift in the method of posing research questions that will, I believe, lead to a clearer picture of the historical dynamics of agrarian classes in Mexico.

Campesinismo *Variants*

Which path the peasants might take to avoid their dissolution as a class depends on which of the two variants of *campesinismo* we are talking about—the reformist or the radical. The reformists propose to change the forms of government intervention (through agrarian policy) to support peasant production rather than capitalist agricultural enterprises (Warman 1976, 1980; Esteva 1980). Most advocates of this policy evince the conceptual influences of dependency theory, but in a clearly nationalistic version. They argue for food self-sufficiency based on peasant-centered government policies such as subsidized lands and technical assistance. In their view, most agricultural enterprises are engaged in production for export (cattle or fruits and vegetables), whereas peasants produce for the internal market. Opposing a comparative-advantage, free-trade approach, reformist *campesinistas* thus propose to achieve food self-sufficiency by consolidating peasant production. The clearest expression of this approach was the *Sistema Alimentario Mexicano* (Mexican Food System), or SAM, a rural development strategy adopted in the 1976–1982 administration of José López Portillo (Fox 1992; *Nueva Antropología* 1981; SAM 1980). This approach is reformist because it intends merely to modify the agrarian sector in the image of the peasantry while continuing with the development of industrial capitalism (on a more nationalistic basis, perhaps).

By contrast, radical *campesinismo* (Armando Bartra 1979a, 1979b) holds that peasant struggles for land are inherently anticapitalist and that increased peasant control of the land must result from the peasant movement's combative struggle rather than from gracious concessions by the bourgeois state. Radical *campesinismo* argues that because its struggles are, by definition, anticapitalist, the peasantry is a revolutionary agent of the first order. This anticapitalist character is, they argue, embedded in the very logic of reproduction of the peasant community, which is distinct from capitalist logic. The political prescriptions of this perspective are twofold: to fight to consolidate the peasant community and, for the peasant movement, to struggle for *all* agricultural land. Logically and practically inimical to integration into an overall process of capitalist development, these struggles are thus assumed to be fundamentally anticapitalist.

I question the assumption of the *inherent* anticapitalism of peasant struggles. We can theoretically conceive of a situation in which the agrarian bourgeoisie is completely expropriated and thus eliminated as a fraction of the capitalist class and replaced by commercial peasant producers. The industrial bourgeoisie could well establish a production pact with such a peasantry for the supply of industrial raw materials and wage goods. But capitalism itself would still remain intact, at least in the industrial sector (Otero 1982, 1983).

Thus, what leads me to label Armando Bartra's approach as radical is that he also advocates an alliance between the peasantry and the working class, a Maoist version of Leninism. In contrast, reformist *campesinistas* do not see industrial capitalism as an essential problem; they merely wish to reform it to render it more beneficial to the peasantry.

Proletarismo *Variants*

Several variants may be discerned within the *proletarista* approach as well, but I will deal with only three, all of them within the Marxist camp. The first holds that peasants no longer exist as a political class, even if there are still some peasant agents at the level of production relations. Therefore, we can only speak of "bourgeois forces" and "proletarian forces" in Mexican society as a whole (de la Peña 1980). The agents of new and old social movements who might expand the definition of the revolutionary subject (such as women and ethnic minorities) are excluded at the outset as significant players in political conflict since everything is interpreted—simplistically and mechanically—in terms of the polar classes of the capitalist *mode of production*. Because this analysis is pitched at such a high level of abstraction, it excludes many colorings and variations of actual societies. In this view the left need only unify and consolidate the so-called proletarian forces in order to form a revolutionary movement. And, since there would probably be no internal differences in class or group interests, the political and ideological discourses would be monolithically geared toward socialism. Unfortunately, this monochromatic perspective is very far from reality: The real-world left is riven with conflicts that go well beyond structural class positions.

The second variant of *proletarismo* is similar to the first but characterizes the agrarian structure differently. The process of depeasantization is seen to have greatly accelerated because of a double crisis: the great world capitalist crisis that appeared in the early 1970s, triggered by increased oil prices, and the crisis of peasant production that in Mexico started in 1965. This double crisis has rendered peasant production incapable of resisting increasing market prices of nonagricultural goods, for it leads peasant households, in a contradictory process, to increase their production to fulfill their subsistence needs while some members of the household must look for wage employment in the capitalist labor market. This contradictory process consists of the following: a dominant tendency toward depeasantization, i.e., toward internal social differentiation or stratification of the peasantry; and a subordinate tendency that drives peasants to increase their family production in spite of declining agricultural prices. Roger Bartra has labeled this process "permanent primitive accumulation" (1974a, 1975a).

While Bartra does recognize that there is a process of repeasantization, he nevertheless proposes that this is only a subordinate tendency and that peasants as such do not have a revolutionary role in today's Mexican capitalism. To the contrary, the peasantry consolidates despotic-bourgeois power as it is coopted into the "mediation structures" that undergird the modern Mexican state (R. Bartra, 1978). The only way in which peasants in the process of dissolution can become revolutionary is by wearing their agricultural proletarian hats and waging socialistic struggles in the countryside; their dual-class personality (petty-bourgeois commodity producers on one hand and sellers of labor power on the other) compels them to choose the proletarian side and struggle accordingly if they are to be revolutionary. The conclusion, again, is that struggles and social conflicts are increasingly reduced to two main contenders: bourgeoisie versus proletariat.[1]

A third variant of *proletarismo* can be found in the work of Luisa Paré. She has most clearly distinguished among the several modes of exploitation in Mexican agriculture at the point of production, most notably as regards what she calls the agricultural proletariat (Paré 1977). She first establishes the classes and factions that make up the agrarian structure: (1) the agrarian bourgeoisie; (2) an agrarian petty bourgeoisie, made up of "rich peasants"; (3) middle and poor peasants; (4) a semiproletariat, torn between peasant production and wage labor, subsidizing the former with the latter; and (5) an agricultural proletariat, which she divides up into a proletariat in a "restricted sense"—all wage workers in agriculture who do not possess land—and a proletariat in a "broad sense"—those *ejidatarios* who sell the largest proportion of their harvest to a capitalist enterprise through a previously established contract. This broad proletariat is therefore made up of peasants who produce commercial crops (such as cotton, tobacco, barley, sugar cane, coffee, wheat, and so on) and whose labor process and finances are largely controlled by capital (state or private). This is the case that Marx called the "formal subordination of labor under capital" (1975) when he referred to the kind of exploitation suffered by cottage-industry artisans during the transition to capitalism in Western Europe. In Mexican agriculture, however, this mode of exploitation is exemplified by *ejidatarios* whose labor process is controlled by the state or by agroindustrial enterprises. When these *ejidatarios* rely more on seasonal hiring of wage laborers than on family labor, they become a part of the petty bourgeoisie, squeezed between capital and wage labor. It is only producers in the first situation—when production is based mostly on family labor—that Paré would include in the broad proletariat. I use the term "peasant-entrepreneurs" to describe those who do hire labor but cannot be considered an agrarian bourgeoisie because of their limited endowments of land and finances (see Chapter 6).

Paré rightly points out that this mode of exploitation in Mexico, in contradistinction to Marx's description of the formal subordination of labor under capital, does not seem to portend a transition toward other more classically capitalistic modes; it appears to be the specific way capitalist development has taken shape in a large part of Mexican agriculture. There are many legal and cultural impediments to transcending this mode of exploitation. And there are also many economic and political advantages to capital in this mode: Capital avoids the risks involved in the agricultural phase of production while reaping all the benefits; at the same time, the producers feel that they have their own land and remain content in most cases.

Paré's distinctions are adequate for clarifying the different economic class locations of direct producers in production relations. The problem, however, is that she then falls into the class-reductionist trap: She assumes that each mode of exploitation has a corresponding set of material interests and that such interests will tend to set the agenda for political struggles. The first part of her interpretation is not reductionist; she correctly establishes a link between material interests and mode of exploitation. Only the second part, in which Paré assumes that such interests will set the agenda for political struggle, is reductionist.[2]

Class Reductionism and the Homogeneity Hypotheses

Class reductionism has thus been a prevalent problem in the Mexican debate to the extent that political implications have been derived from economic class positions, regardless of which criterion—presence of wages or access to land—is viewed as the chief determinant in characterizing the agrarian structure. Another, more substantive, problem is that authors adopting either of the two stances have tended to generalize their hypothesis to the entire Mexican agrarian structure and have thus failed to do justice to its obvious heterogeneity.

Class reductionism is untenable both theoretically and empirically. Moreover, in Mexico there is a heterogeneous mix of determinants in different regions that accounts for differences in the kinds of struggles and movements in which direct producers engage.

I will now present some schemes depicting ideal-typical causal models and hypotheses of the *campesinista* and the *proletarista* views. I present the two positions in the Mexican debate as ideal types and thus exaggerate the causal links contained in their arguments. None of the authors' theories discussed would completely fit such an ideal-typical formulation (see Chart 2.1).

In this ideal-typical causal model, *proletaristas* stress the relation between the commodification of labor power or access to wages and political class formation, while *campesinistas* give primacy to the relation between access to land and political class formation. The following scheme depicts the hypotheses of each approach in light of this difference in emphasis, which is specified within the cells in each chart (see Chart 2.2). It is labeled broadly as either peasant or proletarian, depending on the hypothesized object of struggle and the specified mix of variables and relations.

The difference between the two predictions regards two cells in Chart 2.2: where wage workers have not been totally separated from their means of production and where landless workers are not selling their labor power (or are unemployed). For the first case, *campesinistas* automatically regard these producers as peasants, and thus they are expected to engage in struggles of a peasant nature, i.e., for land. *Proletaristas,* however, would say that if wage income accounts for more than 50 percent of total domestic income, then we have a proletarian family that is expected to engage in struggles of a proletarian nature, i.e., for higher wages, job security, unionization, and so on (ultimately for socialism). This first disagreement is the most important, for it concerns the category of producers we might

CHART 2.1   Class-Reductionist Model

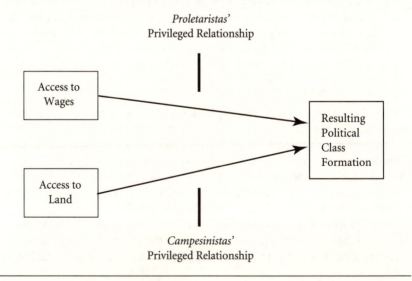

CHART 2.2   Predicted Objects of Struggle from Class-Reductionist Models

PROLETARISTAS
Access to Wages

	+	−
+	Proletarian (Wages)	Peasant (Land)
−	Proletarian (Wages)	Proletarian (Wages)

Access to Land

CAMPESINISTAS
Access to Wages

	+	−
+	Peasant (Land)	Peasant (Land)
−	Proletarian (Wages)	Peasant (Land)

Access to Land

call semiproletarians insofar as they are torn between peasant production and wage labor. They represent the largest proportion of agricultural direct producers, as will be shown in Chapter 4.

The second disagreement is over the landless and unemployed social agents. They have been totally separated from their means of production but there has been no systematic commodification of their labor power. For *proletaristas,* this category represents the unemployed fraction of the agricultural proletariat, a reserve army of labor power that shares the interests of the proletariat. For *campesinistas,* however, to the extent that these producers maintain a link with the peasant community or their kinship group, they are said to maintain access to land and thus they are supposed to struggle for peasant demands. If direct access to land actually exists, it amounts to taking this category back to one of the cells where there is agreement on the two sides of the debate : wageless peasants. The only reason why such agents would appear in the box of the "landless" is that their access to land is not formal-juridical.

Because a huge proportion of semiproletarians do find access to land through various informal means (through kinship and/or community networks), I agree with *campesinistas* on this point. It is not enough, however, to determine that there are multiple forms of access to land in order to then predict struggles of a peasant nature. We have to go further to determine the specific weight of such social relations, which are so important for the material reproduction of agricultural direct producers. Such relations are crucial in maintaining a peasant culture.

Moreover, the wide regional differences in Mexico should be taken into account. Modes of reproduction vary with the degree of capitalist penetration and commercialization. Bowing to the *proletaristas,* the *campesinistas* have apparently felt obliged to frame their discussion in the former's context of class, but only by limiting this concept to narrowly defined *economic* relations.

The difference between *campesinistas* and *proletaristas* thus lies in the way each perspective conceives of class positions. Whereas the former stress access to and struggle for land, the latter are fixated on wages, the prevalence of which (at least 50 percent of total domestic income) should engender proletarian interests and struggles. If not, the *proletaristas* argue, it is because "social consciousness" is "lagging behind": There is a problem of "false consciousness," and revolutionary organizations are thus responsible for unveiling the "truth" to misguided proletarians so that they finally struggle for their "true" and revolutionary interests. Such reasoning clearly leads to a vanguardist view of revolution in which the party cadres lead the masses to the promised land.

Michael Kearney's "Polybians"

Before going into my alternative conceptualization of the agrarian question, let me briefly review the one provided by Michael Kearney in *Reconceptualizing the Peasantry* (1996), a wide-ranging review of most of the anthropological literature on the peasantry. Given the relevance of the Mexican debate in this literature, it represents much of his focus of discussion.

Kearney's review of the anthropology of the peasantry critiques the central problem of an economically based class analysis, arguing that class has rarely been the basis for identity construction. Part of the problem stems from reality itself, he argues: It has produced persons with more than one subject position—"polybians," in Kearney's coinage. Kearney invents this term by extrapolating from *amphibian,* a being that can live both in the water and on the land. By analogy, a polybian is a being that lives in a plurality of situations—wage labor-activities, handicrafts production, agriculture, commerce, and so on. Kearney then asks how polybians can be constituted and mobilized politically. The most promising unifying identity, in his view, is ethnicity, which addresses issues of human rights, global citizenry, and ecopolitics, which is also transnational.

The main limitation of Kearney's argument is that he backs it up by focusing on rural areas with indigenous people. Therefore, one has to wonder about the identity politics of peasantlike populations that are similarly polybian but lacking in indigenous ethnicity. As we learn from de Janvry's book (see Chapter 4 in this volume), less than 15 percent of Mexico's rural population is indigenous.

Similarly, one may wonder, how do peasants in other ethnic regions (such as Chiapas, where peasants do not have the same rates of international migration as those in Oaxaca) become constituted politically? It seems that Kearney, like so many anthropologists before him, tends to generalize certain observations from "his" communities (in his case, particularly from his indigenous areas in Oaxaca state) to rural Mexico as a whole. Cynthia Hewitt de Alcántara warned anthropologists against this bias when she wrote,

> Both foreign academics and Mexican colleagues have gone into rural areas in search of situations which fit their preconceived images of adequate field sites, and have done their best to see local reality in terms validated by a previously adopted set of assumptions (1984, 178).

Kearney is not in thrall to previously held assumptions; rather he tries to debunk them. But in doing so, he creates new assumptions which may not be substantiated by a broader look at rural Mexican reality.

Alternative Research Questions and Hypotheses

What first inspired me to formulate an alternative framework to study political class formation was the general dissatisfaction with economic and class-reductionist versions of Marxism prevalent in the late 1970s and 1980s. Such dissatisfaction generated several theoretical reactions, some of which either rejected or were parallel to the contributions of Marxism. Among the former, there was the perspective of the so-called "new social movements" (NSM), which emerged primarily in Europe. This perspective represented a strong criticism of politics centered on class and political party, favoring instead a politics of identity rooted in civil society (as opposed to focusing on the state or political society). Latin American expressions of this perspective focus on autonomy, meaning, and identity (Escobar and Alvarez 1992; Alvarez, Dagnino, and Escobar 1998).

In the United States, the debate was between sociologists inspired by structural-functionalist theories, which regard social-movement actors as irrational, and those with a social-conflict perspective (primarily Weberian with Marxist influences), for whom mobilization is rational. Among the latter, the "resource mobilization theory" (RMT) strongly emphasises movement organizations as institutional actors. Unlike the NSM perspective, which focuses on civil society, RMT continues to examine group action in the political system to achieve its ends.

Another development that emerged in the United States and became a useful supplement to RMT was the "political opportunity structure" (POS) approach. The main emphasis of this perspective is on whether political institutions allow movements to successfully challenge structural problems. For POS theories, then, the question is whether political institutions are firm, unyielding, and coherent, or whether they are open (intentionally or not) to provide movement opportunities (Cook 1996: 27–32).

As may be seen from my preceding critique of theoretical positions in the Mexican debate, the NSM perspective was an important source. I remained unsatisfied, however, with its overemphasis on identity politics and its almost total discarding of any connection to what I call here "class structural processes," which include not only the social relations of production but also the social relations of reproduction. Therefore, theories of NSM, particularly those of Laclau and Mouffe (1985), provided me with ammunition to reject economism and class reductionism. Furthermore, they were crucial in calling my attention to civil society as the locus of political class formation. They also led me to explore regional cultures as the source for identity and interest formation.

After my alternative formulation was developed, I realized that it had some parallels with both RMT and POS. As will be seen in this section, I stress the formation of class organizations for struggle as a critical aspect of political class formation, just as RMT emphasizes movement organization; moreover, like POS, I regard the character of state intervention as a critical part of that process. While the POS perspective stresses political opportunity structures for group or movement action, however, I focus on two aspects of state policies: First, whether they are favorable or detrimental to direct producers; and second, whether such policies are initiated by the state itself or result from the bottom-up pressure and mobilization of direct producers.

Solving the questions of the agrarian structure (production relations) is thus not enough to determine the directionality or the character of political class formation. Nor is it enough to find an appealing form of identity such as ethnicity. The impact of at least three other factors should be carefully studied in order to adequately account for this process: regional cultures, state intervention, and leadership types.

The central question is as follows: Given the relation between the economic position of agricultural direct producers (peasants, semiproletarians, and proletarians) and their political class formation, what are the mediating determinations in this process? Once identified, in what ways do these determinations shape the political outcomes? These questions imply that a simple economic and class-reductionist approach that derives political behavior from positions in production cannot properly address the process of political class formation (Laclau 1977; Laclau and Mouffe 1985). I hold that examining regional cultures, state intervention, and leadership types is also necessary.

Political class formation thus refers to the process by which groups and classes define their demands (or objects of struggle), construct class organizations to defend and promote their interests, and establish alliances with other groups and classes. These three aspects of political class formation will be discussed at greater length later on in this chapter. Chart 2.3 depicts the causal relations among the various concepts in my alternative formulation.

Whereas the dominant question in the Mexican debate focuses on the *structural* aspect of the relation between class position and political formation, I place a greater emphasis on the *process* itself. Moreover, I do not assume that such a process inevitably leads to the proletarianization of the peasantry, as both modernization and Leninist theories do. While the process is in fact one of depeasantization, the struggle of direct producers may successfully resist proletarianization with either of two results: (1) They may retain or recover a self-employed peasant position, or (2) they may move on to a new form of agrarian struggle centered on the self-management and democratic control of cooperative or collective production units. Neither of these alternatives, however, is intrinsically conservative or revolutionary, coopted or oppositional. Much depends on the class organizations that are constructed and the alliances that are forged with other groups and classes.

Class organizations pose the problem of interest representation. They may be constructed either by the initiative of their class agents as means to struggle for their own material interests, or they may be constructed and/or appropriated by

CHART 2.3 Alternative Causal Model

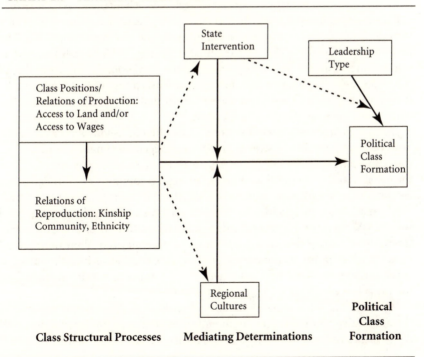

Class Structural Processes   **Mediating Determinations**   **Political Class Formation**

the dominant class or a fraction of it. Such an appropriation of the organizations of subordinate classes is precisely the political content of the process of hegemony in civil society (Gramsci 1971; Laclau and Mouffe 1985), even if this takes place through the mediation of the state apparatuses, as happens in Mexico. This aspect of political class formation pertains to the fact that classes are never formed once and for all. Their formation is a continuous process that involves organization and disorganization, at times subject to appropriation by subordinate classes and at times subject to the hegemony of a dominant class (Poulantzas 1975). Class organizations often constitute the very object of struggle; the state or the ruling class tries to destroy or gain control of the organizations of subordinate groups and classes, while the latter try to gain or regain their control over them.

Furthermore, the process of political class formation is limited in its organizational aspect by the structural capacities for struggle (Wright 1978). These consist of the material environment in which subordinate classes produce their livelihood, including social relations *in* production (Burawoy 1979). Such an environment may conduce to uniting and forming organizations for struggle, or it may encourage the fragmentation of direct producers, inhibiting their organization. Industrial factory workers are often viewed as having structural capacities that facilitate their political class formation (Marx 1981). The factory environment is supposed to enable them to unite and jointly identify their interests as a class, which in turn facilitates the formation of organizations to struggle for such interests (Wright 1978).

Conversely, it has also been common to portray the peasantry as a class with a structural incapacity for struggle rooted in its isolation in the work process. The best-known reference in this regard is that of Marx (1981); he states that while peasants are a class because their position in the work process is similar to that of the landowners, they are unable to form political organizations that transcend the local level because of their great dispersion in that very process. Hence, they would need a Bonaparte to represent them.

Peasants in different parts of the world or in different regions within a country, however, may have diverse structural capacities depending on the distinctive histories and cultures of the villages or regions where they develop. In some of them the social relations of reproduction may knit tight community networks and thus a culture of solidarity that amounts to a structural capacity. The peasants' structural capacities or incapacities for political class formation is thus an empirical issue. In Mexico the ethnic and communitarian traditions of pre-Columbian times, along with contemporary *ejidos* in some cases, may contribute to structural class capacities rather than incapacities. To the extent that such institutions and cultural traditions bring peasants together, the formation of class organizations for struggle is enhanced.

What follows is a lengthier theoretical discussion of the concepts involved in the alternative approach. First, each end of the relationship depicted in Chart 2.3—"class structural processes" and "political class formation"—will be defined.

I then elaborate upon the concepts of the mediating variables in that relationship: culture, state intervention, and leadership types.

Class Structural Processes

With the development of capitalism, there arises an increasing commodification of labor power and a separation of direct producers from their means of production. Because this process will be discussed at length in Chapter 3, I will momentarily take for granted what commodification involves at the structural level in this analysis. The following clarifications are nonetheless necessary.

First, I am not implying that each stratum of agricultural direct producers necessarily constitutes a *class*. My central concern lies not with structural class boundaries as much as with political class formation and how this process confronts determinations beyond the problem of *class position,* as defined at the level of production relations.

Second, I use the term "agricultural direct producers" to refer simultaneously to peasants, semiproletarians (or peasant-workers), and proletarians. It is a broad concept that encompasses all producing agents, regardless of their specific position in production relations. To accurately specify class structural processes, I argue that social relations of *reproduction* should also be systematically studied. Only then can we account for economic interests and cultural processes beyond narrowly defined class positions in production relations.

Third, the difference between class position and reproduction is seen as follows: Class position alludes predominantly to the *relations between exploiters and exploited,* such as that between owners of capital and wage laborers. Otherwise, class position refers to the specific forms in which direct producers produce their subsistence—e.g., peasant production.

Social relations of reproduction, on the other hand, refer mainly to *relations among the exploited.* For peasants, relations of production and reproduction largely coincide, and their exploitation in a capitalist context is generally mediated through the market. Nevertheless, for peasants, production takes place mostly at the household level, while the social relations of reproduction are broader, encompassing kinship and community relations. In the case of wage laborers, relations of reproduction refer to off-work activities in which they reproduce their laboring capacity and that of their family: their relations within the household, the neighborhood or the community, and so on. For semiproletarians or peasant-workers, relations of reproduction are crucial: They entail a whole network of relationships, mostly outside the market, on the basis of which they guarantee important supplements to their subsistence and survival. Whereas peasants guarantee their reproduction through their access to land and workers through their access to wages, in direct link with production, semiproletarians must rely more heavily on the social relations of reproduction.[3]

The structural specificity of semiproletarians is that they are divided between access to land and access to wages, but neither one provides for the full reproduction of their labor power. The relative weight of each form of reproduction shapes the type of culture and political struggles in which semiproletarians engage; each entails different labor and production processes, which in turn involve diverse social relations. The relative weight of each form of production and reproduction is clearly related to the time spent in each sphere and to the relative security provided by each type of production system: wage labor and peasant production. Therefore, simply assigning families with over 50 percent of their incomes to "proletarian" class slots, for instance, is arbitrary and misleading. This method addresses only the quantitative aspect of class position, disregards reproduction, and obscures important cultural processes that influence political outcomes.

Political Class Formation

We can conclude, then, that the process of political class formation of direct producers cannot be deduced from class position alone. Political class formation is an overdetermined process governed by at least three major factors: (1) the varying contents of *demands and struggles,* (2) the character of *class organizations* created to defend and promote class interests, and (3) the degree of *independence and autonomy* of the organizations.

Let us first discuss demands and struggles. Despite the heterogeneity of economic class positions in Mexico's countryside, most rural conflicts have centered on land. Nevertheless, the class or social contents of such struggles may vary markedly, depending on the articulation of other demands: e.g., for other means of production and/or for the appropriation of the productive process. Peasant-type demands, which are often limited to land for autonomous family production, should be distinguished from struggles with a postcapitalist character. The latter also involve struggles for land, but they are accompanied by the demand for control over the rest of the means of production *and* the democratic control of the production process by direct producers (Otero 1989b).

As regards the character of class organizations, this book focuses on three types of political outcomes: bourgeois-hegemonic, oppositional, and popular-democratic. Bourgeois-hegemonic class organizations are those promoted by a political force beyond the class whose interests it formally represents. In Mexico, this political force is best exemplified by the corporatist organizations formed from above by the ruling *Partido Revolucionario Institucional,* or PRI, which in Mexico has been the political arm of the state apparatus itself.

Oppositional class organizations are those that are formed independently of the state apparatus and the ruling class and that represent the interests of their constituencies as manifested in the concrete demands of their struggle or social movement. The oppositional organizations are usually formed in reaction to adverse state interventions. Although their oppositional character is a challenge to the hegemony and control of the state and the ruling class, such organizations are unable to impose their own demands on the state.

Finally, popular-democratic class organizations are a successful variant of the oppositional type when they are able to shape certain state policies in their favor while maintaining (or regaining) their independence from the state and the ruling class. The proliferation of popular-democratic organizations within a capitalist state indicates the consolidation of a counterhegemonic project.

Once class organizations are formed, their degree of independence from the state and ruling class becomes an issue. It is at this point that the factor of leadership becomes important. This is specially the case in a country like Mexico, where *caudillos* (charismatic military heroes) have been abundant and where there is a highly personalistic political culture. There are at least three types of leaders in agrarian movements: (1) the "charismatic-authoritarian" leader, whose fundamental interest is to maintain personal control of the movement; (2) the "corrupt-opportunistic" leader, who, although initially concerned about defending the interests of those he (rarely "she") represents, could compromise their long-term interests, particularly those regarding the strategic autonomy of the organization or movement; and (3) the "democratic" leader, whose principles include concerns over raising the political and ideological consciousness of the masses and training new cadre who might succeed him in the leadership post when this is suitable (due to completion of term or unforeseen causes). The last is the ideal representative, one whose interests (both short- and long-term) fully coincide with those of his or her grassroots constituents. Needless to say, the first two types are the ones most often encountered in practice.[4]

Therefore, in terms of political outcomes since the 1930s, it is important to consider the kinds of demands posited by the direct producers—peasant, proletarian, peasant-entrepreneurial, or postcapitalist—the character of organizations, and the alliances that they have established. Rather than offering an economic argument based on narrowly defined class positions, the explanation suggested here emphasizes the regional cultures, the forms of state intervention, and the types of leadership in agrarian movements. While cultures largely shape the objects of struggle, state intervention mediates in forming the character of class organizations, and leadership types shape the extent to which their organizations remain independent from the state and the ruling class.

Culture and State Intervention

Let us now turn to the determinants of the process of political class formation. State and culture produce their impacts simultaneously, in varying forms, but I will discuss each one in turn for the sake of a simpler exposition. Leadership types, it may be argued, largely depend on regional cultures themselves. But because there are a variety of leadership types within a given regional political economy, the impact of each one of them should be explored. I should add that this is the least-studied variable, and it came to my attention only after the research was completed rather than during the design phase. The impact of leadership types is therefore the least-developed variable.

Culture and Class Structural Processes

The culture concept in anthropology is a controversial one (Keesing 1976, Silverman 1979). Among the many authors who have defined it, there are those like Clifford Geertz who see culture as an ideational realm of norms, values and meanings; and there are others like Julian Steward who define the concept more broadly as the whole way of life, including aspects of social organization. There are several other important differences between these definitions—as well as other definitions, for that matter—, but for my purposes I will adopt Geertz's narrower definition. This will allow me to separate it analytically from social organization, or what I have called "class structural processes." Geertz defines culture and social structure as follows:

> On the [cultural] level there is the framework of beliefs, expressive symbols, and values in terms of which individuals define their world, express their feelings, and make their judgments; on the [social] level there is the ongoing process of interactive behavior, whose persistent form we call social structure. Culture is the fabric of meaning in terms of which human beings interpret their experience and guide their action; social structure is the form that action takes, the actually existing network of social relations (Geertz 1957, cited in Keesing 1976, 143).

Now that I have chosen a definition of "culture" at the most abstract level, I will elaborate more concrete concepts referred to how culture shapes the objects of struggle in historical settings. In Chart 2.3, above, I have posited a causal relationship between class structural processes and culture, although I do not attempt to theorize about it. (This is why a broken line between the two concepts is drawn: because they are related but in an undetermined way.) Only very careful assumptions may be made about this relationship, while maintaining in the definition a relative autonomy of culture from social structure. I will spell out some assumptions with regard to the relation between capitalist development and peasant culture.[5]

It is assumed that, in general, peasant culture *declines* with the development of capitalist social relations. Such decline, however, has a different temporality from that of capitalist development. It is thus not uncommon to find wage workers of a second or third generation who maintain a peasant culture and engage in political struggles to regain a peasant condition. This persistence of a form of peasant culture, nevertheless, does not take place in a vacuum. It generally requires the continued contact of social agents with a peasant environment, if not in their immediate class positions in production, at least in their social relations of reproduction. The latter not only include household and kinship relations, but also community, and ethnic relations.

Several clarifications are necessary about the concept of "peasant culture." First, I assume the existence of more than one type of peasant culture, depending on whether it bears communitarian, ethnic, subsistence-oriented, and/or peasant-entrepreneurial traits.[6] Ethnic and communitarian cultural traits are usually over-lapping in the south-central region of Mexico, while a peasant-entrepreneurial culture developed—albeit weakly—in the North, mainly in the latter part of last century. Therefore, peasant culture may not be thought of as a homogeneous reality.

Second, it is held that the specificity of each type of peasant culture is rooted in the material conditions of production and reproduction in which it develops, and yet it maintains a relative autonomy from them. From a class-reductionist per-spective, it would appear that once peasant production has entered an imminent process of dissolution, the interests of direct producers would be identified with those of the proletariat. Even writers like Luisa Paré tend to push the idea that semiproletarians are closer to the interests of the agricultural proletariat, and that their struggles *should* therefore be centered on this type of demands. When they are not, they explain this absence by a supposed "false consciousness" problem in direct producers (Lara, 1979).

There are many agrarian struggles in Mexico which have been documented as specifically *peasant* struggles in this century, and in most of these cases the strug-gling agents have been proletarians or semiproletarians in terms of class position. Thus, if we have a community or village where a peasant type of economy domi-nates, even if most producers lose their land and become semiproletarians for years (often for more than one generation), because of their peasant social rela-tions and culture they will still be longing to return to their lost peasant condition behaviorally as well as psychologically. Thus, despite changes in class position, the most relevant values of peasant culture can be maintained for long periods of time. And this happens not merely because "values" (in general) are long lasting, but because a multiplicity of aspects of social reproduction continue to constitute a material basis for such peasant values and culture to subsist.[7]

Forms of culture among direct producers, therefore, will vary according to the degree of capitalist development. That is to say, the more capitalism develops, the more class positions with access to wages are created. And this process will gener-ally entail a *decline* of peasant culture, although not in a linear way. The question then becomes: When peasant culture does decline, what is it replaced with among agricultural direct producers? My proposition is that declining peasant culture is not necessarily replaced with what we might call a "capitalist", i.e., either a "bour-geois" or a "proletarian" culture. Instead, in most cases a "noncapitalist" culture will still prevail among the subaltern classes in the countryside.[8]

Noncapitalist culture may be of at least two types: "non-market-oriented," such as peasant, ethnic, or communitarian cultures; and "market-oriented," such as that of simple commodity producers, or what I have called peasant-entrepre-neurs. Also postcapitalist direct producers with self-management, cooperative, and democratic production arrangements may be said to share a noncapitalist, yet market-oriented culture. When I say that peasant culture declines, I am referring to the subsistence, or "non-market-oriented," type of noncapitalist culture.

The emergence of a market-oriented but noncapitalist culture still contains elements of resistance to capitalism, with which direct producers oppose proletarianization. The two main alternatives to proletarianization—peasant-entrepreneurship and postcapitalist production—preserve the value of autonomy in production from the state and the agrarian bourgeoisie. The main difference between these alternatives is that peasant-entrepreneurs also value production organized by the individual household, while postcapitalist producers value self-managed cooperative or collective forms of organization. My argument is that the latter cultural value may arise at a point when cooperation in the capitalist labor process has become part of everyday experience of direct producers for extended periods of time, across several generations.

I will briefly refer to James Scott's theories on hegemony and peasant culture (1977); his mistake is the opposite of Leninism's: He mystifies the role of culture in the peasantry. Although his substantive analysis of cultural elements of Third World peasants is often quite insightful (Scott 1976, 1990), he proposes that peasant culture, among subcultures of subordinate classes, is potentially more revolutionary than that of the proletarians. Scott contrasts proletarians' and peasants' material basis for cultural independence and concludes that proletarians' dependence on wages, and on capitalists generally, renders them more vulnerable to hegemonic culture. In contrast, peasants' relative economic autonomy facilitates the creation of a strong class subculture outside the normative sway of ruling institutions (1977, 277). Scott then goes on to equate peasant values with peasant radicalism: "Far from being handicapped, the 'obsolete' values of peasants and their local orientation may well be the source of their radical action" (1977, 281).

The problem here is that Scott does not analyze the aftermath of rebellions to see whether peasants actually manage to transcend capitalism or are coopted after obtaining some concessions. When he does talk about aftermaths, in a couple of sentences, he is forced to recognize that most peasant rebellions and revolutions fail, but he attributes this outcome to a problem of tactics and strategy, not culture. In sum, for Scott the condition for rebellion and revolution is an isolated culture that may be shielded from hegemony, even if, paradoxically, rebellion will end up in defeat. From this approach, then, the more capitalism develops and commercialization processes set in, the less viable revolutions become, insofar as peasants become more subject to bourgeois hegemony. Conversely, however, revolts inspired by an independent peasant culture will probably lead to defeat.

I believe that the Mexican cases we will analyze here clearly speak against Scott's cultural theory: There is no requirement of isolation for noncapitalist cultures to emerge and develop. As I have argued, market-oriented yet noncapitalist cultures are also conducive to successful resistance to capitalism and even to transcending it, at least within the immediate realm of production relations if not societally.

My perspective attempts to provide a synthesis between views that see economically defined classes as crucial and those that stress culture in their explanations. With regard to the peasantry, Hamsa Alavi was one of the first contemporary scholars to suggest the cultural mediation in his theoretical contribution to the opening issue of *The Journal of Peasant Studies* (1973). James Scott later became the main proponent of culture as a key dimension in peasant studies (1976, 1985).

For Mexico, Claudio Lomnitz-Adler has produced a materialist response to poststructuralist analyses of culture and identity; his analysis is rooted in the empirical and spatial existence of classes and ethnic groups at the regional level. One of the key concepts he proposes is that of regional culture, which he defines as "the internally differentiated and segmented culture produced by human interaction within a regional political economy" (1992, 22). Unlike a more general concept of "class culture," this concept of culture is bounded by space. The concept of class culture is an aspatial concept that rarely corresponds to any specific set of cultural practices observed on the field. Lomnitz-Adler situates classes in a complex spatial relationship with other classes that varies with the culture of the class. Based on his case study of Morelos, a neighboring state to the west of Puebla, Lomnitz-Adler identifies which types of culture are residual, emergent, or dominant in that region: "From the perspective of the regional political economy, peasant cultural cores are residual, working-class cores are emergent, and petit-bourgeois cores are dominant" (1992, 39).

In rural Mexico, despite the heterogeneity of economic class positions that exists among land cultivators, most conflicts have centered on land as an object of struggle, though often under the ethnic guise (Schryer 1990). This struggle may nevertheless develop very different class or social contents, depending on the articulation of other demands shaped by regional cultures. Demands of a peasant type, for instance, limited to land for autonomous family production, should be distinguished from struggles accompanied by the demand for control over the rest of the means of production *and* the democratic control of the production process by direct producers. The latter demands involve expanding the realm of democratic struggle to the sphere of production, both in terms of decision-making and the distribution of economic surplus.

Character of State Interventions

In postrevolutionary Mexico, the state apparatus has had a major role in orienting capitalist development in the countryside. It has combined its coercive and repressive power with means to gain consensus. The agrarian policies of the Mexican state have had two major goals: enhancing capitalist development in agriculture as a means to support industrialization and allaying political unrest in the countryside while gaining consensus and legitimacy for the postrevolutionary regimes. The different emphasis given to these contradictory goals has depended on several factors, but the most important one has been the correlation of class forces in the different regions of Mexico. That is to say, depending on the contending groups and classes and their relative strengths, the state apparatus has devised different types of state intervention, often introducing regional variations to a national pattern of state policy.

As I will show, state interventions sometimes strengthen the agrarian bourgeoisie, even at the expense of direct producers and a loss of legitimacy; and in other cases the state is forced to respond to the demands of agricultural direct producers, even if the interests of some agents of the agrarian bourgeoisie must be negatively affected. Thus, the state should not be seen as a monolithic entity that always has the same effects through its interventions.

The ambiguity of these interventions is determined by the contradictory nature of the state's goals. As mentioned above, the state apparatus has to be concerned not only with enhancing capitalist development, but also with maintaining consensus and legitimacy for the postrevolutionary regimes. Thus, it is not always possible to apply outright repression to political unrest in the countryside, even if this option would enhance capitalist development. Moreover, the state apparatus is sometimes *forced* to respond favorably to the agrarian struggles and demands of subordinate classes, and to implement agrarian policies, such as land redistribution, that favor them. More often than not, such favorable policies are explained by the strength of mass mobilization rather than by the populist attitudes of state regimes. In other words, the determinants of state policy are not only the agents who control the state apparatus, but also those involved in popular mobilizations.

In contrast to my perspective, some authors consider the state as unduly autonomous in devising its policies. Steven Sanderson (1981), for instance, generally posits a state initiative for land redistribution during Luis Echeverría's regime (1970–76). The beginning of this period, however, saw the rise of agrarian mobilizations in several regions of Mexico (A. Bartra, 1979b). Yet for Sanderson favorable state interventions are usually seen as populist policies of concession, as if the state were an invincible force impervious to popular mobilization.

In operational terms I see state interventions as either favorable or unfavorable to the reproduction of direct producers. They are unfavorable when they are oriented toward enhancing capitalist development at the expense of direct producers. Such cases tend to spawn class organizations with an oppositional character, as has been suggested above. In contrast, favorable policies are those geared to support or enhance the basis for livelihood of direct producers. They may take the form of land redistribution or an extension of wage-employment opportunities. These latter variants are clearly compatible with capitalist development while favoring direct producers. Thus, favorable policies are not always implemented at the expense of the agrarian bourgeoisie (another example is distributing "federal" lands to direct producers). Favorable state interventions, therefore, should be further broken down into two kinds, which should be considered separately: (1) state policies that favor direct producers at the expense of their losing control of their class organizations, which become coopted by the state and consolidate bourgeois hegemony; and (2) state policies that are imposed on the state from below, through the initiative, strength, and mobilization of direct producers who are able to maintain independent control of their class organizations, which gives them a popular-democratic character.

Popular-democratic organizations assume a certain level of political class formation prior to the mobilization. In this case our dependent variable actually becomes an independent one. This is what I call the "subjective moment" of political class formation: a politically formed class is able to impose its will on the state. Obviously, classes constituted as popular-democratic social agents are not immune to cooptation or bourgeois hegemony. A key future task for these classes is to maintain their organizational independence and establish alliances with other subordinate groups and classes of a similarly popular-democratic persuasion.

Notes

1. I should point out from the outset that I agree with much of R. Bartra's characterizations of the Mexican agrarian structure but not with his political conclusions. In his early work (e.g., 1974a, 1978) his Leninist class reductionism was evident. During the 1980s he became greatly influenced by Eurocommunist writers and went well beyond Leninism in both his political analysis (1981, 1986) and in his interpretation of the agrarian class structure itself (R. Bartra and Otero 1987).

2. Catherine LeGrand (1984) has also questioned unilinear perspectives in Marxism that posit the inevitability of peasants' transformation into wage laborers. First, on a structural level, she argues that class formation is quite fluid and partly depends on economic cycles, so that repeasantization processes may appear. Second, as regards rural revolt and protests, she argues that approaches that have focused too closely on productive organization to derive political behavior have drawn too sharp a distinction between peasants and workers (e.g., Stinchcombe 1961; Alavi 1965; Paige 1975). While she thinks this approach is an advance from unilinear ones, she argues that we also need to admit that workers purposefully struggle not only for wages but also to regain a peasant condition. Thirdly, she argues that legal forms are important ideologically.

3. Drawing on previous work on simple commodity production (SCP), which uses political economy to specify its characteristics, Gavin Smith (1985) attempts a similarly general theorization of the noncommodified social relations of SCP to mobilize labor. He argues that noncommodified relations are at least as important as commodified ones for specifying the character of SCP. Therefore, I contend that these relations of reproduction must be systematically accounted for in any analysis of "class structural processes."

4. My classification of leadership types has an obvious parallel to Max Weber's classic formulation (1978, 941–1157). One difference is that I constructed the types inductively, drawing on the Mexican historical experience.

5. Margaret S. Archer has identified three basic forms of conflation in cultural analysis (1996). The first one, "downward conflation," originated in anthropology but was carried over to sociology and consists in thinking that culture sets the boundaries within which human action takes place. The second type of conflation originated in simplified versions

of Marxism. Archer calls it "upward conflation" because it basically inverts the order of determination. In this case the cultural system is supposed to be basically a reflection or epiphenomenon of sociocultural interaction. Marx himself actually allowed for a more nuanced analysis that allowed for the possibility that the cultural system might influence sociocultural interaction. The third conflationary approach to culture and agency is represented by Anthony Giddens's theory of structuration (1976, 1984). Archer calls it "central conflation" because of its tendency to negate the independent action of the cultural system and sociocultural interaction by amalgamating them. By amalgamating culture and agency, we forego the possibility of examining the *interplay* between them over time. Thus, while upward and downward conflationism amount to conceptualizing either culture or agency as an epiphenomenon of the other, central conflationism denies their autonomy or independence by its assertion of mutual constitution. Some autonomy or independence must be assigned to each, culture and agency, in order to come up with an adequate theoretical stance that captures the interplay between the two entities of social life.

6. Peasant-entrepreneurs are autonomous, simple commodity producers who are self-employed and use limited amounts of hired labor. The concept is inspired by Ivan Szelény's (1987) notion of "peasant-burghers." The concept is equivalent to Lenin's kulaks (1967), minus the satanic connotation that the term *kulak* acquired in the early years of the Russian Revolution.

7. Ann Swidler has provided a persuasive argument in favor of culture's independent influence on action. She argues that action is neither governed by interests or values. Both views that sustain these propositions are flawed by excessive emphasis on the "unit act," she says. Instead of viewing actions as decided upon piece by piece, Swidler proposes the following: "Action is necessarily integrated into larger assemblages, called here 'strategies of action.' Culture has an independent causal role because it shapes the capacities from which such strategies of action are constructed." (1986, 276–277). Strategies of action, says Swidler, incorporate and depend on habits, moods, sensibilities, and views of the world. I would add that all of these are sustained mostly by the specific social relations of reproduction in which social agents are immersed.

8. Alastair Davidson has convincingly argued that during the 1920s, but mostly in the 1930s, Gramsci modified his developmentalist interpretation of the peasantry. Also, he saw that popular culture contained elements of hegemonic culture, but also of noncapitalist culture on which Marxists could build to incorporate the peasantry in a new hegemonic project of allied subaltern classes. His new strategy assumed the following: "(1) the peasantry would remain in the foreseeable future as a significant political force; (2) their ethos and values would therefore have to be incorporated in any Marxist theory of transition to socialism; and (3) developmentalism and modernization would have to be re-examined as a core part of Marxist strategy" (Davidson 1984, 139). Although Gramsci has been regarded as the Lenin of advanced capitalist formations, I believe that these general observations are especially relevant to Third World societies as well and are clearly a revision of Leninist theory.

3

Agrarian Reform: Capitalism, the State, and Neoliberalism

The Mexican agrarian reform is often touted by government officials as the product of a peasant revolution that brought justice to the rural masses. In contrast to this view, the critical history I present here argues that land redistribution in Mexico was the way chosen to develop and entrench capitalism in Mexico. Mexican agrarian reform has resulted in a pauperization of rural people that has brought both peasant and capitalist agriculture to a crisis. The end of redistribution in the 1970s weakened the relationship between the peasantry and the state, undermining the viability of the state in the corporatist form it assumed after the revolutionary period from 1910 to 1920. In fact, the changes in agrarian legislation introduced in 1992, along with the neoliberal policies that have been pursued since the mid–1980s, present a dramatic change in the menu of available policy choices for the state vis-à-vis agriculture and the peasantry. This chapter discusses the agrarian reform in historical perspective as a background to these recent changes, the legal end of agrarian reform in 1992, and the new agricultural policies brought about by neoliberalism.

Social Origins of the Agrarian Reform

The social and political origins of the agrarian reform may be traced to Articles 27 and 123 of the Mexican Constitution of 1917. These two articles embody the revolution's approach toward the peasantry and the working class, respectively. They represent advanced social thought when seen in relation to postrevolutionary Mexican society. Indeed, they became the basis for future peasants' and workers' struggles, and most of the resulting organizations were folded into the PRI, the dominant political party (with several name changes) since 1929.

More specifically, Article 27 was a negotiated settlement between two predominant political factions in 1917, one led by Alvaro Obregón and the other by Venustiano Carranza. These two factions represented the constitutionalists, and their goal was to deprive the more radical revolutionary peasant factions—led by Emiliano Zapata and Francisco Villa—of their original demands. With the completion of this move, the radicals lost a final political battle against the reformist constitutionalists, coupled, as it was, with the military defeat of both Zapata's and Villa's armies. Thus, the Constitution of 1917 marked the rise of a new reformist regime from a bloody revolution.

The Mexican revolution was a costly social process in which one million people died. Those who gained from it were not the ones who sacrificed the most. The revolution primarily helped the agrarian bourgeoisie of the north, not the peasantry who had been the primary revolutionary force. On the other hand, the reformist leadership managed to form an alliance between the working class and the constitutionalist movement. Thus, some Mexican political scientists conceptualize the revolution as a political rather than a social revolution because it did away with a highly exclusionary regime in which political power was based on land ownership. Nonetheless, the main trajectory of the new society was still capitalist development; notwithstanding reformed property relations in the countryside, private ownership remained the foundation of the economic system. Thus, while the revolution eliminated the barrier to capitalist development in agriculture that had been erected by the large and inefficient landholders, it did not modify property relations fundamentally (Córdova, 1972).

The Reform Laws of the Porfirio Díaz Regime

The diverse histories of the various regions that make up the Mexican republic reflect a heterogeneous agricultural population. The rural people of central Mexico had an important precolonial cultural heritage, while the north was significantly settled only in the last century.

Before the revolution, the Roman Catholic Church was the largest landowner, representing a type of feudal ownership that contrasted markedly with the liberal ideology that had emerged in other sectors. A clash resulted from the emergence of an industrial bourgeoisie that demanded the development of agriculture so that its own growth would not be stunted by increased wage demands and falling profits. Meanwhile, the Church continued to maintain large areas of uncultivated land and represented a major fetter to development.

The liberal reforms of 1857 provided the legal instruments to expropriate the Church's landholdings. But the same law, aided by further legislation passed during the *Porfiriato* (the prerevolutionary period, 1876–1910, during which Porfirio Díaz ruled Mexico), was applied as well to Indian community land. Thus, after the liberal reform laws and during the *Porfiriato,* the Indian communities were deprived of 90 percent of their land.

Land monopolization continued at a brisk pace during the *Porfiriato,* abetted by the *baldío* laws of 1883 and 1884, which provided for the surveying and sale of "vacant" lands. For these purposes, surveying companies (*compañías deslindado-*

ras) were created. These companies were given the right to keep one-third of the surveyed land as payment for their work; the rest was sold by the government. The surveying companies eventually owned 49 million hectares, or one-fourth of Mexico's territory; once surveyed, the companies purchased much of the land sold by the state. They also surveyed the Indian and peasant towns and communities, arbitrarily deeming the land to be "vacant" or eligible for surveying as they went. When Indian communities lost their land, their members were converted into laborers or peons, working for the resultant *haciendas* or the surveying companies; many became unemployed.

The immediate outcome of the liberal reforms was thus a transfer in landownership from the Church and the Indian communities to existing and new *latifundistas*. Large holders in the private sector of Mexican agriculture saw that they could enlarge their farms at little cost. For decades that followed, they satisfied their voracious appetites for land by putting their fences around Indian communal land. They also devised ways of attaching newly landless Indian peasants to the land—for example, through various debts the workers would incur with the landowner (credits for wedding feasts, goods advanced at *tiendas de raya* or *hacienda* stores, and so on). These debts were inherited by the peons' children, who were not able to give up their "jobs" until they had completely paid any past-due accounts to the landlord (López Cámara 1967; Hansen 1974; Meyer and Sherman 1979).

The *Porfiriato* saw the development of the infrastructure for industry (for example, a large railroad network). But, paradoxically, the *Porfiriato* also maintained and reinforced feudal and even slave forms of labor relations in farming. It was only through a ruthlessly repressive dictatorship that these contradictions in economic structure were maintained for so long. In the end, the contradictions between capitalist development and the archaic land-tenure pattern sharpened into a revolution that sought to alter the entire system.

Industry was still a nascent sector during the *Porfiriato*. As of 1910, the main capital investments were concentrated in railroads (40 percent), mining (17 percent), industry (6 percent), and oil (5.9 percent). Most of this investment—77 percent—was made up of foreign capital (Gilly 1974, 21).

The *Porfiriato* promoted a massive flow of North American investments into Mexico; this was a decisive step for Mexican integration into the world economy, one viewed by Friederich Katz (1982) and others as a prime mover of the revolution. The second motivating factor was the expropriation of Indian communities, and the third was the pacification of nomadic Indians on the northern frontier, which transformed the area into a peaceful and permeable border with the United States (Aguilar Camin 1977). The flow of North American capital into the Mexican economy followed soon thereafter, and the downturn of the world economy in 1907 had dramatic effects in Mexico's northern states.

The revolutionary movement coalesced in different ways in the various regions of Mexico. In central Mexico the main social rift was between the expropriated Indian communities and the *hacendados*. In the north, revolution was led by the *hacendados*, who were excluded from political power during the *Porfiriato*. They formed a broad and unlikely alliance with their own peons, small farmers, ranchers, and urban middle classes. In central Mexico, specifically in Morelos, Indian peasants had been organized to oppose the *Porfiriato* since 1908, before Francisco I. Madero had even called for the revolution's first shot (Womack 1969). Unlike the broad alliance in the north, which was represented by *hacendados* (like Madero), the Morelos peasantry chose their leader, Emiliano Zapata, from their own community. Zapata earned his livelihood from training horses on a *hacienda* in exchange for a wage. Thus, strictly speaking, he was not a peasant. Yet he was a respected member of the community. Followers of Zapata decided to ally themselves with Madero and the northern *hacendados* because an effort to air their grievances had been repulsed at the state level.

By the time of the *Zapatista* uprising, sharecroppers and poor farmers were ready to join with the revolutionary movement. *Peones acasillados* (peasants resident on haciendas) preferred their current lives to the uncertainty of revolt:

> Only rarely did they [the *Zapatistas*] recruit rebels among the *gente de casa* [resident peons], who anyway preferred their bonded security, and nowhere evidently did they excite these dependent peons to rise up and seize the plantations they worked on" (Womack 1969, 87).

The most militant and combative of *Zapatistas* were poor peasant producers and share tenants. In 1911, once *Zapatistas* began to implement local land reform according to the *Plan de San Luis Potosí*, Madero's revolutionary manifesto, "armed parties of sharecroppers and poor farmers began invading fields. . . . The defenseless plantation managers and peons resident on the lands the squatters claimed had no alternative but to meet the revolutionary demands." (Womack 1969, 87).

The prerevolutionary situation in the north was distinct. La Laguna, located in the north-central region, was settled only in the last century; it did not harbor an extant, sedentary Indian population as did so much of the highlands of central Mexico. Among the difficulties faced by settlers were repeated attacks by warrior and rootless Indian tribes of the north. These "Apaches," as they were generically called, had always been outside of Aztec influence prior to the Spanish Conquest (1521). Whereas the *Laguneros* had been the native settlers before 1750, their population was so decimated by the struggles against Spaniards and smallpox that, by the turn of the twentieth century, there was hardly a trace of Indian culture in La Laguna (Beals 1932).

In contrast to peons from central *haciendas*, who tended to remain loyal to their patrons and spurn the revolution, peons and *hacendados* in the north rebelled *together* against the central government. Francisco I. Madero, a *hacendado* from the state of Coahuila, led the rebellion. Such an alliance was possible partly because, in the north, debt servitude had lost its sway since mid-nineteenth century because of the development of mining and even some industry, which offered alternative employment opportunities (Katz 1982, 28–29; Knight 1986). Even the *tiendas de raya* were different in the north. In the center of the country they were the *hacendado*'s instrument to keep peons indebted and thus attached to the hacienda; in the north, by contrast, peons were not forced to purchase goods at the *tienda de raya*. Indeed, *hacendados* usually sold products there at lower prices as an additional incentive to attract labor. Also in La Laguna, agricultural wages were the highest in the country (Katz 1982, 31).

In addition to those involved in the resident peon-*hacendado* relationship in La Laguna, there were the colonists. They usually held greater amounts of land and more livestock than free peasants of other regions (Landsberger and Hewitt de Alcántara 1970, Craig 1986). In the state of Chihuahua, communities of colonists were established specifically to defend the frontier against Apache incursions. They had a greater internal autonomy and felt that they had not only the right but also the duty to arm themselves against Apache attacks (Nugent 1985; Wasserman 1980). Although they were not a large percentage of the rural labor force, they did get land from President Benito Juárez in 1864 after helping him fight against the French invasion. Later on, during the *Porfiriato*, the La Laguna colonists struggled with livestock *hacendados* who had deprived them of water by altering the flow of the Nazas River (Eckstein 1966, 132). Considering that the colonists had lost their land under Porfirio Díaz, it was not surprising that they became combative in the revolution and were among the first land reform beneficiaries in 1917. In Chihuahua, compared to ordinary peasant communities, colonists had become accustomed to privileges usually accorded Spaniards and Creoles; they were land proprietors and could sell their land. But by 1910, they had been dispossessed of their land and deprived of municipal autonomy. These aggrieved colonists were easily organized for combat (Katz 1982, 24–26).

Another important revolutionary group developed in the northwest state of Sonora. Most of the leaders of the constitutionalist movement, in fact, came from Coahuila and Sonora (Cumberland 1975). Initially headed by Venustiano Carranza, a former governor of Coahuila, the Sonora group seized control of the revolutionary state by 1920 (Matute 1980). Generals Adolfo de la Huerta, Alvaro Obregón Salido, and Plutarco Elías Calles are closely associated with the triumph of this faction of the revolution; they helped to legitimize the emerging agrarian burgeoisie of the north. These three generals held the presidency of Mexico between 1920 and 1928, and Calles extended his reign through "puppet" administrations from 1928 to 1935 (Loyola Díaz 1980; Medin 1982). At the time of the revolution, Obregón was a small farmer, whereas Calles came from a family of well-off merchants. Nevertheless, they soon embodied the spirit and character of what today is the northern agrarian bourgeoisie (Aguilar Camín 1977, 1982; Sanderson 1981; Cartón de Grammont 1990).

Revisionist historians have pointed out enormous regional differences in kinds of revolutionary leadership and involvement. Barry Carr (1973, 1980), for example, has challenged the supposedly "popular" character of the first decade of the revolutionary period. He emphasizes "the hegemony exercised by bourgeois groupings over most of the revolutionary coalitions" (Carr 1980, 7). In the Sonoran case, argues Carr, "an exceptionally high percentage of the state's revolutionary leadership emerged from the ranks of the hacendado community or from the class of prosperous capitalist farmers and ranchers that occupied such an important place in northern society." (Carr 1980, 8)

In sum, the social origins of the Mexican revolution were as varied as Mexican society itself. The key contrasts between the revolutionary alliances in the north and south corresponded to diverse regional social structures and political cleavages.

Article 27: A Reformist Compromise

Article 27 of the 1917 Constitution was designed to fulfill the demands of the many peasant farmers who had been dispossessed during the *Porfiriato* while preserving the possibility of private landownership. Indeed, the land reform article of the Constitution was a reformist compromise. One of its central features was that it declared all land to be owned by the nation. The nation, in turn, had the right to transmit this land to individuals and to constitute "private property." Also, the nation had the right and the obligation to expropriate any private property when the land was deemed necessary for "public use." This article provided the postrevolutionary state with the legal instrument to carry out land redistribution. The methods for carrying out an agrarian reform were to be determined in a set of enabling laws designed by the national Congress (Sanderson 1981, 67–69).

The *ejidatario*, legal holder of an *ejido* land grant, is a producer independent of large landowners. Like the *minifundista* (or private proprietor of a tiny plot of land), the *ejidatario* might transform himself into a capitalist or might become proletarianized; he might accumulate capital or lose his means of production; he might maintain himself in the market or be eliminated. Such polar alternatives existed for *ejidatarios* after the inception of the 1917 agrarian reform. Whether they became capitalists, peasant-entrepreneurs, or proletarians depended largely on state policy.

Structural Reforms Under Cárdenas

From 1917 to 1935 some land was slowly redistributed. During Carranza's mandate (1917–20), much of the land that had been given out under the *Zapatista* laws was returned to its previous owners. Zapata himself was murdered by an officer of the Federal Army at a meeting in which the two were expected to negotiate terms for surrender of the peasant armies (Womack 1969). Without its beloved leader, the peasant movement in Mexico gradually became impotent.

The period from 1920 to 1935 was one of economic reconstruction and ruling-group consolidation. Because the "revolutionary family" was becoming fragmented, especially after the assassination of Obregón in 1928, Calles in 1929 sponsored the organization of all revolutionary forces into a political party called the National Revolutionary Party (*Partido Nacional Revolucionario,* or PNR, the first precursor of the PRI). The 1920s saw the "Sonora Group" rise to the top of the nation's hierarchy. The agrarian bourgeoisie was establishing its hegemony over postrevolutionary development.

The outstanding features of the 1920–35 period were a leadership based on *caudillos* (charismatic military leaders), an ideological radicalism expressed in heavy anticlericalism, and a halt to land redistribution. Anticlericalism led to the *Cristero* rebellion in west-central Mexico, while the absence of significant land redistribution led to a radical agrarian movement in the eastern state of Veracruz. This movement was headed by Governor and General Adalberto Tejeda, one of the revolutionary caudillos (Falcón 1977; Fowler Salamini 1979). These two threats, one from the right and the other form the left, explain why the congress of the dominant PNR chose Lázaro Cárdenas as its presidential candidate in 1933 (Medin, 1982). Calles, the *Jefe Máximo,* or highest chief of the revolution, agreed to nominate Cárdenas for at least three reasons: Cárdenas had proved himself loyal to him, political factors predominated over ideological or economic factors (i.e., the "revolutionary family" was becoming consolidated within the PNR), and he felt that Cárdenas's record as an agrarianist during his stint as governor of Michoacán would offset the pressures from radical *Tejedismo* in Veracruz.

In order to consolidate the power of his office against Calles, who attempted to retain his informal rule even after the election, Cárdenas organized the peasantry and the working class into mass organizations. Rather than allowing peasants and workers to organize independently, he incorporated their organizations into the official party, which became the Party of the Mexican Revolution (*Partido de la Revolución Mexicana,* or PRM, second and last precursor of the PRI). This obviously required making several concessions. Cárdenas encouraged workers— within certain limits—to struggle with the other "factor of production" (i.e., the capitalists) to attain an "equilibrium." His intention was not to promote class struggle but to encourage a "class conciliation" in which the state was the "impartial" mediator (Córdova 1974; Hamilton 1982; Medin 1972).

Before Cárdenas's administration, most land in the agrarian reform had been distributed to *ejidatarios* as *individual* plots to each *ejido* member. But Cárdenas confronted, for the first time, the need to distribute the land of highly productive *haciendas* in irrigated regions where the agrarian movement was intense; he felt there were scale economies in these units. In order to preserve the productivity of large units and to maintain an uninterrupted flow of agricultural raw materials and wage-goods to industry, Cárdenas's policy was to create "collective" *ejidos,* which appeared very similar to producer cooperatives. Ultimately, about 12 percent of all *ejidos* assumed this collective form of organization (Eckstein, 1966).

Although Cárdenas obliged the large-acreage ex-owners to transform themselves into capitalist agriculturalists, he also respected the principle of "small private property ownership." Each time a farm was expropriated, the owner could retain the *hacienda* core, not to exceed 150 hectares (1 hectare = 2.47 acres) of irrigated land; in land-reform jargon, which often involves a euphemistic turn of phrase, this is a "small property," or *pequeña propiedad* (sometimes called a *rancho*). An important number of *latifundistas*, frightened by the climate of violence in which agrarian reform was being carried out, divided their lands themselves and sold them as "small properties." In some cases this was done through trusted *prestanombres* (name-lenders). The *prestanombre* might be a family member or a former employee. These cases usually implied that the original owner retained control of land that was formally "sold."

At the end of his presidential mandate, Cárdenas had granted more land to the peasants than all his predecessors together: 17,891,577 hectares had been distributed among 814,537 peasants (Gutelman 1974, 109).

The Collective Ejidos: *La Laguna, El Yaqui, and Atencingo*

The *Cardenista* plan for La Laguna's collective *ejidos* set the example for future collectivization in other regions of modern capitalist agriculture; the government hoped it would serve as a model of the political viability and the economic superiority of collective farming as compared to private property. Furthermore, enough popular strength had to be mobilized to offset the reaction of *hacendados* when their farms were threatened with expropriation. After land redistribution, beneficiary-producers had to maintain a solid organization to resist attacks from ex-*hacendados* and to produce at an exemplary level.

The plan aimed at achieving self-management by ejidatarios. In La Laguna, this goal was to be achieved through the organization of beneficiaries into fifteen regional unions, which would eventually substitute for the *Banco Ejidal* (Ejido Bank), a state credit-granting agency. The fifteen unions would be coordinated by the Central Union of Collective Credit Societies, which was intended to perform the *ejido*'s economic and marketing functions.

This plan was proposed and elaborated through the interaction of the *Ejidatarios'* Central Union and government technicians. The initial impetus for the fifteen regional unions and the Central Union came from below, from beneficiary-producers; Cárdenas not only approved the plan but also helped to convert the organization into a legal entity. President Cárdenas was so impressed by the La Laguna organization that he thought all future collectives should adopt a similar pattern (Rello 1984).

After months of preparation and labor mobilization, La Laguna agricultural workers finally were awarded *ejido* land grants on October 6, 1936. In the first few years, the La Laguna collectives were well supported by government agencies. Thus, their productivity was comparable and, in many cases, superior to that of former capitalist *haciendas*. This tendency lasted only through 1947 in La Laguna. (For more on this region, see Chapter 5.)

As in La Laguna, the collectives organized in the Yaqui Valley of southern Sonora also illustrate that production in the initial period was satisfactory. The confluence of widely available credit, technical assistance, and water resources in the first few postreform years pushed per-hectare yields from collective *ejidos* past those of private farms (see Chapters 5 and 7).

A collective *ejido* was also organized in Atencingo, Puebla. But here the story differs from that in the north. Those pressuring for land were not landless agricultural workers who lived as *peones acasillados* on their *haciendas;* they were peasants like those who had rebelled in Morelos under Zapata. In Atencingo peasants were still demanding redress for the dispossession of communal lands in the late 1800s.

The sugarcane-producing lands in question in Atencingo included nine villages that belonged to William Jenkins, a former U.S. consul in Puebla. Indeed, he had built an agroindustrial sugar empire of sorts: The harvested cane was destined for a sugar mill that he owned. In order to end the struggle of the *Zapatistas,* Jenkins decided to circumvent the problem by "donating" his cropland to the resident peons on his farm (Ronfeldt 1973; Paré 1979a).

The new *ejidatarios* were obliged to produce sugarcane and sell it to Jenkins's mill, thus guaranteeing him a continued supply and, perhaps, a more comfortable living than before. The Atencingo *ejidatarios* remained the mill's de facto peons as Jenkins played fast and loose with loopholes in the law. They were hired and fired as before and had no real rights over the new collective *ejido*. They lived from their wages only, since no profits were distributed to them between 1938 and 1947. Any grievances they had could be repressed, and corporal punishment was common. (The Atencingo region is discussed at length in Chapter 6.)

Cardenismo: *The End of the Agrarian Bourgeoisie?*

The 150 irrigated hectares (or the equivalent in lower-quality land) left to the former owners at the time of reform were always the best on the ex-*haciendas*. They left the proprietors with a precious enclave complemented by latent contacts with at least some of the agrarian-reform beneficiaries. It did not take long, therefore, for many landlords to renew their patron-client domination. Additional leverage was provided to them by the fact that *ejidatarios* often lacked the infrastructure, resources, and credit that, for a price, the *pequeños propietarios* could supply. The ensuing concentration of land and power often resulted in so much landlord domination that some observers have labeled this phenomenon *neolatifundismo* (Stavenhagen et al., 1968; Warman, 1975).

Thus *Cardenismo* did not really mean an end to the agrarian bourgeoisie; it did mean a restructuring of the power bloc (Contreras 1977). In a sense, *Cardenismo* created an opening into which the industrialists stepped with investment; they were abetted by an agreeable state. The state adopted its contemporary form and structure at that time. Personalistic politics of yesteryear were left behind in favor of more impersonal and institutional forms. For example, the man wearing the presidential sash could have extraordinary power, a situation that could last for only six years, however. (González Casanova 1964; Hellman 1983; Otero 1996a).

After 1938 the consolidated Mexican state geared up in earnest to promote industrialization. Because this meant acquiring large quantities of foreign exchange, agriculture had to be modernized rapidly; crops were to be exported to pay for industrial machinery, raw materials, and technology. The consolidation of this industrial hegemony in the power bloc was one of the new features of the two administrations which followed that of Lázaro Cárdenas, especially that of Miguel Alemán.

Alemanismo: Restructuring the Power Bloc Under the Hegemony of the Industrialists

The end of the peasant-oriented agrarian reform came in 1938. Cárdenas's reformism was limited by negative foreign reactions to the expropriation and nationalization of the petroleum industry and the resultant discontent of the internal bourgeoisie (Hamilton 1982). Thus, a development philosophy geared to the private sector set in before the end of the Cárdenas administration. Because World War II called for a policy of "national unity," Mexico awoke after the war to find that its working class and mass organizations had been coopted by the state. In particular, the National Peasant Confederation (*Confederación Nacional Campesina,* or CNC) and the Workers Confederation of Mexico (*Confederación de Trabajadores de México,* or CTM) were converted into governmental political arms so that the state could control peasants and workers, respectively. One additional target was the collective *ejido:* It had become a stronghold of opposition and socialist organization, and its example was threatening to private firms.

In the late 1940s the government's productivity drive was combined with a commitment to individualism. Collectivism was equated with the "threat of Communism," an epithet of the Cold War. This was a global change and, reflecting it, "the CNC took an increasingly individualistic position toward land tenure and exploitation during the 1940s, even joining with private property-owners in some states to pressure the regime for stabilization of land tenure." (Sanderson 1981, 138)

All this was anticipated in 1942 with two *ejido*-policy laws that sanctioned the individualistic tendencies: the Agrarian Code and the Law of Agricultural Credit. The former placed great emphasis on granting individual *ejido* title (which fell short of full ownership and a fee simple title) to each beneficiary.

The emphasis on security of possession and on titling accompanied bourgeois pressure for government to extend *certificados de inafectabilidad* (certificates of immunity) to landlords. These certificates were guarantees that holders would never be expropriated. To protect the livestock industry, the government granted to owners of large acreages certificates for "enough grazing land for 500 head of cattle" (or the equivalent in smaller livestock) or for "land without irrigation." When owners eventually improved their land, the immunity certificates still held, leaving some with substantial farms. Providing these certificates was central to the free-market spirit of the Alemán government. Clearly, several paragraphs of the Agrarian Code were amended to promote commercial agriculture. For this reason Alemán's presidential term has been called a "period of counterreform." His initiatives were further strengthened in later administrations. Under Alemán alone 11,957 certificates of immunity were granted to private landholders, safeguarding over a million hectares of privately held cropland. Also 336 certificates were granted to protect 3,449,000 hectares of grazing land. During the same period 56,108 peasants received only 3 million hectares of land, much of which was marginal and infertile (Gutelman 1974, 115–19).

Dismantling the Collective Ejidos

Although the legal strictures meant to dismantle collectives were in place by the end of 1942, government agencies did not generalize their campaign against them until 1947, at the beginning of Alemán's term (1946–52). Representatives of the Ejido Bank, the Ministry of Agriculture, and other governmental departments tried to convince *ejidatarios* that they could earn more by working their own plots without paying technical and managerial functionaries or contributing to a machinery fund (Hewitt de Alcántara 1978, 174).

Mexico's involvement in World War II resulted in its forging close economic and political ties with the United States during the wartime administration of Manuel Avila Camacho (1940–46). As we saw above, however, it was his successor, Miguel Alemán, who carried out the Cold War's extension in Mexico. The manner in which this hardening of ideological positions shaped state policy toward rural Mexico was dramatic. Not only was financial and technical support withdrawn from the collectives, but the *ejidos'* efforts to become self-managing enterprises were ignored by the government. During this period there was heavy federal expenditure for irrigation infrastructure (much of it to transform former pasturelands into cropland); large-scale, capitalist agriculture was given strong impetus under *Alemanismo*. Not by accident, irrigation was chosen as a primary vehicle for modernizing agriculture: It was the infrastructure most needed by the strongest agricultural pressure group in the country, the entrepreneurs of northwestern Mexico (Sanderson 1981, 154; de Grammont 1990; Mares 1987).

One of the more lamentable consequences of the crusade against the collective *ejido* was that even formerly productive ones began to disintegrate, a process that was never reversed. From 1938 to 1943 period, *ejidos* (both individual and collective) outproduced private farms by 9 percent. After the state withdrew its support from collectives (and indeed began a boycott against them), a dramatic reversal in production occurred. Hewitt de Alcántara (1978) and Silos-Alvarado (1968) present similar figures, which show deteriorating production yields for the post-Cárdenas period. From 1951 to 1955, the private sector began to show superior yields when compared with those on *ejidos* financed by the Ejido Bank. For 1956–60, the advantage of the private sector was accentuated (Silos-Alvarado 1968, 27–44). By 1960 private properties had a 25 percent yield advantage over *ejidos* (Hewitt de Alcántara 1978, 191).

The strength and type of attack on collectives varied regionally; the offensive was most severe where there was a local agrarian bourgeoisie pushing for counterreform. In La Laguna, the state eventually controlled most *ejido*-sector production, mainly through the Ejido Bank (now called Banrural, *Banco Nacional de Crédito Rural*). In El Yaqui, the agrarian bourgeoisie was consolidated, aided by huge public investments in irrigation infrastructure, while such infrastructure was largely denied to *ejidos*. Atencingo was the only collective *ejido* under state control in the entire state of Puebla. It represented a sort of state-capitalist island within a sea of peasant subsistence-production units, most of which were farmed only with family labor.

Alemán's policies consolidated the private-sector orientation that still prevails in Mexico, though there was a brief hiatus during Echeverría's administration. In addition to providing heavy investment in large-scale irrigation projects to benefit large farms, Alemán's presidency shifted a good deal of rural credit from the *ejido* to the private sector; gave strong impetus to the seed- and yield-improvement centers, which eventually became the linchpin of the Green Revolution; and emphasized production for export by downplaying the provision of ample foodstuffs for the domestic market (Sanderson 1981 145, 1986). All of these policies were consistent with the consolidation of the industrial bourgeoisie and the transformation of a tight alliance with its agrarian counterpart.

In the mid–1970s, the state tried to revitalize the *ejido*, but under the strict control of the state. During Luis Echeverría's presidential term (1970–1976), a few more collectives were established, but they were far from the self-managed, democratic cooperatives that Cárdenas had supported. Instead, they were a form of state-run enterprise (Warman 1977).

The *ejido* policy treated thus far has referred predominantly to those *ejidos* organized originally as "collectives" during *Cardenismo*. However, this kind of organization was implemented only in those places where modern *haciendas* had been expropriated. By 1970 collectives constituted only 12 percent of all *ejidos*. What happened to the vast majority of *ejidos*, which were organized on an individual basis form the outset?

A few *ejidatarios* managed to prosper from their individual *ejido* plots, often renting land belonging to their peers. But these were exceptions. Because most individual *ejidos* were in areas of rain-fed agriculture, they usually fared worse than the collectives. Individual *ejidos*, in fact, constituted a *minifundio* sector.

Ann Craig (1983) has documented the agrarian history of Los Altos de Jalisco as a case in point. She argues convincingly that the *ejidos* in this region are representative of most in the country. As Craig notes, Los Altos de Jalisco is a region "characterized by poor soil and highly variable rainfall, devout Catholicism, conservative politics, and an economy based on dairy farming and small scale cultivation of maize, beans and chile." (1983, 13)

Unemployment in Los Altos is still a major problem, and today there are more landless young men and families than *ejidatarios* in most municipalities of the region (Craig 1983, 245). Agriculture has provided so few rewards and so much hardship that young men now speak more about the need for sources of nonagricultural employment in the countryside than about land. Such perceptions are reinforced by short-term work experiences in Mexican urban centers and in the United States. Thus, in this kind of agricultural region, wage labor is highly valued by rural people, but not enough is offered. The region's *hacienda* class, in contrast, adapted quickly to new conditions after land reform; today, its members are still wealthy.[1]

Are Small Peasant Operations Economically Productive?

Several economists have defended the Mexican agrarian reform, arguing that the "social productivity" of small holdings was greater than that of large landholdings (Barchfield 1979; Dvoring 1969). They assume that family labor costs can be calculated at zero for the *ejido* sector and for private holdings of 5 hectares or less, where family members provide the bulk of the required labor power. Thus, they calculate an inverse relationship between size of the farm and land productivity; they apply "social productivity" labor costs only to capitalist enterprises, where wages are monetary and an actual operating cost to the employer. Their justification for this assumption is that, in societies such as Mexico, where there is an "unlimited" supply of labor, opportunity costs are close to nil. Dvoring acknowledges that the greater production per hectare in *ejidos* and *minifundios* is due to greater labor-intensiveness.

This approach, which focuses only on the macroeconomic or "social" productivity aspects, disregards the economic consequences for the individual economic unit. As recent Mexican experience can attest, such an approach has proved myopic, even at the macroeconomic level. In the long run what appeared to be macroeconomically productive resulted in agrarian crisis.[2] For the peasant economy, providing free labor to society has had its limit—witness the agrarian movement of the early 1970s and the renewed activity of the 1990s.

Thus, the agrarian reform has not been able to solve the problems of the rural poor in Mexico. Capitalist development in agriculture expelled a large number of workers, while industrial growth has been insufficient to absorb them. In fact, the optimistic expectations that politicians had in the 1940s about industry and employment never materialized at the required levels. Large numbers in the countryside have been forced to confront counterreform and an industrialization process incapable of absorbing their labor power productively. The result, as we will see in Chapter 4, has been social polarization. Before going into this topic, though, I will turn to the most recent agrarian-reform legislation in Mexico.

Neoliberalism and the New Agricultural Policies

Chapter 2 discusses state intervention as one of three major variables determining political class formation in Mexico's countryside. Depending on whether it favored the social reproduction of agricultural direct producers or not, bourgeois-hegemonic, oppositional, or popular-democratic organizations would arise. This pattern was clearly true from the 1930s to the 1980s, as we will see in Chapters 5 to 7. Toward the end of the last decade, however, new national and international winds effected major changes in the state's approach toward its own intervention. Abandoning an inward-looking economy based on heavy protectionism, state intervention in the economy, subsidies, and deficit financing, Mexico's technocratic governments since 1982 have done a dramatic about-face to reposition the country in the international economy. Now the key goals are to eliminate direct state intervention in the economy, subsidies, and protectionism, and to promote market forces, international competition, and foreign investment. "As the economy makes the transition from a state-guided and paternalistic economy toward a more ruthless and market-driven one, high rates of joblessness and income inequality will be facts of life." (Bremner and Ihlwan 1998, 47) Much of this "neoliberal" reorientation of economic policy toward market-led dynamics has been imposed from the outside through the "structural adjustment" packages that Mexican officials had to sign with the International Monetary Fund and the World Bank in order to resolve the debt crisis of the early 1980s (Otero 1996a). Yet it is clear that much of Mexico's private-sector and government officials have supported and indeed promoted such reorientation (Valdéz Ugalde 1996).

By 1991 Mexican agriculture contributed only about 7 percent of GDP with over 25 percent of the economically active people, a disparity that reflected a tremendous technological lag and the deep fragmentation of land tenure. The rural development strategy that had been followed by the Mexican state was predicated on an overwhelming and pervasive presence of the state, which intervened through diverse means—including selective indirect subsidies—that were usually regressive (i.e., deepened social and economic inequality). The *ejido*, as discussed above, was the main form of land tenure assigned to the beneficiaries of agrarian reform, who could not rent or sell the land. But the *ejido* also functioned as a means of corporatist political control since the 1940s and was heavily subsidized until the late 1980s. This form of corporatism also ceased to be efficient after democratization winds began to blow following the student and popular movement of 1968.

Hence, President Carlos Salinas de Gortari (1988–94) set out to introduce another agrarian reform in 1992. Its three main components were as follows:

(1) Land in *ejidos* could now be sold or rented; (2) the state no longer had the responsibility for redistributing land; and (3) while limits for individual landholding were kept to 100 hectares (1 hectare = 2.4 acres), corporations could operate as much as 2,500 hectares as long as at least twenty-five individuals were associate members and none exceeded the individual landholding limit of one hundred hectares. This agrarian reform was combined with other neoliberal policies, including deregulation of the agricultural economy; the transfer of former state enterprises to the private sector; the elimination of most subsidies; a severe restriction of agricultural credit and insurance; and a swift unilateral trade opening in basic crops such as sorghum, soy, and other processed and semiprocessed food products (Cornelius and Myhre 1998; Encinas R. de la Fuente, Mackinlay, and Romero 1995; García Zamora 1997). Therefore, this neoliberal reform as a whole represents a new model for the *ejido:* It is now free of state tutelage, but it is also deprived of nearly all state support. Nevertheless, the *ejido* could still become an organization of peasant support around which peasants could mobilize to obtain state support, but this initiative would have to emerge from below.

Established under the agrarian reform, the *ejido* sector was where the state intervened in most phases of production and distribution—from planning and provision of inputs to marketing. Such intervention is now being replaced by the market as the main mechanism for resource allocation. All subsidies for crop prices and agricultural inputs will be gradually eliminated by 2009. Credit has been substantially reduced, most marketing agencies of the state have been phased out, and direct price regulation has been replaced by trade liberalization for most crops.

The rest of this chapter explores the socioeconomic implications of these changes for Mexican rural society. Abandoning the state-led approach, the new policies single out market forces, productivity, and profitability as the key criteria for producers' decisions about resource allocation. The new policies seek to enhance Mexico's competitiveness in the global economy and to line up Mexican agriculture with the requirements of both the North American Free Trade Agreement (NAFTA) and the World Trade Organization (WTO). But the new agricultural policies are likely to promote a profound social polarization (see Chapter 4), since it is unlikely that the rest of the economy will grow quickly enough to absorb the labor force that will become redundant in agriculture.

Even though the state has traditionally expected agroindustries to conform to capitalist criteria, most land cultivators became accustomed to compensatory state intervention in agriculture. Now most Mexican land cultivators confront increasing pressures to meet the test of the market even though they lack capital and are not accustomed to the rigors of market forces and profit margins. The new agricultural policies can thus be expected to promote a new wave of bankruptcies that will force peasants to sell their lands and will expand the reserve army of unemployed workers in the cities. In fact, the labor surplus resulting from agricultural bankruptcies will far exceed the usual "function" of a reserve army of labor in capital accumulation.

Such "liberation" of workers from agriculture will have a threefold effect. First, there will be a process of land concentration in fewer hands; marginal lands might be abandoned indefinitely, while other peasants will continue to cultivate at greater social and environmental cost. Family members normally involved chiefly in household reproduction will be forced to take part in remunerated agricultural tasks; hence, the "feminization" of agricultural production—a growing phenomenon since the 1970s (Arizpe 1989; Preibisch 1996)—will no doubt increase, as will the intensification of the labor of school-age children and elderly persons.

Second, the expansion of unemployed workers will allow market forces to replace political repression as the chief means of exerting downward pressure on wages. In turn, low wages will continue to lure new waves of direct foreign investment into the NAFTA framework of industry and services. Third, the excess of unemployed population beyond the functional needs for an "industrial reserve army" in capital accumulation is likely to heat up already-simmering social tensions, possibly discouraging new foreign investment. One countervailing trend to the effects of neoliberalism, however, is that many peasants are taking refuge in subsistence agriculture, even if it means greater impoverishment (de Janvry, Godrillo, and Sadoulet 1997).

Mexico's Second Agrarian Reform by Alain de Janvry et al. lays a firm quantitative foundation for many widely held views on the peasant economy. Although the land market was legally opened only in 1992, some activity was captured by the 1994 survey—one of two on which this book is based (the other was conducted in 1990): Of the five regions into which Mexico was divided, the land market was most active in the gulf, center, and north; and it was least developed in the south Pacific, where very small farms dominate. There was also a slight increase—from 2.5 to 4.8 percent—in the percentage of *ejidatarios* holding private land.

Even though NAFTA has introduced a comparative advantage for the production of fruits and vegetables on Mexico's farms, the *ejido's* ability to adapt is limited by lack of access to credit and technical assistance. Hence, corn and beans, which remain the only crops with some state subsidy, are by far the most important crops: They occupied 57 percent of the total cultivated land in the *ejido* in 1994. State support for farmers has fallen off sharply: By 1994 only 8.6 percent of *ejidatarios* had some technical assistance, down from 59.6 percent in 1990. They were left in an institutional vacuum just when they needed to diversify and modernize to take advantage of NAFTA. Unless this vacuum is filled, neoliberal reforms threaten the competitiveness and solvency of the *ejido* (de Janvry, Godrillo, and Sadoulet 1997, 86).

The state dramatically decreased its support to farmers in credit and insurance between 1990 and 1994; access to loans increased through Pronasol (*Programa Nacional de Solidaridad,* or National Solidarity Program), a social assistance program. But the mass of credit to the sector declined, and access to credit was thus diluted over a larger number of users. This trend is confirmed by David Myhre's studies of the financial system in rural Mexico (1998; 1996). Myhre says, for instance, that the

> reorganization of the rural financial system has simply replaced one 'sad story' with another. Until reorganization strategies are implemented that do not a priori exclude half of Mexico's rural population from financial services, the prospects for a happy ending are few (1996, 136).

The most ironic social trend observed in the book by de Janvry et al. is the emergence of an entrepreneurial peasantry in the *ejido* sector, something that should have resulted from the original agrarian reform but was stifled by an overly interventionist state. With the neoliberal reform, entrepreneurship in the countryside is bolstered by peasant strategies that offer the prospect of survival if not success: monocropping corn in the fall-winter cycle, diversifying into fruits and vegetables, increasing cattle raising, and reinforcing the migration strategy. The first strategy was most concentrated in the north Pacific region; the second in the gulf; while cattle raising was more spread out into gulf, south Pacific, and center; and migration concentrated in the north and center regions. The determinants of success, however, were access to credit, irrigation, pastures and common lands, increased education, access to technology, and access to migration social networks. Since most of these were in short supply—especially credit—only a small percentage of farmers managed to pursue entrepreneurial strategies.

De Janvry's inequality chapter contains a sophisticated quantitative analysis that reaches a number of strong conclusions:

> The ejidos with the smallest internal inequality compared to external inequality were those in the Center and North, those with a mestizo majority, and those with the oldest [land] endowments. In contrast, it was the indigenous communities that had the highest internal inequality. In this case two-thirds of total inequality was internal to the community, and only one-third external. The communities thus have the dual characteristic of consisting of very small farms with large internal differences (de Janvry, Godrillo, and Sadoulet 1997, 167).

The End of Agrarian Reform

Under the state-led period of agriculture, most Mexican peasants gave their loyalty to the ruling PRI and the government in exchange for social guarantees and minimum incomes (Fowly 1991; Gates 1993; Bartra 1993; Singelmann and Otero 1995). Until 1992, article 27 of the Mexican Constitution (1917) had reflected a solid state-peasant alliance for over seven decades. It provided for the agrarian reform by granting the state the right to redistribute land to poor peasants and rural workers. Through a series of state-run agencies and programs, most land cultivators came to depend on state intervention in agriculture, from technical assistance and loans to marketing and the transformation of agricultural products. It was the *ejido* sector that came to depend most closely on the state, thus reinforcing the historical state-peasant alliance (Warman 1976).

Through the agrarian reform program, 28,058 "*ejidos*" or "agrarian communities" had been formed by 1988.[3] Other than private property, these were the two forms of land tenure that emerged in the wake of article 27 and its enabling laws. Together, *ejidos* and agrarian communities made up the agrarian reform or the "social" sector, comprising 3,070,906 individuals who held rights to 95,108,066 hectares (one hectare = 2.47 acres). This land surface amounts to nearly 50 percent of the grazing, agricultural, and forest land in the country. However, only 21 percent of this land is suitable for agriculture. Because of the poor quality of land distributed, as much as 73 percent of total land in the agrarian reform sector is held communally, whether in *ejidos* or agrarian communities, in such forms as shared pasture or forest land (DeWalt, Rees, and Murphy 1994, 4; Mackinlay 1994, 18).

While Mexican agriculture experienced a relative boom from the late 1930s to the mid-1960s, a severe crisis emerged both in peasant and in capitalist agriculture by the late 1960s (Bartra and Otero 1987; Bartra 1993; chapter 4 in this volume). In view of this crisis, some organizations in the private sector became quite vocal in proposing the privatization of the *ejido* lands, arguing that this would provide landholders with security of tenure: Private holders would no longer feel threatened by agrarian reform, while *ejidatarios* themselves would no longer feel dependent on the state.

But it was not until 1992 that a revision of article 27 formally declared an end to agrarian reform. It allows for the privatization of *ejido* land, permits rental of land and its use as collateral for loans from private banks, and promotes the formation of associations between *ejidatarios* and private enterprises (Barry 1995; Cornelius 1992; DeWalt, Rees, and Murphy 1994). To supplement these legal changes, the government has launched a new set of policies to eliminate agricultural subsidies, redefine criteria for rural credit by the official bank (Banrural), and dissolve or drastically reduce the funding of state-regulatory agencies in agriculture.

In practice, the Mexican state all but ended agrarian reform during the administration of José Lopez Portillo (1976–82), when agricultural policy was geared toward increasing production. But this administration also inaugurated two agricultural policies with different implications for promoting peasant production: the Mexican Food System (*Sistema Alimentario Mexicano*, or SAM) and the Agricultural and Livestock Promotion Law (or *Ley de Fomento Agropecuario*, LFA). The SAM tried to increase production by supporting peasants in rain-fed agriculture, while the LFA promoted the association between *ejidatarios* and capitalists who would modernize agriculture through new investments. The main beneficiaries of the SAM were medium and large farmers, not the small peasants of rain-fed agriculture who were originally targeted (Redclift 1981; Fox 1993).

In contrast to the SAM, the LFA openly established the legal conditions for private capital to enter agriculture decisively. This law was supposed to complement the official discourse on agrarian reform and declared that there was no more land to redistribute. Consequently, the rural population was supposed to concentrate on making its landholdings more productive with an infusion of capital investments from the private sector. Throughout the 1980s, however, no more than 110 associations emerged under the LFA along these lines (DeWalt, Rees, and Murphy 1994, 57).

Changing Role of the State

The Mexican state made its presence felt and controlled agriculture through multiple forms until recently. Besides the cabinet secretariats dealing with this sector, there were a number of other key "economic apparatuses of the state" devoted to agriculture. These included the Rural Bank (Banrural), Conasupo (the agency controlling the purchase of basic crops and distribution of popular foods, including basic crops), and Anagsa (the agricultural and livestock insurance state company) (Rello 1986). During the Echeverría administration, these agencies became large and notoriously corrupt bureaucracies. Rather than helping peasant production, they became effective means of economic and political control in the countryside (Gordillo 1988).

Along with the elimination of or fundamental change in most agencies related to agriculture, subsidies to crop and inputs prices are being phased out. According to the Salinas government assessment, with the policy of subsidies, farmers with the best lands tended to benefit disproportionately, a circumstance that often resulted in higher crop and food prices. Thus, consumers were also negatively affected by past forms of subsidies, which often resulted in higher crop and food prices. Because agricultural prices tended to be higher than international prices after the 1970s, past subsidies introduced an important market distortion, sustaining too many producers who had high production costs. Such policy-created distortion became clearly inconsistent with the trend toward globalization and North American integration in which the main logic is increased efficiency, reduced state intervention, and international competitiveness.

Another kind of distortion introduced by support prices (*precios de garantía*) had to do with crop choices: Some farmers tended to adopt subsidized crops in lands that could be better used for other, more profitable, crops—for example, in the north and northwest regions, which have an abundance of irrigated land, the surface dedicated to corn increased from 451,000 hectares in 1989 to 907,000 in 1992 (SARH n/d, 20). Conversely, poor farmers went into corn production through deforestation or by planting on slopes and other marginal lands with extremely low fertility.

In the past few years many state agencies have seen their regulatory roles fundamentally altered or eliminated. Banrural has become merely one more bank that can grant agricultural loans (using clear market and profitability criteria) alongside all the other commercial banks. Its former "social" function, expressed in routinely forgiving peasants in default (Gates 1993, 1996) has been absorbed by Pronasol. This new program was initiated on the first day that Carlos Salinas de Gortari took office as president of Mexico on December 1, 1988. It was designed to combat poverty through direct handouts given by the executive through municipal presidents (Cornelius, Craig, and Fox 1994). This program replaced much of the former action of corporatist organizations affiliated with the PRI and linked the urban and rural poor directly to the head of the federal executive, the president. As a political strategy, the program represented a response to the hotly contested presidential elections of 1988 and the rise of the opposition headed by Cuauhtemoc Cárdenas (Mackinlay 1994, 109; Otero 1996a).

Likewise, Conasupo is still engaged in the marketing of agricultural products, but state policy has now shifted to favor producer initiatives to cover such functions. Furthermore, Conasupo will no longer absorb distribution and transportation costs, as in the past; these will be charged to the producers as an additional incentive for them to organize their own distribution efforts.

Other state agencies have been completely eliminated—witness the dissolution of Imecafé, once involved in the planning and marketing of coffee production (Downing 1988), and of Azúcar, S.A., which centralized the planning, production, and distribution of the sugar industry, including the management of most sugar mills (Singelmann 1993, 1995). The agricultural and livestock state insurance company has been renamed Agroasemex, and its insurance functions now match the commercial criteria of private companies.

New Agricultural Policies: Procampo

Procampo (*Programa de Apoyo a la Comercialización Ejidal* or Support Program for Ejido Marketing) was launched in 1993 to support producers' income through direct subsidies, thus reversing the past logic of indirect agricultural subsidies through supported crop prices and lower input costs. With the latter forms of subsidies, all producers benefited regardless of their capital or land endowments, with the better-off farmers benefiting disproportionately. The goal of Procampo is thus twofold: to promote the production of crops in which Mexican farmers have a comparative advantage and to funnel subsidies only to those producers that need them the most.

The first goal is addressed by providing a fixed, per-hectare support to those producers who have been planting one of nine basic crops in any of the three years prior to the initiation of this program in 1993: corn, beans, wheat, cotton, soybeans, sorghum, rice, safflower, and coffee. Supports go directly to producers' income rather than to crop or input prices, thus reducing market distortions.

Producers were declared eligible for support for fifteen years after the 1994 implementation, regardless of whether they continue to plant the same crop or change the productive activity on their land. One condition is that the land remain dedicated to a productive activity that creates employment. The hope is that by not ordaining the crop to which the land should be devoted, farmers will choose crops in response to market signals and to the "natural vocation" of the land. During the first ten years the per-hectare support will be fixed in real terms, and thereafter it will gradually decrease until the fifteenth year. In 1994 all price subsidies disappeared in Mexico, except for corn and beans (de Janvry, Gordillo, and Sadoulet 1994). On January 1, 1999, even the longstanding tortilla subsidy was eliminated. As is well known, corn tortillas are a staple of the Mexican diet.

The second of Procampo's goals is to address an acute dilemma of previous subsidies: Out of over 3 million agricultural producers, 2.2 million were being left on the margin of price supports because they usually dedicate a significant proportion of their production—over 58 percent—to self-consumption. Therefore, to the extent that their products did not become commodities bearing a price, subsidies in the form of price supports could not reach this kind of producer. The new form of subsidy has involved increased federal expenditures, absolutely and relatively: In 1994 Procampo had a budget of 11.7 billion new pesos, in contrast with 5.3 billion spent in 1993.

A central objective of this policy change was to make the adjustments necessary to put Mexico in line with international accords and its international trading partners. Most of the nine crops included in Procampo are also subsidized in North American and European countries. But in line with international accords such as NAFTA and the WTO, two basic principles had to be respected: (1) that subsidies do not involve a transfer from consumers, and (2) that the new support does not have the effect of becoming a price support for producers. Meeting these two criteria is supposed to guarantee that international agricultural markets will not be distorted by the support policy (SARH n/d, 25).

Other expectations of Procampo are that producers will switch to the most rational forms of land use. Those currently overexploiting marginal lands are expected to switch to the more "natural vocation" of such lands (such as forestry) to avoid deforestation and land erosion. Conversely, those producers with better lands will switch to more profitable crops with comparative advantages to increase Mexico's export capacity while reducing the amount of agrochemicals used in the production of corn in good lands. In both cases it is expected that the change will result in environmentally sounder practices.

In spite of the fact that both Pronasol and Procampo represent substantial expenditures for the Mexican state, they both act more as welfare safety nets rather than as spurs to production (Covarruvias Patiño 1996, 110). For example, while Pronasol covers about 2.5 million hectares of corn cultivated by poor small producers, it still represents a per-hectare loan several times lower than that assigned by Banrural (Appendini 1994; de Janvry, Gordillo, and Sadoulet 1997). Furthermore, Procampo is incapable of redressing income inequalities stemming from unequal access to land endowments. According to a survey conducted in 1994 by INEGI (*Instituto Nacional de Estadística, Geografía y Informática,* or National Institute of Statistics, Geography, and Information), 70.5 percent of *ejidatarios* who received Procampo assistance were concentrated in the range of 1–5 hectares plots and got an average of 2.6 times the program assistance. *Ejidatarios* with an average plot of 6–10 hectares, 20.9 percent of the total, received an average of 7.7 times; while those with over 21 hectares, representing only 1.5 percent of *ejidatarios,* received 39 times the program assistance (Covarruvias Patiño 1996, 109). Procampo nevertheless reaches those corn producers growing corn for subsistence who did not benefit from support prices in the past. But the paltry amounts of assistance cannot transform a production process, much less significantly cushion the blows felt by Mexican peasants from the restructuring of agriculture and the economy as a whole through their links to labor and commodity markets.

Conclusions

Neoliberal policies in Mexican agriculture have introduced sweeping changes for land cultivators. Agricultural direct producers have had to face a rude awakening from the decades of protectionism and state intervention in agriculture. This does not mean that they had been particularly privileged in the previous decades, for Mexican agriculture had been geared to subsidize industrial expansion since the 1940s by keeping urban costs of living low. This urban bias signified an increasingly unbearable cost-price squeeze, with rising input costs and declining relative crop prices.

By the mid–1960s, Mexican agriculture entered into a period of severe crisis from which it has yet to recover, resulting in high degrees of social differentiation. Today, few cultivators are adequately prepared to compete by international standards. Therefore, one should expect to see tremendous challenges in the era of NAFTA for the Mexican agricultural semiproletariat. For the state, the main challenge will be political, to the extent that the new policies have, de facto and de jure, dissolved the basis for the long-standing "state-peasant" alliance.

Procampo was designed less than a year before the 1994 presidential elections, primarily as a continued safety net for the poorest peasants in exchange for their political loyalty. Thus, at least two doubts have been raised about the state's success with Procampo: (1) It is quite unlikely that the supports of Mex$250 per hectare on a yearly basis (starting in 1994) will become a production-enhancement program for small producers, who are generally at an infrasubsistence level. It is more likely that this program will supplement Pronasol, with the assistance-oriented and electoral overtones that have been assigned to this program by analysts (A. Bartra 1996; Cornelius, Craig, and Fox 1994; Dresser 1991); (2) contrary to expressed intent, both small and large farmers are likely to remain involved in environmentally damaging practices (DeWalt, Rees, and Murphy 1994). In the case of small farmers, there is no reason to believe that the small-income support will be enough to deter them from producing in degraded or deforested lands. Likewise, medium and large farmers might simply transfer and even increase the use of agrochemicals in switching from corn to more commercial and export-oriented crops.

Thus, new dilemmas will emerge for the state when the assistance-oriented and political face of such programs becomes evident and once it is clear that a majority of rural producers are being left on the margins of mainstream economic development. As new government programs prove insufficient to turn them into peasant-entrepreneurs or provide feasible alternatives to land cultivation within the countryside, new government challenges will also arise in the area of employment insufficiency in industry and services. Such insufficiency is likely to become socially explosive, especially after nearly two decades of declining real incomes for the majority of the Mexican population and an official poverty rate of about 50 percent that runs even higher in the countryside and was aggravated by the economic debacle that started in December 1994 with the devaluation of the Mexican currency. It remains to be seen whether the next decade will represent a rerun of this one, but this time starting from a lower floor of poverty for most Mexicans.

Notes

1. Monique Nuijten (1998) provides a detailed account of the actual organization and functioning of the *ejido* in southern Jalisco and its relations with the state. Her story largely resembles that of Los Altos de Jalisco. For his part, Gabriel Torres (1997) offers a microsociological analysis of "everyday forms of resistance" by tomato workers in southern Jalisco. For the state of Michoacan, John Gledhill (1995) discusses migration strategies to the United States by impoverished peasant farmers.

2. For a more extended critique of this position, see R. Bartra (1974a, 1993), and R. Bartra and Otero (1987).

3. "Agrarian communities" was the legal tenure form divised to "restitute" Indian communities that had been displaced from their lands during the *Porfiriato*. In the end, however, many Indian communities received land in the form of *ejidos*, and many *mestizos* received land in the form of "agrarian communities."

4

Agrarian Transformations:
Crisis and Social Differentiation

The purpose of this chapter is to show how the process of depeasantization has proceeded in the Mexican countryside, both nationally and regionally. I will address the main causes and outcomes of this process: A double crisis of capitalist agriculture and peasant economy has resulted in an important social differentiation (or stratification) among the peasantry. Such differentiation, however, has not resulted in a proportionate proletarianization. Instead, a large semiproletariat, torn between wage-labor and peasant production, has arisen as the largest rural group. Thus, as the peasant economy continues to deteriorate, creating a process of depeasantization, capitalist agriculture and industry have been unable to fully proletarianize the increasingly land-deprived masses.

The first section outlines the basic contours of what I call the double crisis of Mexican agriculture, one referring to the capitalist sector, the other to the peasant economy. A close insight is provided into this double crisis through an analysis of cash crops in contrast with subsistence crops. This analysis is divided into two main policy periods. The first is 1940–83, when import-substitution industrialization policies prevailed within a relatively closed economy that featured protectionism and subsidies for several industries and some basic crops. The second period is 1984–95, when neoliberal economic policies were introduced involving an open market toward international trade and investment and the elimination of most subsidies (except for maize and beans in agriculture). The second section presents a spectrum of social differentiation of agrarian producers in Mexico, based on the 1970 census data. Then, by contrasting the 1970 situation with that of 1960, I show the extent to which the peasant economy had been eroded by that year and how the semiproletariat constitutes the largest agrarian group. Next, the census data from 1960 and 1970 are plotted in a graph, along with those data from a survey of the *ejido* sector, conducted by the CEPAL in 1990 and 1994 (de Janvry et al. 1997). This analysis will reveal that the basic structure of differentiation is still there but that some land reconcentration is beginning to take place among the middle strata of direct producers, while many of the poorest are abandoning agriculture. Finally, a brief overview is provided as to how capitalist development has affected the spectrum of social differentiation regionally: A contrast is presented among the states in which our three regions are located.

The Double Crisis of Mexican Agriculture

The crises of Mexico's rural economy, with capitalist agriculture on the one hand and peasant farming on the other, have resulted in social differentiation among the peasantry within a capitalism that has not expanded the proletarian class proportionately. As the peasant economy continues to deteriorate, depeasantization occurs: Increasing numbers of peasants are separated from their means of production and pushed onto a wage-labor market that is incapable of productively absorbing them (Coello 1981).

The first problem for the peasant economy emerged with increased commercialization of agricultural production. From 1940 to 1970, the proportion of output sold by all production units in the country rose from 53.6 percent to 87 percent. If this jump seems impressive, it is all the more so considering that most of the change took place during the first decade of the period. In fact, the percentage of production sold in the market increased from 53.6 percent in 1940 to 82.1 percent in 1950. After the *Cardenista* agrarian reform, most agricultural production passed through the national market.

Of course, there are differences in the proportion of total output sold by the various land tenure types (see Table 4.1).[1] In general, private production units with more than five hectares always sold a greater percentage of their output than any other type of producer; performance on these private farms was closely followed by *ejidal* units. Private operations of five hectares or less, the vast majority of them being peasant units, show more erratic behavior. In 1950 they sold a greater proportion of output than did the *ejidos* (78.7 percent versus 72.4 percent), but in 1960 the percentage fell to 67, only to increase again in 1970 to 81 percent.

Reliance on the market, especially after the late 1960s and early 1970s, made the peasant economy more vulnerable than before. Increased commercialization

TABLE 4.1 Percentage of Production Sold by Land-Tenure Type, 1940–70[a]

Tenure Type	1940	1950	1960	1970
Total	53.6	82.1	82.0	87.0
> 5 hectares	55.7	89.4	87.0	88.2
≤ 5 hectares	40.0	78.7	67.0	81.0
Ejidos	54.2	72.4	77.0	86.2

[a] *SOURCE:* Elaborated from Dirección General de Estadística, *Censo agrícola-ganadero y ejidal, 1940; 1950; 160; 1970* (Mexico: DGE, n.d.).

in agriculture demonstrated the contradictions of a peasant economy developing in a capitalist context.

The decade of the 1970s began with decreases in production in most crops. Corn production (which stagnated in the mid-1960s) collapsed in 1972, and crop output was not really satisfactory again until the early 1980s—and then, only briefly. A similar pattern occurred with beans (Bartra and Otero 1987, 342–50).

Commercial crops such as cotton, sesame, sugarcane, and tomatoes also were in crisis in the early 1970s. For cotton and sesame, there was no recovery during the early 1980s. The cash crops that did best were directly linked to agribusiness with export interests: citrus, pineapples, and strawberries. "All these commodities grew rapidly, while the basic foodstuffs sector barely grew at all." (Sanderson 1986, 279) The growth of these cash crops, which might be referred to as "luxury foodstuffs," along with the growth of grain production for feeding livestock, reflected the internationalization of Mexican agriculture (Sanderson 1986; Barkin and DeWalt 1988).

Mexican cities absorb major quantities of corn, making it possible for peasants who produce and sell it to purchase industrial products indispensable to life in the countryside. On farms, corn is usually stored as insurance against bad times. Thus, when corn prices rise, less of it is required to achieve a balance between work and consumption (Chayanov 1974). But if corn prices fall, then peasant families must expand their labor efforts to obtain more corn. For given capital scarcity and low land quality, peasants cannot shift their production to other crops easily. And since access to land is usually restricted, peasants can rely only on extending the use of the single resource over which they have control: domestic labor power.[2]

In a few years, Mexico's agriculture went from providing ample foreign exchange necessary for industrialization to an inability to feed its own population (Sanderson 1986). For this reason, the José López Portillo administration (1976–82) implemented the Mexican Food System (*Sistema Alimentario Mexicano,* or SAM) in 1980, a strategy to gain self-sufficiency in basic grain production (*Nueva Antropología* 1981; Fox 1992). Although the official declarations presumed that self-sufficiency would follow from strengthening the peasant economy in rain-fed agricultural zones, most production increases really took place in irrigation districts. This result indicates that government subsidies for some inputs were so high that members of the agrarian bourgeoisie seized the opportunity to profit from basic grains. In fact, production rose markedly for both beans and corn in 1980 (Redclift 1981).

Mexicans were paying dearly for these production increases, it turns out; for they involved massive subsidies. And, while there was some progress in food self-sufficiency, it was transitory—the results in 1982 were disappointing, partly because of a lower-than-normal rainfall. When Miguel de la Madrid took office in December of 1982, SAM was abandoned.

Despite the fact that the 1960s witnessed a large redistribution of land, the erosion of the peasant economy was considerable. Part of the reason was that poor land was distributed during the Gustavo Díaz Ordáz presidency (1964–70). While

25 million hectares were distributed, a larger quantity than under Cárdenas, only about 10 percent (2.4 million) was arable. In contrast, Cárdenas distributed close to 18 million hectares of which almost 5 million or 28 percent was arable. Thus, the Díaz Ordáz agrarian reform reduced the proportion of arable land in *ejidos* from 23.2 percent in 1960 to 18.3 percent in 1970 (Gutelman 1974).

By 1970 many small agricultural producers were no longer able to sustain themselves by relying only on their farmland. The process of semiproletarianization was already under way: Increasing numbers of rural producers were caught between insufficient peasant production and a wage-labor market offering few alternative employment opportunities.

Hence, the 1970s saw the beginning of a simultaneous explosion of two crises: an accelerated retrogression in the living standards of small peasants and a fall in export prices that profoundly affected the commercial sector. Politically, these trends sparked renewed struggles for land among peasant producers (A. Bartra 1979b; Otero 1981, 1983).

Structural Differentiation of Agricultural Direct Producers

The purpose of this section is to present an analysis of peasant social differentiation in Mexico between 1960 and 1994. The empirical information comes from several studies specified below. The methodological discussion, though, focuses on the study carried out by a group of researchers from The United Nations Economic Commission for Latin America and the Caribbean (*Comisión Económica para América Latina y el Caribe,* or CEPAL), using the 1970 Mexican census of population and agriculture (CEPAL 1982). The project was led by the economist Alejandro Schejtman. Although the data are old, this study demonstrates the extent to which the peasantry was already differentiated by 1970, when Mexico's agricultural crisis was already evident to policy makers and analysts alike. Furthermore, by comparing this study to a previous one based on the 1960 census, I will show that the middle sectors of the peasantry were disappearing.

The methodology of this study has also been the basis for two more recent surveys conducted by CEPAL: one in collaboration with the Ministry of Agriculture and Water Resources in 1990, and the other with the Ministry of Agrarian Reform in 1994, as reported by de Janvry, Gordillo, and Sadoulet (1997).

One of the goals of the 1982 CEPAL study was to device a typology in order to distinguish between peasant and entrepreneurial farms and then to specify the various strata within these broad categories. CEPAL's assumption was that small peasant farms work under a different rationality from capitalistic agricultural enterprises. The latter seek to maximize profits as the prime motive of production, whereas peasant units seek to maximize the economic return to family labor power, since subsistence is the peasant family's prime objective. Therefore, peasant farming operations are usually much more labor-intensive than those of capitalist enterprises.

TABLE 4.2   Mexico: Distribution of Agricultural Direct Producers in CEPAL's Typology, 1970 (percentages)

Type of Production Unit*	Stratum Within Type	Percent
Peasant	I infrasubsistence	55.6
	II subsistence	16.2
	III stationary	6.5
	IV surplus-producing	8.2
Transitional	V transitional	11.6
Entrepreneurial	VI small	1.2
	VII medium	0.4
	VIII large	0.3

SOURCE: CEPAL. 1982. *Economía Campesina y Agricultura Empresarial (Tipología de Productores del Agro Mexicano)*, by Alejandro Schejtman, Mexico: Siglo XXI Editores, 118–19.

* Total Number of Units = 2,557,070

Table 4.2, above, depicts the summarized distribution of agricultural production units in Mexico, according to CEPAL's typology. The figures of the *ejido* and private land-tenure sectors have been merged, because the pattern of social differentiation is similar in both tenure systems (CEPAL 1982, 278–281). Entrepreneurial producers are concentrated in the private sector. Merging the data for the two systems gives the best overall picture of social-structure differentiation in rural Mexico, but, when the two are combined, the proportion of "entrepreneurs" declines.

CEPAL used two central criteria to distinguish between peasant and entrepreneurial categories in its typology: (1) Did the farm unit hire wage labor? (2) Did the farm attain or exceed subsistence production levels? "Peasant units" were those that worked with family labor and occasionally hired wage labor. "Hiring" was measured by wage payments which were not to exceed the equivalent of twenty-five working days per year (calculated by the yearly expenditure in wages and divided by the daily legal minimum wage in each region or state). Most peasant units do hire some workers beyond the family during a few days at harvest. And members of such *minifundio* farms usually sell their own labor power to other peasant households for a few days a year. This exchange of labor power is, in many cases, the monetized form of previous reciprocity relations in peasant communities.

In order to build the various strata, several types of needs were defined for peasant units to determine which units were able to meet what type of needs. Two such types were subsistence needs and needs for the replacement of means of production. Food requirements were thus defined as the main priority for peasant families, which averaged 5.5 members each. Calculations were made to specify the minimum nutritional needs in terms of calories and proteins. Their costs were then converted into an equivalent measure in corn per year, estimated at 3.8 tons for each average family (of 5.5 members). Given the national mean for corn output per hectare (1,036 kg), and having calculated this according to a national land surface equivalence in terms of rain-fed land, CEPAL's study established the minimum surface of land needed to produce the minimum food requirements for the average family. This minimum land surface turned out to be 3.84 hectares, which was rounded up to 4 hectares.

Infrasubsistence Peasants or Semiproletarians?

By CEPAL's criteria, infrasubsistence production units do not meet household food requirements. Their livelihood is thus predicated on an increased level of off-farm economic activity by those members of the family who hire out.

We might ask at this point: Are families in infrasubsistence farms really "peasants"? The notion of the peasantry is a very fluid one, an abstract mean, a tendency, but not a quantifiable reality. CEPAL's classification is predicated upon the notion of subsistence, which refers both to the reproduction of labor power, and the replacement of the means of production. Infrasubsistence means not even meeting subsistence requirements, let alone those for replacing the means of production. I would prefer to call this group of families semiproletarians, since they must complement their incomes with other economic activities, namely wage labor.

The notion of surplus product may be linked to the notions of subsistence and replacement in the following way: Subsistence is the minimum production level required to achieve the reproduction of labor power used up in a production cycle and to reconstitute the labor power of the whole peasant family. Moreover, it is necessary to replace the means of production used up or consumed during the cycle. Finally, surplus product would be the production over and above subsistence and replacement. If both subsistence and replacement are allowed for in a production cycle, then the peasant unit achieves a scale of simple reproduction but not necessarily a surplus, which could be the basis for capital accumulation.

The main characteristics of peasant production, as a theoretical construct, are that the direct producer is owner of or has access to land and other means of production, controls the labor process, and uses his/her own labor power and that of other household members. These resources should allow the peasant domestic unit to reproduce itself on a simple scale, i.e., covering the costs of both subsistence and replacement but lacking a surplus. In capitalist enterprises the owner of capital appropriates surplus product (in the historical form of surplus value) directly in the production process; the capitalist exploitation of peasants is more complex, however, since it is generally mediated by the commodities market through the sale of their products.

What we are interested in discussing at this point is the partial dissolution, not the total disintegration, of the peasant economy. This process of dissolution may move peasant households down to a semiproletarian position, where some of their members partially or completely proletarianize. Because of its subordinate position, the peasant economy within capitalism might attain a level of simple reproduction, but even this level might prove unattainable. What I am suggesting is that, although the unit might be able to produce enough for reproducing itself on a simple scale, capitalists, through unequal exchange, appropriate part of the peasant unit's subsistence and/or replacement funds. Such a situation would necessarily lead to a depeasantization process for some or all of the members of the peasant family, depending on the extent and prevalence of unequal exchange. For most members who manage to get a wage employment, the result will probably be only a partial proletarianization, with the peasant domestic unit and/or the community still partly responsible for the reproduction of these members of the community. This is what Claude Meillassoux has called the "social function" of peasant economy for capitalism. The community reincorporates workers idled by layoffs, illness, or old age (Meillassoux 1972, 1977). Adding this mechanism for surplus-labor extraction to unequal exchange, we can see that the peasant economy is doubly exploited by capitalism: When members of the household sell their labor power, peasant production subsidizes the unpaid wages in periods of layoff, illness, or old age; and when peasant products are sold in markets, they are usually subject to unequal exchange.

Eric R. Wolf speaks of the above situation as taking place in contexts where peasants are engaged in asymmetrical relations of exchange determined by external conditions, a common circumstance for peasants under capitalism. He writes,

> where exchange networks are far-flung and obey pressures which take no account of the purchasing power of a local population, a cultivator may have to step up his production greatly to obtain even the items that are required for replacement [or simple reproduction, in our terms, G.O.]. Under such conditions, a considerable share of the peasant's replacement funds [which include both of our subsistence *and* replacement funds, G.O.] may become somebody else's fund of profit (Wolf 1966, 9).[3]

Given the fact that infrasubsistence units do not really fulfill minimum theoretical requirements for their inclusion in the peasantry, I will place them in the category of semiproletarians. I have opted for this term rather than, for instance, "peasant-workers," (Szelényi 1987) because the dominant tendency in Mexican agriculture is clearly toward depeasantization. The concept of peasant-workers seems to imply that there are equal chances for this type of social agent to enter (or reenter) either a peasant or a proletarian class trajectory, i.e., repeasantization or proletarianization. Although I admit that both possibilities exist, I prefer to name the concept in accordance with the dominant tendency: depeasantization without full proletarianization. This formulation implies the expansion of the semiproletarian position rather than its contraction. (As we will see from the surveys of the 1990s, semiproletarian positions have increased quantitatively and also in terms of their intensity, in the sense that larger proportions of more *ejido* households' incomes depend on wages rather than agricultural income.)

Subsistence Peasants

The second stratum in CEPAL's typology is subsistence-level units. It was devised on the basis of whether production units were able to produce enough not only for food requirements, but also for replacing inputs and means of production used up in the production period. Cost calculations determined that such units should be within the range of four to eight hectares of ETN (National Rain-Fed Arable Land Equivalent). By CEPAL's own account, however, units between four and eight hectares tended to experience a deterioration in their production conditions and/or were forced to subsidize the fund for replacement with off-farm incomes. Clearly, then, this category does not achieve the level of simple reproduction if it is to rely exclusively on farming activities.

Nevertheless, subsistence units warrant classification as part of the peasantry even if those in the infrasubsistence category do not; although the former are deteriorating, they are able to sustain an essentially peasant operation. Selling some labor power might be a strategic means of preventing the unit's consumption levels from falling to bare subsistence or less.

Stationary and Surplus-Producing Peasants

The third stratum in CEPAL's typology is made up of "stationary" units, and they must fall in the eight-to-twelve-hectare range of ETN land to be able to produce at a simple reproduction scale. Those exceeding twelve hectares were classified in a fourth stratum called "surplus-producing" units or, more precisely, units with a surplus-producing potential. For the third stratum, stationary units, the costs of reproducing means of production and inputs were calculated on the basis of farming on a plot of ten hectares. As can be seen, not all the units in this eight-to-twelve-hectare range will necessarily be successful in achieving simple reproduction. Some of them are also subject to a deterioration of their production capacity, unless they supplement their costs with off-farm economic activities.

Before moving on to discussing nonpeasant units, let us briefly analyze the political economy of surplus production in a peasant economy. Theoretically, once a surplus product is present within a peasant unit, at least four things can happen to it.

1. First, surplus product might be appropriated by merchant or usury capital through unequal exchange or outright theft. Alternatively, if peasant products are competing not with capitalist enterprises but only with other peasants, the indirect beneficiary may be the industrial bourgeoisie. This circumstance has prevailed in Mexico with some basic grains, where

the state has fixed prices at low levels. The industrial bourgeoisie has benefited from getting cheap agricultural raw materials and cheap "wage goods," which allow it to pay low wages to industrial workers. Through this mechanism of cheap food production, the industrial bourgeoisie can realize greater rates of profit, and the peasant unit maintains its peasant character instead of accumulating capital.

2. Second, the surplus product might be so small that peasants choose merely to increase their consumption level, in which case what was initially a potential surplus product ceases to be one, and the scale of simple reproduction takes place at a higher level of consumption. Thus, the peasant unit retains its character without having to bestow gratis its surplus labor to capital, as it did in the first case.

3. A third way in which the peasantry could achieve simple reproduction is through cultural redistributive mechanisms typical of some peasant communities with an Indian tradition—for example, the possession of *cargos* for religious ceremonies (Cancian 1972, 1992; Vogt 1966, 1973). In this case, most or all of the initially potential surplus product will be spent on a traditional fiesta or some other redistributive mechanism, thereby merely increasing the consumption of the peasant community.

4. In the fourth and last alternative, the surplus product could be retained by the unit, opening the possibility for expanding the level of production by hiring some wage labor and/or investing in additional means of production. In this case, the peasants would gradually become peasant entrepreneurs and eventually, perhaps, an agrarian bourgeoisie. This is the social category that Lenin called kulaks, or rich peasants.[4]

Nonpeasant Units

The remaining four categories of production units were defined by the CEPAL study as nonpeasant units. The fifth one falls between the peasant and the entrepreneurial sector: hence the name "transitional units." The defining criterion for this latter stratum is merely the payment of between $25 and $500 in daily minimum wages per year. There is no specification about the land size, but we can assume that it is beyond the ETN level of twelve hectares, which was the minimum for surplus-producing units. These units are transitional in the sense that some might acquire entrepreneurial traits while others might fall back toward the peasant sector.

On the entrepreneurial side we have three strata that are demarcated by a purely quantitative criterion: They are "small," "medium," and "large" enterprises, depending on the range of hired wage labor. Small units pay between 500 and 1,250 daily minimum wages per year, medium units pay between 1,250 and 2,500, and large units pay over 2,500 minimum wages per year.

A different definition was given to livestock-raising units, which make up 11 percent of entrepreneurial units, but since the peasant units fall mostly outside this category, they will not be discussed here. Suffice it to say that all livestock-raising units were also operationalized as "small," "medium," or "large" capitalist enterprises.

Problems with CEPAL's Data

CEPAL's typology is derived from the agricultural census. Thus, if we are to have an idea about the agrarian classes in Mexico from these data, we should inquire into the degree of overlap between the information for agricultural production units in this census and the one on the general population census. According to the latter, rural population in Mexico in 1970 was roughly 19.9 million, which corresponds to about 3.6 million families. In an attempt to address the above question, CEPAL assumed that we can equate families with production units. By so doing, we would have a little over 405,000 heads of households who would not simultaneously be heads of agricultural production units, since the corresponding census registers only a little over 3.2 million units (CEPAL 1982, 111–12).

Of these 3.2 million agricultural production units registered by the agricultural census,

> 87,000 lacked land in general, and another 185,000 lacked arable land, thus leaving slightly over 2.9 million heads of households who would have arable land. That is to say, somewhat over 80 percent of rural families would be incorporated in the typology to some degree. To some degree, because close to 12 percent of those units (about 340,000), judging by the census data, correspond to *ejidatarios* from collective and mixed *ejidos* on which no direct information was obtained from census cards (CEPAL 1982, 112).

As we can see from the above contrast between the general population census and the data from the agricultural census (*Censo agrícola-ganadero y ejidal*) of 1970, the vast majority of the rural population (80 percent or more) has been accounted for in CEPAL's typology. One major limitation in CEPAL's study remains, however: It excluded formally landless households from consideration. Such households must be part of the nearly 20 percent of the omitted rural population. Thus, 20 percent would be the maximum conceivable estimate for the rural proletariat, assuming there were no merchants, artisans, urban proletarians with rural residence, and so on included in this figure.

Nevertheless, it is difficult to measure the regional distribution of proletarian households. We thus have no choice but to study the rural proletariat indirectly, through the general population census. The latter census has its own limitations, however: Its information is presented in terms of individuals, not households, as in the CEPAL study. Thus, many (perhaps most) of the individuals registered by the census as landless peasants or workers in fact belong to semiproletarian or peasant households, i.e., have at least a minimal access to land. But at this point, these are only speculations. The following section briefly addresses the question of rural proletarian households.

Structural Differentiation: A Disappearing Middle?

Thus far I have presented a profile of social differentiation in 1970, but we have no idea whether the peasantry has proportionately expanded or contracted. The only way to find out would be to address the problem historically: How has this profile changed over time? Addressing this question is one way of concluding whether the peasantry is shrinking or growing. Unfortunately and surprisingly, this question went unaddressed in the CEPAL study. Despite—or, perhaps, because of—the study's intent to substantiate the *campesinista* position no analysis has been provided on the previous history of the various producers in CEPAL's typology. Thus, one is unable to determine from its analysis alone whether peasant producers are being consolidated or going bankrupt.

To find out whether peasant producers are becoming more viable or are failing, one can compare the proportion of agricultural producers in the various categories between 1960 and 1970 by consulting a study by the Center of Agrarian Research (*Centro de Investigaciones Agrarias,* or CDIA) of the 1960 census (CDIA 1974). While the CDIA study classifies rural producers into only five categories (infrasubsistence, subfamily, family, medium-sized multifamily, and large-sized multifamily), the CEPAL study defines eight types of production units. To achieve some comparability, I have merged CEPAL's three entrepreneurial types into one to form six categories: infrasubsistence, subsistence, stationary, surplus-producing, transitional, and entrepreneurial. A graphic comparison is presented in Figure 4.1.

These data show the decline of the peasant economy between 1960 and 1970. Specifically, the middle units appear to be going bankrupt, thus reinforcing the polarization of agriculture; both the semiproletarian and the bourgeois sectors are increasing, while there is a disappearing middle group. Moreover, a large proportion of former peasants or semiproletarians simply fall out of the analysis: They are ex-peasants who cannot hold onto at least a semiproletarian position and have become day laborers or have moved to the cities.

Plotting the more recent data from 1990 and 1994 yields flattening curves, leaving the impression that the polarization trend is diminishing. Before speculating about the reasons for these new shapes in the curves, let me first clarify some of the data. First, they refer only to the *ejido* sector and do not include the private farms of 5 hectares or less, which constitute the *minifundia* sector. As mentioned above, however, based on the CEPAL 1970 study, the profile of social differentiation is very similar in both the *ejido* and the private sectors, although the latter is slightly more polarized. This greater degree of polarization in the private *minifundio* sec-

Figure 4.1   Social Differentiation Among Mexico's Rural Producers: 1960–1994

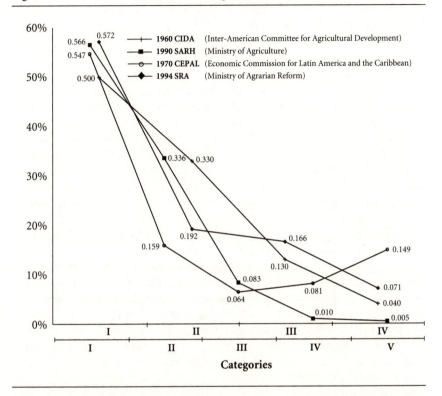

SOURCE: Elaborated with data from: Alain de Janvry, Gustavo Gordillo, and Elisabeth Sadoulet (1997). *Mexico's Second Agrarian Reform: Household and Community Responses.* Transformation of Rural Mexico Series, Number 1. La Jolla, CA: Center for U.S.–Mexican Studies, University of California, San Diego, pp. 27–29.

tor is undoubtedly due to the fact that small private owners of land have been able to sell legally all along, while *ejidatarios* have not (at least as of 1992).

The interesting new trend in the 1990s, though, is that the better-off sectors of the peasantry are expanding by purchasing land from the worse off, many of whom are simply abandoning agriculture. Nevertheless, neoliberal reforms (as discussed in Chapter 2) have resulted in the following historical paradox: They are creating the conditions for an entrepreneurial peasantry to emerge while also eliminating the middle farmers and confining large masses of rural dwellers to marginal conditions as agricultural producers. The paradox lies in the fact that the original agrarian reform of 1917, which was touted as a peasant triumph, resulted in proletarianization. Conversely, the neoliberal reform of 1992, which was labeled antipeasant by its populist critics, is actually setting the conditions for a small but vigorous peasant-entrepreneurial class to consolidate.

The dark side of the 1992 reform, though, lies in the intensification of the semiproletarian condition. Indeed, the extent to which rural producers depend on nonfarm incomes is staggering. De Janvry's study indicates that 81.9 percent of total income in the smallest farms comes from off-farm activities, including 46.7 percent from wages and microenterprises, with the rest coming from migration, i.e., also from wages. If income data are disaggregated by quintiles, off-farm income is most important for the middle quintiles, while on-farm income is most important for the poorest and the richest quintiles (de Janvry, Gordillo, and Sadoulet 1996, 178). Other studies that have quantified this phenomenon of the increasingly semiproletarian character of the rural direct producers are Appendini and Salles (1976, 1980), and Bartra and Otero (1987).[5]

Furthermore, poverty was found to be extensive and deep in rural Mexico: "Overall, 47 percent of the households are in poverty and 34 percent in extreme poverty" (de Janvry, Gordillo and Sadoulet 1996, 197). In contrast, 25 percent of individuals are below the poverty line in the urban sector and 34 percent nationally. It is conclusively demonstrated that being a member of an indigenous community brings an increased probability of being poor or extremely poor, even after controlling for access to land, education, and weaker migration networks. Indigenous communities make up 14.8 percent of the poor in the so-called social sector, which includes *ejidos* and agrarian (indigenous) communities, though they represent only 11.9 percent of the social-sector households. In fact, 71.2 percent of households in indigenous communities were poor compared to 44.7 percent in the *ejidos*.

De Janvry's main policy conclusions revolve around filling the institutional vacuum left by neoliberal reform. Measures in this direction would include a favorable macroeconomic environment, the promotion of organizations through the *ejido* system, and public investment in irrigation and education. Continuously stressed throughout de Janvry's book is the need for differential policies that reflect the regional and social heterogeneity of rural Mexico. This policy, however, seems antithetical to neoliberalism, which prescribes homogeneous policies regardless of the sharp inequalities of rural conditions.

Let me now briefly discuss the question of the agricultural proletariat in quantitative terms. Table 4.3 categorizes the economically active rural population, using census terminology. This table depicts the evolution of the categories of workers, peasants, and employers in the countryside between 1960 and 1970.

The absolute numbers of the agricultural workforce decreased from 1960 to 1970, continuing a trend of several decades. Similarly, it is not surprising that workers decreased in absolute numbers. This decrease reflects the secular decline of the agricultural sector as the economy develops: Rural-to-urban migration brings it about, and agricultural technological mechanization hastens it along. It

TABLE 4.3   Economically Active Rural Population, 1960 and 1970[a]

	1960		1970	
Sector	millions	percent	millions	percent
Workers	3.40	57.5	3.00	59.3
Peasants	2.50	42.2	2.00	38.2
Employers	0.02	0.3	0.13	2.5
TOTAL	5.92	100.0	5.13	100.0

[a] *SOURCE:* Dirección General De Estadística, *Censo General De Población, 1960; 1970* (México: DGE).

should be noted, however, that the peasant category decreased more drastically than that of workers,—from 2.5 to 2 million people, a 20 percent decline. Workers declined from 3.4 to 3 million people, a 12 percent decline. On the other hand, the relative number of workers increased from 57.4 to 59.3 percent, whereas that of peasants decreased from 42.2 to 38.2 percent.[6]

Regional Social Differentiation

I have translated the regional profile of social differentiation (in Table 4.4, below) into the economic class categories developed above while critically presenting CEPAL's typology. The differences between my economic class categories and CEPAL's typology are as follows: (1) Infrasubsistence units are now called semiproletarian; (2) transitional units have been placed under the social category of peasant-entrepreneurs; and (3) small, medium, and large entrepreneurial units are now labeled agrarian bourgeois. Given that the basic structure of social differentiation has been maintained through the present, I prefer the CEPAL data to the more recent study by de Janvry et al. (1996) because they are comprehensive, including both the *ejido* and the private sectors.

CEPAL's allocating procedure has been basically respected except for the case of infrasubsistence units, given that such units have few chances of reentering a peasant-class trajectory. Torn between land and wages as their material basis for reproduction, semiproletarian households are really the most dynamically growing sector. This statement was substantiated by contrasting the 1960 and 1970 data above.[7]

Table 4.4 depicts significantly diverse regional class structures in terms of social differentiation of the peasantry: Contrary to what may be expected intuitively, though, there is a larger *proportion* of peasant population in northern than in central Mexico. In central Mexico, the plots of land available to direct producers are in most cases insufficient for them to fall into the peasant category. Thus, most of them must complement their reproduction with off-farm activities, including wage-labor employment, although many of these wage earners do not be-

TABLE 4.4   Agrarian Class Structures in Puebla, Coahuila-Durango, and Sonora by Class of Household, 1970 (percentages)

State	Semiproletarian	Peasant	Peasant-Entrepreneur	Agrarian Bourgeois	Total
Coah./Dgo.	47.1	29.4	21.5	2.0	118,278
Sonora	13.7	54.1	21.8	10.4	29,224
Puebla	79.7	14.9	5.0	0.4	231,262

SOURCE: Elaborated with data from: CEPAL. 1982. *Economía campesina y agricultura empresarial (Tipología de productores del agro mexicano),* by Alejandro Schejtman, Mexico: Siglo XXI Editores, 118–119.

come sellers of labor power in the central region itself but in the northern regions and the United States through temporary migrations (Arroyo Alejandre 1989).

Agricultural production units from the peasant sector in the north tend to produce commercial crops to a much greater extent than those in the center, which concentrate on typically subsistence crops, i.e., corn and beans. While this cannot be taken as a direct indication of the degree of commercialization in each region, since corn and beans are also produced for the market, it is indeed an indirect hint that serves as a starting point for decoding the more qualitative aspects of the dynamics involved.

In fact, Kirsten Appendini and Vania Almeida Salles (1976) have demonstrated with the 1960 data the existence of a significant correlation between *municipios* (municipalities or counties) producing corn and beans and those states with commodification rates lower than 50 percent. Conversely, in *municipios* in the northern states of Baja California Norte, Baja California Sur, Chihuahua, Coahuila, Sinaloa, and Sonora there is the opposite correlation: low production of subsistence crops and commodification rates of over 80 percent of each unit's product. Furthermore, these scholars found similar correlations regarding wage labor: The highest incidence of units hiring wage labor was found in northern states and vice versa for central and southern states. The exceptions in the latter states were very localized *municipios* where tropical cash crops are produced. The region of Atencingo, Puebla, which produces sugarcane, is such an exception. Appendini (1983) has applied the same methodology of the earlier study to the 1970 census data, obtaining similar results, except that the polarization trends showed up more acutely.

The key point is that the bulk of cash crop production concentrates in the northern regions, while subsistence crops are produced mostly in central and southern Mexico. Yet there is a larger proportion of peasant units, properly speaking, in the north, in contrast to the center and the south. Therefore, it seems that the semiproletarianized direct producers in the latter two regions tend to concentrate on subsistence food production. And, conversely, northern peasants, peasant-entrepreneurs, and the agrarian bourgeoisie concentrate on cash crops production.

Semiproletarians from central Mexico nevertheless appear to produce under a peasant-type logic, focused on subsistence crops and based on family labor.

Let us briefly address the specificities in the patterns of structural differentiation in our three regions. At this level of aggregation we do not have data on the specific municipalities of our regions. Yet the data on the states where they are located generally describe their most salient features (see Table 4.4).

One can infer from the figures in Table 4.4 that the process of capitalist development has had diverse regional impacts, leading to significant differences in class structures among the three regions compared. Instead of indicating a greater peasant population in the center (Puebla) than in the northern states, it is exactly the other way around: There are proportionately more peasants and peasant entrepreneurs in the north and more semiproletarianized agricultural producers in the center. Conversely, however, there must be more fully proletarianized direct producers in the north, particularly in Sonora, who do not appear in our agricultural census data simply because they do not have formal ownership or possession of land. Thus, the sellers of labor power seem to be concentrated in the northern regions, where there is a large proportion of peasants, peasant entrepreneurs and agrarian bourgeois who can hire them for a wage. This interpretation is consistent with the findings of Appendini and Almeida Salles (1976) mentioned above, and with Appendini's (1983) more recent study of the 1970 census.

Clearly, then, Sonora has proportionately the most capitalistic structure of the three regions (with 10.4 percent of agrarian bourgeoisie), followed by Coahuila and Durango in a sort of middle point in the road (2 percent). Puebla, however, appears to have experienced a very low degree of capitalist development in agriculture, with only 5 percent of peasant entrepreneurs and a mere 0.4 percent of agrarian bourgeois (which may, nevertheless, concentrate very large extensions of land). The bulk of rural producers (79.7 percent) are in a semiproletarian position in Puebla, with access to so little land or of such poor quality that they cannot even achieve subsistence, much less a scale of simple reproduction. In contrast, Sonora has a very low proportion of semiprolatarians.

There is a significant difference on this count between Coahuila-Durango and Sonora. The proportion of semiproletarian households in the former is 47.1, whereas it is only 13.7 for the latter. We might speculate from these data that Coahuila-Durango's peasant entrepreneurs and agrarian bourgeois enjoy having a large pool of workers from their own semiproletariat, while in Sonora an agricultural proletariat proper must be in formation. It may still be the case, however, that a significant proportion of hired wage laborers in Sonora are seasonally migrant workers from other Mexican regions. Therefore, the wage labor force in Sonora is made up of both a local agricultural proletariat in formation and migrant workers (i.e., semiproletarians) from other regions, as has been documented in the literature (Cartón de Grammont 1990; Mares 1987; Posadas and García 1986). Puebla, for its part, relies mostly on its own semiproletariat, although such reliance might involve internal migrations within the state itself and occasionally from the states of Oaxaca and Guerrero (Lara 1979; Paré 1979a; Ronfeldt 1973). An agricultural proletariat proper must be nearly nonexistent or very small in Puebla.

Conclusion

The census data do reflect the extent to which the double crisis has resulted in the deterioration of peasant economy. They also reflect the type of class structural differences that one might expect to find among the various regions of Mexico.

The current crisis seems to have incubated in the 1960s. To the already advanced dissolution of peasant economy the state responded with a largely ineffective and insufficient agrarian reform. Redistributing land that was mostly useless for agricultural production merely served the political purpose of pacifying land-hungry peasants and semiproletarians—for a few years. But this reform was an economic failure: It fell short of reversing the demise of peasant economy. Politically the explosion was postponed only temporarily, reappearing in the early 1970s and then again in the 1990s as a result of the formal end of agrarian reform and economic integration with the United States and Canada.

On the other hand, the agrarian bourgeoisie seems to have been very infatuated with productivity increases brought about by the Green Revolution in the 1950s. This productivity hike followed the special treatment received from the state during the preceding decade, which took the form of price incentives above those of the international market. Capitalist profits were large in those two decades. By the 1960s, however, international prices for most cash crops began to fall dramatically without additional compensation from productivity increases: The romance with productivity and high profits was over. Thus, after an overproduction phase, capitalist agriculture also entered a prolonged crisis in the early 1970s that continues today.

The result has been a decimated peasant economy marked by increasing semiproletarianization and a fragile capitalist sector incapable of providing full employment for agricultural workers. Thus, the most dynamically growing position in the rural social structure is that of semiproletarian households. New agrarian struggles and the character of class organizations that emerge will depend on which political direction this semiproletariat takes. This direction will in turn depend on the specific cultures and forms of state intervention prevalent in each region. Such specificities are the focus of the regional case studies in the next three chapters.

Notes

1. I am referring to the land-tenure classification of the Mexican census, which is made up of three categories: private production units with more than 5 hectares, *ejidos*, and private units with 5 hectares or less. The latter category corresponds to the *minifundio* sector.

2. Use of this resource also has a limit, however, when its productivity drops below zero. When hired labor is used, such a limit is reached when labor's productivity equals the wage. Those who assume the value of labor power to be zero in the peasant unit are actually looking at its lower limit, below which agricultural production makes no sense to peasant farmers. Whereas peasants usually sacrifice their ground rent and often part of their imputed "wage," assuming the latter to be zero from the outset actually places the analysis at the point of peasant bankruptcy.

3. Also Marx mentioned the consequences for peasant production of being dominated by capitalism. He argued that peasants' surplus product sold in the capitalist market was hardly ever realized at its value, since prices are set by the production costs and average rate of profit, determined by the more efficient capitalist units of production. It is by this mechanism of price formation that "one portion of the surplus labor of the peasants, who work under the least favorable conditions is bestowed gratis to society . . ." Marx, I 1967:806). For a discussion of more specific mechanisms of appropriation of peasant surplus labor by the different fractions of capital, see Zamosc (1979).

4. For the classic discussions on peasant differentiation in Marxism, see Lenin (1967) and Kautsky (1974). For a contemporary account, drawing on the Latin American experience, see De Janvry (1981).

5. This article with Roger Bartra contains our agreements with regard to how to characterize the agrarian structure economically. Our main disagreements on its political implications, however, are contained in Otero (1989b) and Chapters 2 and 7 of this volume.

6. As mentioned above, there is one crucial difference between the General Population Census (GPC) and the rest of the figures provided previously in this chapter: the GPC refers to *individuals,* while the CDIA and CEPAL studies refer to *family units.* The figures of the GPC do depict the general trend nonetheless.

7. The distinction between peasants and peasant-entrepreneurs is that the latter are fundamentally oriented to market rather than subsistence production, although both are self-employed and hire few people seasonally. Peasant-entrepreneurs, however, have greater chances of entering an agrarian bourgeois class trajectory, although they are also subject to the erosion of their economic units. A similar distinction has been proposed by Harriet Friedman, regarding what she calls "household production" (peasants) and "simple commodity production" (SCP, or family farmers). She defines household production as that "whose reproduction occurs through non-commodity relations (whatever the proportion of production for sale to production for use)" (Friedman 1980:161). SCP, in contrast, is fully integrated into both the "factor" and "product" capitalist markets, even though both forms of production basically rely on family labor power. Clearly Friedman's concept of SCP is designed to depict family farmers in advanced capitalist countries. Nevertheless, I would argue that peasant-entrepreneurs in Third World social formations share most of their defining features, except that the latter may rely more on hired labor, at least seasonally, than family farmers (who have access to more technology than to cheap labor power).

5

La Laguna: From Agricultural Workers to Semiproletariat

The history of La Laguna involves combative agricultural workers who advanced labor-type demands in the 1930s but got land instead. After a period (1936 to 1947) of postcapitalist organization of production centered on self-management and the democratic control of a cooperative production process, the state converted direct producers into a "broad proletariat." This proletariat "in the broad sense" (Paré 1977) became subordinated to the economic apparatuses of the state, although many observers have classified it as peasantry because of its access to land. The direct producers' resistance to this subordination ended up converting them into a semiproletariat with small subsistence crop parcels alongside cotton, the predominant cash crop in La Laguna. Distribution of more than 75 percent of irrigated land into 311 collective *ejidos* in 1936 was a significant setback for the agrarian bourgeoisie. Thus, it was the state itself, through its economic and political apparatuses, that controlled the destinies of direct producers in La Laguna agriculture.

The Agrarian History and Cultural Setting

Before addressing the agrarian struggles in the region, I will present an outline of its agrarian history and cultural setting. La Laguna is a region located in north-central Mexico, which includes nine municipalities of the states of Coahuila and Durango (some classifications encompass fifteen municipalities). An oasis in the desert, all of its significant agriculture is irrigated. Rainfall is only 300 to 500 mm per year. Thus, irrigation is largely dependent on the Nazas and Aguanaval rivers and the Lázaro Cárdenas and Francisco Zarco dams. After land reform in 1936, however, the number of deep water wells increased enormously and now irrigate about a third of the land in normal years (up to two thirds in drought years) (Otero San Vicente 1986; Salinas de Gortari and Solís González 1994, 12).

Capitalist origins in La Laguna can be traced to 1846, "when Leonardo Zuloaga and Juan Ignacio Jiménez . . . built dams across the Nazas river at the place where

Torreón now stands." (Wilkie 1971, 11). The industrial-agricultural connection began also in 1846, when the Sánchez Navarro family installed a cotton gin in Monclova, Coahuila. They were also among the large landholders who had cotton fields irrigated by the Nazas river (del Castillo 1979). By 1936 the "La Laguna region was one of the few areas in Mexico where corporate farming became dominant. . . . Foreign corporations owned large tracts of land before the expropriations." (Senior 1958, 54). During this time, La Laguna accounted for half of Mexico's cotton production, and it was third in the production of wheat.

TABLE 5.1   Contrasts Between Northern and Southern Haciendas

La Laguna Hacienda	*Traditional Hacienda*
1. Highly capitalized	Low investments
2. Administration by land-renting companies	Absentee ownership
3. Payment of wages	Indebted peonage, in kind or tillage
4. Most supplies from outside	Economic self-sufficiency
5. Cash crops dependent on world market	Subsistence crops
6. Wage labor characterized peon-owner relations	Paternalistic relations
7. Bipolar class structure	Highly segmented class structure, including middle strata
8. *Not* a political unit	Formal political unit with government posts inside hacienda
9. "Ties between husband and wife do not seem to have been strong, judging from the large number of separations. Ritual kinship was extensive, but the bonds did not have great importance in terms of rights and duties."	"migration was impossible for the resident peons, so the communities inevitably became closely related."
10. No church within hacienda, only baptism was universal	A church inside hacienda, with priest exercising much ideological control
11. First- or second-generation immigrants in region	Families long settled in localities

SOURCE: Elaborated from Wilkie (1971, 13–16).

The distribution of registered *haciendas* by size in 1928 was as follows: Seventy-five *haciendas* of 1,000 to 10,000 hectares each, nineteen of more than 10,000 hectares, and three of more than a 100,000 hectares. Many of these *haciendas* belonged to foreign companies and were efficiently managed (Eckstein 1970, 273). In fact, the contrasts between La Laguna *haciendas* and the traditional ones from central and southern Mexico are remarkable. Table 5.1 above, where the criterion for comparison is self-evident in each case, summarizes such contrasts.

Although haciendas definitely dominated the agricultural scene in La Laguna, there were small parts of the population producing under different relations from that of resident peon-*hacendado,* and this had its own cultural impact. There were sharecroppers and small holders: "Their number was extremely limited, but their role in the agrarian struggle was nevertheless an interesting one" (Landsberger and Hewitt 1970, 5). Sharecroppers obstructed the agrarian movement for fear of losing their superior position.

In contrast to communities in central Mexico, where kinship and religion are rather strong institutions (Nutini, Carrasco, and Taggart 1976; Nutini and Bell 1980), in La Laguna life is more secular and individualistic. As we will see, this is closely related to differences in the production and social reproduction processes.

An Agricultural Proletariat Is Awarded Land Grants

Given the profile of La Laguna *haciendas* and agricultural workers, it is not very surprising that the mass movement in 1935–36 centered mostly on labor demands rather than land. There were about 104 agricultural labor unions struggling for such demands and only twelve groups petitioning land grants. In 1935 legislation was formulated in such a way that most of La Laguna direct producers were excluded from the possibility of agrarian reform, since resident peons were not eligible to obtain land grants. Only eleven *ejidos* had been formed in La Laguna before 1936, with 2,318 members and 5,000 hectares.

After the depression of the early 1930s, the *hacendados* further mechanized their operations to cut labor costs, "to which workers reacted by renewing their efforts to organize unions and obtain *ejido* grants." (Wilkie 1971, 18). In response, *hacendados* offered to buy land and create some *ejidos* to silence demands, on the condition that the president of Mexico give them "unaffectability" titles to avoid land reform thenceforth. Only 3 percent of the workers got land in this way, i.e., by *hacendado* initiative.

When Cárdenas came to power in 1934 and encouraged the organization of labor unions, La Laguna workers responded immediately: In 1935 there were 104 strikes by agricultural laborers. In May of 1936, urban unions joined the rural ones in a general strike protesting previous repression in former strikes, such as the firing of union leaders by *hacendados.* The president then requested a postponement of the strike in exchange for appointing a commission of experts to study the La Laguna situation. The strike's goal was a collective contract for

28,000 agricultural workers in the region. By August the State Labor Services of Coahuila and Durango declared the strike illegal and protected 10,000 strike-breakers from outside the region, who had been brought in by the *hacendados*. In view of this local stalemate, Cárdenas asked the strike leaders to end the strike with the promise of applying agrarian reform laws in La Laguna and modifying impediments to resident peons' receiving land. Then, on October 6, 1936, Cárdenas decreed the expropriation of about three-fourths of the irrigated land in the region. This land was turned over to approximately 38,000 workers organized into 311 *ejidos* (Senior 1958; Whetten 1948; Restrepo and Eckstein 1979).

Most observers agree that unions played the leading role in the La Laguna agrarian reform and that their struggle centered on labor demands. Although Senior misnames *hacienda* peons or workers as peasants, his own description makes it clear that they were structurally wage laborers:

> Their demands included the signing of a collective bargaining contract, increases in wages to 1.50 pesos (42 cents) a day, reduction of hours to eight per day, and the right to name a checker when cotton delivered by peasants was being weighed (Senior 1958, 65).

For his part, Eckstein also points out that "the syndicalist [labor union] movement played a predominant role in bringing about the reform. At a later stage the same unions were instrumental in persuading the emancipated *ejidatarios* to adopt the collective system." (1970, 275) The same point was made later by Restrepo and Eckstein (1975).

Fernando Rello (1986) explained that agricultural workers in La Laguna were totally dispossessed of land. And although they had formerly struggled for land, they had to shift to labor demands, given the ferocious response of the agrarian bourgeoisie. In 1935 many working-class organizations were being created in order to defend *Cardenista* reforms from the reactionary threats of *Callismo* (Loyola Díaz 1980; Medín 1982). Many of these organizations were heavily influenced by Vicente Lombardo Toledano (then secretary general of the Workers Confederation of Mexico, CTM) and the Communist Party of Mexico (PCM). Rello argues that, on the whole, the principal actor and crucial force were organized agricultural workers, linked with other sectors of the national proletariat (1986).

A slightly different account has been provided by Henry A. Landsberger and Cynthia Hewitt (1970). According to them, fifty unions posed formal labor demands, while only twelve groups were organized as agrarian committees whose demands centered on land. Based on statements by one of the leaders, however, these authors suggest that such labor demands may have been only tactical ways of weakening the *hacendados* while pursuing the ultimate goal of land reform for the direct producers (1970, 15).

Landsberger and Hewitt also suggest an important difference between Durango and Coahuila regarding both *haciendas* and demands. In Durango *hacien-*

das were more traditional, and demands more clearly centered on land, while in Coahuila direct producers confronted large companies, and thus labor demands appeared easier to carry out vis-à-vis the impersonal capitalists. In addition, Durango agrarianists were supposedly more combative than those in Coahuila.

The accuracy of this account is difficult to assess because it is based mostly on one leader's interpretation and was done some forty years after the fact. It is not that the interpretation seems unreasonable. In fact, it is quite plausible that the labor demands, centered on wages and working conditions, were tactical demands; yet it is possible nonetheless that the ultimate desire for all the land was in fact a postcapitalist rather than a peasant demand. What appears first as a possibility was later confirmed by the actual struggle immediately after land redistribution, which centered on a self-managing, democratic, and collective agriculture in which a great deal of independence was gained with respect to the Mexican state. The unions were not only struggling for collectivization but also for control over various aspects of the agricultural production process, such as the purchase of inputs for agricultural production, credit, insurance, and the marketing of produce.

Initially, then, the La Laguna struggle had a popular-democratic character in its demands, the nature of organizations, and the kinds of alliances formed by direct producers. Unfortunately, this character changed because of stern and repressive opposition by the state.

From Postcapitalist Self-Management to Productive Disappropriation

The *Cardenista* plan for La Laguna collectivization was definitely crucial for this administration (1934–40). Designed to set an example for future collectivization in other regions of modern capitalist agriculture, it had to demonstrate the economic superiority of the collective system and make it politically viable at the same time. The latter objective entailed organizing enough popular strength to offset the reaction of the *hacendados* facing expropriation of their lands. After land redistribution, direct producers also had to maintain a solid organization to resist the attacks from ex-*hacendados* and to fulfill the productivity levels expected by the state.

The plan that emerged from the bottom up was to achieve a self-management arrangement by *ejidatarios* in order to develop both economic and political strength in the newly created collectives. This goal was to be achieved through a web of fifteen regional unions that would eventually replace the administrative presence of the Ejido Bank. Moreover, the fifteen unions would constitute and be coordinated by the Central Union of Collective Credit Societies (henceforth, Central Union), which was intended to perform the following economic functions:

> sell the cotton crop . . . ; purchase of supplies including machinery; own and operate machinery stations; [operate] cotton gins and embark on other industrial enterprises; engage in extension, general education and agricultural research activities;

and supervise the expenditure of the so-called "social funds" of each *ejido* to provide wells, new schools and clinics (Landsberger n/d, 16–17).

This plan took shape through the interaction of the Central Union practices and the collaboration of government technicians, whose agencies had the official duty of fully supporting the collectives. Cárdenas not only approved of this initiative from below but also converted this organizational form into law so that all future collectives would take the same shape. This organizational format was incorporated into the Credit Law in 1940, one year after the de facto constitution of the Central Union, as the state-preferred model.

Land, Water, and Credit

In 1936, the total land in the region was 1.5 million hectares, out of which 190,000 hectares were irrigated and 1.31 million were unimproved. Under the new legislation passed in 1936 for La Laguna, resident peons became eligible for *ejido* grants. Thus, the La Laguna work force now included the following groups of workers, all of whom were eligible for land grants: permanent or resident peons, 15,000 to 16,000; temporary workers from nearby villages, 10,000; and seasonal migrant workers, 5,000. Additionally, there were still about 10,000 strikebreakers who had been brought in by the *hacendados* in 1936 (*Liga de Agrónomos Socialistas* 1940, 57). Thus, there were about 40,000 workers ready to receive land in a region that usually supported up to 30,000.

In the end, the total *ejido* grants consisted of 468,386 hectares, of which 147,710 were irrigated (nominally). This means that 31.2 percent of agricultural land was granted to *ejidatarios*, which included 77.7 percent of irrigated land. The number of beneficiaries totaled 38,101 *ejidatarios* (Whetten 1948, 216–17).

By 1944 35.4 percent of all loans granted nationally by the Ejido Bank were assigned to La Laguna *ejidos*, where only 7.6 percent of all *ejidos* were located at the time (Whetten 1948, 216–17). This indicates the extent of modernization in La Laguna agriculture, which required huge capital investments by the state lending agency. It also reflects the fact that collective *ejidos* were a fundamental piece in the overall *Cardenista* capitalist development project. In fact, commercial agriculture in the reformed sector concentrated in the collectives. Even though only 14 percent of *ejidatarios* operating with the Ejido Bank were in collective *ejidos*, they received 57 percent of all funds lent in 1944 by that bank. Collectives concentrated in five regions: La Laguna, the Yaqui Valley (in Sonora), Los Mochis (Sinaloa), Lombardía and Nueva Italia (Michoacán), and El Soconusco (Chiapas) (Whetten 1948, 215). Other sugar-producing collectives such as El Mante (Tamaulipas), Zacatepec (Morelos), and Atencingo (Puebla) were financed directly by the sugar mills they supplied.

By 1948 the government had withdrawn support to collectives and had actually staged a tremendous boycott to their economic success and their political strength.

The Ejido Bank classified *ejidos* into three categories, based on their capacity to repay loans: "A" for those *ejidos* in La Laguna that were normally able to repay the loans, or 59 percent of the total; "B" for those in arrears but that still managed to pay, 29 percent; and "C" for insolvent *ejidos,* 12 percent of the total (Senior 1958, 115).

In percentage terms, the evolution of credit assignments to La Laguna collectives in the early years is as depicted in Table 5.2.

Although incomplete, these figures begin to hint at the withdrawal of official support or actual boycott to collectives. These figures can be updated indirectly with information from Banrural, which was providing loans to a substantial number of *ejidatarios* once they had dismantled their collective *ejidos* and came under the bank's grip as individuals. According to the bank's own figures, during the 1988 spring-summer season the institution granted financing to a bit more than 34,000 producers (that is, 88 percent of the total number of *ejido* producers in La Laguna) covering 76,619 hectares, with 93 percent of these resources being channeled towards cotton cultivation. By 1992 credit was granted to only 13,000 producers (33 percent of the total number of *ejido* producers) covering 30,000 hectares, and the resources were channeled towards the production of basic grains and other crops that were not cotton (Salinas de Gortari and Solís González 1994, 14–15).[1]

The official boycott in the 1940s only compounded several original problems—technical and political—of agrarian reform in La Laguna: (1) the rushed land distribution into *ejidos* without sufficient planning, (2) legislative barriers to developing a thorough collectivization program that would enable the actual maintenance of the productive unity of *haciendas;* and (3) overpopulation in the region at the time of reform (Eckstein 1966, 138). The distribution of land within each *ejido* was also quite problematic. Some of them had plots of land separated from one another by private properties. In addition, the quality of land distributed was very heterogeneous, particularly with regard to availability of irrigation facilities.

> Some [*ejidos*] have almost 100 per cent of their area in first-class lands; others have almost their total area in lands practically worthless agriculturally. Some ejidos were cut off from irrigation ditches and roads. . . . In computing the total area of irrigable land, serious errors were made, and lands which had been irrigated only during seasons of exceptional river flow were classified as irrigable (Senior 1958, 91–93).

TABLE 5.2   Official Loans to La Laguna Collective, 1940–1961

Year	Percent of Ejido Bank Loans
1940	40.0
1944	35.4
1961	20.0

SOURCE: Elaborated with data from Eckstein (1970, 273) and Senior (1958, 115).

Overestimation of irrigable land at the time had a very negative effect on *ejidos*, given the legislative structure. Since *hacendados* were allowed to choose which hundred hectares they would keep, they invariably picked the most fertile land, and that which included water wells and buildings. Moreover, they kept all the farming machinery. The consequence of this is that *ejidos* had to become quickly indebted to the state bank for the purchase of fixed capital in order to keep modern agriculture going. After a few years much of the new indebtedness was due to the installation of water pumps for underground water irrigation, which was the only way to get additional water. The problem for *ejidos* is that underground water irrigation is twenty times costlier than gravity irrigation! (Restrepo and Eckstein 1975).

Thus, postreform *hacendados* had a comparative advantage from the outset in three crucial fields: irrigation, machinery, and finances. By 1950 "66 per cent of the land possessed by the private owners was irrigable land while only 37 per cent of that of the ejidos was so rated" (Senior 1958, 96). The per capita distribution of irrigated land by land-tenure system was 4.4 hectares in *ejidos* and 25.7 hectares in private properties. But these per capita figures should not lead us to overlook the concentration process within the private sector. Of private owners, 5 percent held 26 percent of private land, and 14 percent owned 55 percent. Furthermore, as Senior rightly points out, "even these data underestimate the amount of concentration because they do not reflect the *simulated sales* which took place widely on the eve of and immediately following the expropriations [emphasis added]" (1958, 96). In fact, there are several huge fortune-holders nowadays in La Laguna who purchased land during the Cárdenas administration at extremely low prices. It is also widely known that many *hacendados* rushed to change the title of their lands to artificially "divide" them up among their children and other close relatives in order to avoid land reform. This phenomenon of land reconcentration was later called *neolatifundismo* in the Mexican literature (Stavenhagen et al 1968; Warman 1975).

By the 1970s concentration of land and water resources could be seen in the following figures, published in one of Torreón's local newspapers: *Ejidatarios* controlled practically 85 percent of river water (*agua rodada*) and 35 percent of pumped water, and they made up 95 percent of producers. On the other hand, private owners controlled 15 percent of river water and 65 percent of pumped water, and they made up 5 percent of producers. Furthermore, the 5 percent of private owners controlled 25 percent of total irrigated land, while *ejidatarios*, 95 percent of producers, controlled only 75 percent of irrigated water (*El Siglo de Torreón*, 1 January 1977, 11.) On average, then, *ejidatarios* only had 1.7 irrigated hectares each from river and wells by 1985.[2] Water from the river, though, which was the cheapest source, has been sharply curtailed by the Ministry of Water resources (SARH). The following table depicts a tremendous drop from an average of 2.8 hectares per plot in 1936–63 to 1.0 hectare in 1984.

TABLE 5.3   Evolution of Average Surface Cultivated with Cotton and River Water Alloted to *Ejido* Plots in La Laguna, 1936–1984

Years	Average Annual Surface per Plot
1936–63	2.8
1964–70	2.0
1971–82	1.5
1983	1.3
1984	1.0

SOURCE: (Pucciarelli 1985,57)

The Ejido Bank and Productive Disappropriation

There have been three major epochs in the relationship between *ejidatarios* and the Ejido Bank (henceforth referred to as the bank), one during and immediately after *Cardenismo,* another one consolidated during the 1950s, and a third that began only in 1990 and is still taking shape. Only the first two are discussed at some length here. The first is characterized by considerable margins of autonomy by direct producing *ejidatarios,* and the second resembles more of a state-controlled agriculture. As Wilkie puts it, however, the bank's presence has been crucial since the beginning.

> The majority of the *Ejido*'s transactions were made through the *Ejido* Bank, which had to approve major expenditures, and since all crop loans were obtained from the bank, *it exercised almost total control over important financial decisions* (1971, 43).

There was an elected work chief in charge of planning and assigning all agricultural tasks. In the initial years of the *ejido,* the work chief directed all field labor and was one of the most important officials for the economic success of the community. He merely directed the implementation of decisions previously taken by the general assembly of the *ejido,* however. The treasurer of the *ejido* paid weekly wages (*anticipos*) to each *ejidatario* and checked the fields to see if the work had been done. In the beginning the major problem that work chiefs had to deal with was worker motivation. But such a problem apparently ceased to be an issue after land was subdivided in 1944. Consequently, the work chief position became less crucial. With land subdivision, *ejidatarios* were now evaluated and paid according to productivity in their assigned plots.

The process of subdivision started by allowing each *ejidatario* to grow corn in one or two acres. Later on, each member was assigned a number of hectares for which he was responsible in growing cotton. "The primary change effected by this subdivision of the land was that incomes of the *ejidatarios* . . . became proportional to the production of their parcelas" (Wilkie 1971, 57). The principal goal of reorganizing work was to avoid the so-called problem of "free riders." With partial individualization of parcels, the new work method "rewarded individual effort and ability in the irrigation and cultivation of cotton" (Wilkie 1971, 58).

There was also the development of a *libre* group of laborers "that competed for employment in the collective work [which remained]" (Wilkie 1971, 46). *Libres,* which literally means "the free ones," were agricultural workers who did not have an *ejido* parcel but lived in the *ejido* village in a piece of land lent to them by the *ejido* assembly. Some of the *libres* were kin of *ejidatarios,* while others were migrant workers who had asked for permission to stay in the village.

Apart from the individual labor devoted to each parcel, there were many tasks that remained collective: Some were the administrative tasks of elected officials and the work chief; others were those of truck drivers, well keepers, mechanics, employees of the cooperative, mule herders, and the school caretaker. Most of the nonelective tasks were held by *libres.* "Non-collective work was performed or directed by the individual *ejidatario,* and *the wages paid for it were loans* [*anticipos* or cash advances], which the *ejidatario* repaid to the Ejido Bank from the sale of the cotton from his parcela [emphasis added]" (Wilkie 1971, 63).

The economic and political success of direct producers became too threatening for the state and the newly consolidated agrarian bourgeoisie. Thus, the bank began to promote dismantling the collectives in 1941. By 1944 the San Miguel *ejido* had subdivided all its land into permanent parcels assigned to individual members. In Wilkie's view this decision did not necessarily mean that the *ejidatarios* were entirely opposed to the collective system; it seemed to be simply a reorganization of the labor process to allow more adequate compensation of individual productivity. The main policy decisions, however, remained subject to a vote in the *ejido* assembly. In Wilkie's view San Miguel *ejidatarios* did not value collective or individual work as such, "but only as one or the other resulted in specific and observable advantages" (Wilkie 1971, 71).

Promoting *ejido* subdivision and individualized work methods was the chief tactic used by the state, nonetheless, to weaken the independent economic and political organization achieved by direct producers in La Laguna. This interpretation was quickly held and publicized by the Central Union:

> The Central Union has denounced officials of the Bank for promoting dissension which leads to the formation of several sectors within an *ejido.* . . . The individual working of plots has made cotton theft and the illegal traffic of unginned cotton much easier. It has made the bookkeeping of both bank and *ejido* more involved (Senior 1958, 114).

New Ejido Credit Societies proliferated with subdivision. Their legal statute gave great powers to the bank, such as dictating the internal rules of each society. Although the statute also foresees the possibility of important *ejidatario* participation, little by little the logic of bureaucratic and vertical control began to impose itself (Rello 1986). Such new functioning resulted in a number of social structural changes in the relationships among the *ejidatarios,* the bank, and other workers. The bank became the virtual employer of *ejidatarios,* who came to rely increasingly on hiring *libres* to do their work while searching for other paid jobs for themselves.

Fragmentation and Decline of the Ejido Economy

Because the La Laguna *ejidatarios* were committed to modernization, they had to become heavily indebted to purchase machines for a modern agriculture after land reform. Between 1936 and 1950 Mexican peasants increased ownership of mules by 339 percent, while in La Laguna the number of mules dropped from 21,731 in 1940 to 9,195 in 1952. In contrast, the number of tractors owned directly by *ejidos,* excluding the ones in machinery centers, grew to 610 in 1952 from none in 1936. In addition, by 1952 there were "141 combines, 506 pumps, 286 trucks, 155 auto-mobiles, 452 tractor-drawn harrows and 461 animal drawn, 2,078 seeders, 6 electric light and power plants, 4 gins, and 2,624 horses" (Senior 1958, 124).

Fragmentation of credit societies led, among other things, to underutilization of equipment bought by members of the same *ejido.* Fragmentation began quickly after *Cardenismo* and made La Laguna *ejidos* look like most others in Mexico (which were not "collective"), except that fragmentation in La Laguna occurred to an even greater degree. In 1940 there were 296 credit societies with an average of ninety-nine members each. That is, 29,279 *ejidatarios* were "served" by the bank out of 38,000. By 1967 the number of credit societies had soared to 1,182, with an average of fifteen members each, and only 17,316 *ejidatarios* of the original 38,000 were being served (Landsberger and Hewitt de Alcántara 1970).

These data partially reflect the tremendous deterioration suffered by the *ejido* economy in La Laguna. Quite unfavorable developments in prices and costs for cotton had taken place by 1967. In fact, 1954 was the year of a turning point in which costs increased faster than prices. The gap between prices and costs only worsened for *ejidatarios* in the following decades (Landsberger and Hewitt de Alcántara 1970).

In spite of such adverse circumstances, both *ejidatarios* and the bank kept hanging on to cotton as the main cash crop. The reasons were different for each party, however. For *ejidatarios,* cotton was the most labor-intensive crop and thus the one that enabled them to "milk" the bank through weekly cash "advances" (wages). For the bank, holding on to cotton was the easiest way to maintain social equilibrium in a potentially volatile region (Rello 1986).

Contemporary Productive Process

Although much of what has been said about the labor process in La Laguna has not changed, it is worthwhile to look at the productive process as a whole through the 1990s. The balance and programming assemblies had ceased to exist many years earlier, having become a mere facade. Starting in the early 1980s, the bank established stricter conditions to grant loans. *Ejido* groups had to organize as the bank told them to or they got no credit. If loans are not paid, the bank has the right to take over the harvested crop and commercialize it to secure payment. In the bank's operation plan, which specifies tasks and costs for the full agricultural cycle, the bank now tends to reduce loans to their minimum, even at the price of diminishing the work for cultivation. The bank's field inspector has become tantamount to a foreman for *ejidatarios*.

By the mid-1980s, sometimes *ejidatarios* did not complete the soil preparation tasks, given the extremely low wages assigned to them in the operation plan. Seeds were imposed by the bank and were produced by another state-owned company, Pronase (*Productora Nacional de Semillas,* or National Seed Company), which often provided low-quality seeds. The same happened with fertilizers, which were produced by state-owned Fertimex (*Fertilizantes de México,* or Mexican Fertilizers). Pest management was usually standardized by the bank, and pesticides were handed to *ejidatarios* with delays and in lower quantities than needed, with terrible implications for productivity. For instance, per-hectare yields for private landholders, who had control over inputs, were five tons of cotton in the mid–1980s, while those for *ejidatarios* were only three tons. Agricultural insurance, which was mandatory in order to obtain a loan, was purchased from another state company, Anagsa (*Aseguradora Nacional Agrícola y Ganadera, S.A,* or National Agricultural and Livestock Insurance, Inc.) and only covered 70 perecent of total losses. Marketing, in turn, was carried out by yet another state company, *Algodonera Comercial Mexicana* (Mexican Cotton Company).

In sum, the *ejidatarios* lost control of their productive process as a whole, although they retained some margin of decision-making in the immediate labor process. But even at this level they must face the bank's field inspector, who acts as the *ejidatarios'* foreman. According to Rello, the bank is the true director of the *ejidatarios'* economic life. Bureaucratically controlled by an economic state apparatus, its organization of production closely resembles that of statist agriculture (1986).

Rello argues that through "productive disappropriation" the bank deprived *ejidatarios* of their own accumulation fund. In order to achieve this end, the bank extended the disappropriation process and control of the reproduction of labor power. Thus, the bank controlled both necessary and surplus time of direct producers—not only their source of surplus, but also the source for simple reproduction. Furthermore the bank's policies nearly precluded the possibility of producing surplus labor. What the state was most concerned with, therefore, was not control of surplus product but political control of *ejidatarios* through hampering their economic strength.

Some elaboration on the mechanisms by which the bank came to control the reproduction of labor power is necessary, for they give a clue to the kind of social relationships and regional culture that developed in La Laguna's *ejidos*. The bank normally grants two types of loan, *refaccionario* and *avío*. The former is for mid-term investments in fixed capital, while *avío* loans are for circulating capital, chiefly wages. Thus, *avío* is the main instrument the bank uses to control the reproduction of labor power and takes the form of *anticipos*, or cash advances. The production of subsistence crops—corn and beans—was forbidden by the bank until the early 1990s because direct producers began to divest funds granted for cotton into subsistence crops. Even some irrigation went to corn, beans, and watermelon, since all cotton would at most simply pay back the *ejidatarios'* debts. Rello (1986) has characterized this practice as one of resistance to the bank's dictates.

The *ejidatarios'* relationship to the bank is thus rather ambiguous. In some ways *ejidatarios* function like slaves, in others like serfs, but can also be seen as simple wage laborers working for the state bank. This ambiguity is reflected in the existence of the "statement of freedom" (*carta de liberación*) awarded by the bank to *ejidatarios* who wish to sever ties to it. Before being able to work on other crops or occupations, the *ejidatario* must obtain a "statement of freedom" from the bank. The requirements for this document, says Rello, are so stringent that in practice it is all but unobtainable. Thus, *ejidatarios* are kept incarcerated in a bureaucratic network. It is quite symptomatic that the name for *ejidatarios* working outside the bank is "free *ejidatarios*" or "independents."

Ejidatarios who have lost control over their labor processes to the bank have also fallen into the trap of a determinate technological paradigm, highly intensive in the use of agrochemical and mechanical inputs, very costly, and therefore, not very profitable. In fact, they stay in this network for lack of better options. This is a state network with a double trap: One represented by the official bank, usually the only source of credit for *ejidatarios*, and the other represented by monopolistic control over river water for irrigation by the Ministry of Agriculture and Water Resources. The state was determined (until 1990) to support the domestic textiles industry with domestically produced cotton, a crop that requires extensive water resources. The problem is that, in order to support industry, cotton had to be offered at international prices even though domestic production costs ran so high that there was barely any margin for profit.

Based on a study conducted in La Laguna in 1984, Alfredo Pucciarelli (1985) estimated that 80 percent of 43,811 *ejidatarios* made up the semiproletariat of bank-dependent producers. The rest consisted of what the author calls middle and enriched peasants. These data are consistent with those presented in Chapter 4 with regard to the North region. This is how Pucciarelli describes the La Laguna producers in social terms:

> They are no longer peasants in the strict sense of the concept, they do not plan or control their production process, they cannot fix the destination of their surpluses, when they have any. The natural evolution of the new regime has deprived them of their peasant condition but has not transformed them into simple wage workers.

They form part of an expanding universe of new subjects, socially hybrid, located in various regions of the country, a new form of labor power in a state-controlled agriculture that has not received an adequate name and has not yet been adequately studied [author's translation] (Pucciarelli 1985, 48).

One consequence of depriving peasants of the control of their labor process is the atrophy of peasants' skills as cultivators: They have become very dependent on the bank's decisions on what to plant, when, how, and so on.

Because cash advances through *créditos de avío,* or short-term credits, have become de facto wages for these "peasants," they have lost any consciousness of being part of a peasantry and instead have developed a quasi-proletarian culture. For instance, they struggle for increasing the amounts of *créditos de avío,* the weekly advances that are tantamount to wages, but there is no correlation between these payments and productivity increases because the direct producers no longer see the crops as their own. Moreover, because these *ejidatarios* have also been deprived of any consciousness of being independent workers, they usually try to find ways to trick the bank: for example, trying to sell some inputs such as seeds or fertilizers, renting out their water allotment, irrigating their corn and bean crops rather than cotton, not performing certains tasks that require their own labor, and so on, all of which results in lower total yields, which, in turn, deepens their indebtedness to the bank.

One way in which *ejidatarios* have tried to resist the bank's domination is by diversifying their crops in order to overcome the water limits imposed for cotton. The vast majority of *ejidatarios* in La Laguna, over 74 percent, were still specializing in cotton by the end of the 1980s, with an additional 12.8 percent having diversified crops as well as cotton. The other 12 percent are divided into those specializing in alfalfa (4.79 percent) and dairying (7.83 percent). Table 5.4 below, with figures for 1983, is representative of most of the 1970s and the 1980s.

After a major abandonment of cotton in the early 1990s, the proportions reflected in this table are probably true again today. From a high of 47,000 hectares

TABLE 5.4   La Laguna *Ejidatarios* by Type of Economic Activity, 1983

Type of Activity	Number of Average Ejidatarios	Total Cultivated Crop Size (hectares)	Surface (hectares)
Cotton Growers	32,568 (74.4%)[a]	1.5	48,852 (64.4%)*
Alfalfa Growers	2,098 (04.8%)	2.9	6,084 (08.0%)
Dairy Producers	3,432 (07.8%)	2.4	8,237 (10.8%)
Diversified Growers	5,613 (12.8%)	2.3	12,910 (17.0%)
Total	43,811	1.7	76,083

SOURCE: (Pucciarelli 1985, 54)

[a] (Percentages do not add up to 100 because of rounding error.)

devoted to cotton in 1990, La Laguna dipped to less than five hundred in 1992. The cultivation of basic grains increased from 16,000 to 63,000 hectares in the same period. This change of crop patterns was due not only to Banrural's new policies of not financing cotton in order to favor basic crops, but also to the fact that maize and beans had become (and remain) the only crops with subsidized guaranteed prices, which are relatively high (Salinas de Gortari and Solís González 1994, 10 fn).

The only *ejidatarios* who have managed to escape the state cotton network (about 26 percent) have liberated themselves from the technical conditioning to which the bank subjects cotton growers, an example of which is that the *ejidatarios* can get irrigation water for a maximum extension of 1.5 hectares, a restriction that limits production severely. With pumped water, diversified or noncotton producers are able to irrigate an average of 2.4 hectares each, or 60 percent more than specialized cotton producers. In these cases they can diversify their agriculture or specialize in alfalfa, which is very profitable because of the regional deficit of alfalfa in the midst of a booming dairy industry, or they can also go into alfalfa and dairy production combined. The latter have also adopted the private sector's highly modernized technological paradigm, which is predicated on heavy use of purchased inputs. While yields are quite high, so are costs, and profit margins are not very high, although absolute income is comparable with that of the better-off cotton-producing *ejidatarios* (Pucciarelli, 1985).

If one compares the productivy of *ejidatarios* with plots of similar size, one sees that association with Banrural yields worse results. In contrast, private producers have the highest yields, followed by "independents," *ejidatarios* freed from Banrural (Pucciarelli 1985) .

The costs for dairy *ejidatarios* are four and a half times those for cotton growers; yet their net incomes are similar because of very high production costs and the monopolistic control exercised by the milk processor over milk prices: There is only one major milk processor in La Laguna, *Leche LaLa*, (which means "La Laguna Milk"). Since the 1970s *LaLa* has become a major nationwide milk producer and a major supplier for Mexico City. Dairy production, therefore, does not represent a stable long-term alternative for La Laguna *ejidatarios* for two main reasons, one technical the other social.

Technically, alfalfa consumes more water than cotton, a critical consideration in a semiarid region. Socially, it would be very hard to break the monopsony of the milk processor in order to get better prices. And because all dairy farmers are wedged into the technological paradigm created by the large transnational corporations that supply agricultural inputs from the United States, costs will only continue to increase.

The credit situation changed dramatically with the advent of neoliberal policies starting in the late 1980s. Close to 80 percent of *ejidatarios* received credit for cotton in 1990, but this proportion dropped to only 33 percent by 1992. Most other *ejidatarios* continued to receive other loans (*crédito a la palabra* or loans on their oral commitment to repay) from the welfare program Pronasol, a program that was characteristic of Carlos Salinas de Gortari's administration (Salinas de Gortari and Solís González 1994,14–15). The problem with these loans is basically that they were too small to cover any form of investment expenditure. The *Banco Rural*, in contrast, now operates only with *ejidatarios* and private cultivators that are clear of debt. In other words, in conformity with neoliberalism, only prosperous peasant-entrepreneurs and agrarian bourgeois are now credit-worthy.

Class Organizations in La Laguna

The history of class organizations of direct producers in La Laguna is that of an overwhelming attack and eventual appropriation by the state. The state could not tolerate the possibility of self-sustaining growth by democratic, self-managed cooperatives with substantial economic and political independence. Thus, the state implacably deployed its mighty economic and political forces against direct producers. It turned the bank against the Central Union, and at times it even used police armed forces against organized workers. The CNC (*Confederación Nacional Campesina,* or National Peasant Confederation), initially democratic and representative, was confiscated by the state and turned into a corporatist state apparatus for political control of the peasantry. The result was one of a major split in La Laguna agrarian organizations, with most taking a bourgeois-hegemonic direction by affiliating with the PRI, while a minority remained in oppositional or popular-democratic organizations and/or alliances.

The CNC was born in 1935 and initially became truly representative of peasants and agricultural workers despite the fact that it was created after the state's initiative. In fact, neither the *Liga National Campesina* (National Peasant League, or LNC) or the *Confederación Campesina Mexicana* (Mexican Peasant Confederation, or CCM) succeeded in unifying local peasant organizations in 1935, precisely because they attempted to do so without Cárdenas's approval, consent, or support (González Navarro 1968, 140). Cárdenas also opposed Lombardo Toledano's initiative to organize peasants and agricultural workers within the CTM, arguing that such a move would incubate germs of dissolution and division that would prove fatal to the "industrial proletariat" (Medin 1972, 85). In fact, he wanted to prevent Lombardo Toledano from accumulating so much power. Thus Cárdenas ordered the PNR (*Partido Nacional Revolucionario,* or National Revolutionary Party, the first incarnation of the current PRI in 1929) to carry out the unification of peasants and rural workers based on the existing CCM, the organization that had proposed him as the presidential candidate in 1933.

The Central Union saw its de facto birth in 1939 in the "Consultative Committees," all of which were articulated in the "Central Consultative Committee." It represented all of La Laguna *ejidatarios,* and its initial results included debureaucratization, decentralization, conciliation of internal conflicts, betterment of social services, design of internal rules, and an accounting system. SICAs (*Sociedades de Interés Colectivo Agrícola,* or Agricultural Societies of Collective Interest) were soon formed to control the purchase and use of agricultural machinery and gins. An Agricultural Insurance Company (_Comarcana de Seguros Agrícolas_) was also organized by the Central Union.

The history of the Central Union is closely linked to that of the bank and the CNC. As Rello has suggested, the state faced two options regarding La Laguna collectives in the 1940s. One was to strengthen the _ejidos_ so that they became wholly independent from the bank; the other was the economic subjection of _ejidos_ by the bank (1986). The state chose the latter, bureaucratic option. Rello suggests that the state feared the possibility that _ejidos_ might achieve economic independence and self-sustaining growth outside the corporatist control of the bank and the CNC.

The process was neither smooth nor fast. It took about thirteen years for the state to take control of the majority of La Laguna _ejidatarios_ after it began its boycott in the 1940s. And even into the 1990s the Central Union survives, although with a different name: _Asociación de Sociedades Locales y Grupos Solidarios de Crédito Ejidal de la Comarca Lagunera, de R. L., 40–69_ (Association of _Ejido_ Local Societies and Solidarity Groups of the La Laguna Region, Ltd.), or simply "The 40–69." The last number used to change with every calendar year, and 40 is the year of its formal beginning as Central Union. The year 1969 marked the organization's break with the Communist Party, when it became a more strictly economic organization, independent from the state and politically autonomous.

The state's fear was sparked chiefly by the Communist influence. In the beginning several of the highest posts within the local CNC had been won by members of the Communist Party through democratic elections. Thus, Communist leaders were truly representing the _ejidatarios'_ aspirations and interests, at least as reflected in their electoral choices. Landsberger (n/d) provides a slightly different interpretation, though. He suggests that the state's intervention was more a matter of power than of fears of Communist influence. In his view, the leadership could just as well have been a rightist one, and the state would have moved to clamp down on the regional political situation.

I tend to favor an eclectic interpretation on this issue. Both Rello and Landsberger probably exaggerate their positions, yet both are partially correct. Communist affiliation was undoubtedly taken as the ideological excuse by the state to justify its attack. As the 1940s advanced, the administrations of Manuel Avila Camacho (1940–1946) and Miguel Alemán (1946–1952) drew closer to the United States, and after World War II, anti-Communist rhetoric was quite fashionable. Nevertheless, Rello might overemphasize Communist influence as the main spur to state action.

In any case, the Central Union managed to constitute a powerful economic and political organization based on broad participation in democratic mechanisms of decision making by its rank-and-file members. Such participation started at the _ejido_ level, where the important production and political decisions were made in a general assembly.

Initially the Central Union was chiefly concerned with coordinating and promoting the economic interests of La Laguna collectives, while the original CNC was supposed to pursue political interests. Almost as soon as Manuel Avila Camacho assumed the presidency in 1940, the Central Union was accused of espousing Communist tendencies. By 1943, the independent elements were removed from the state league of the CNC, and official authority was extended from the national level of CNC to the regional level. "The original peasant officers of the Regional Committees (some of who were members of the Communist Party) were removed and *new appointments made without election*" [emphasis added](Landsberger and Hewitt 1970, 39).

By 1942 the bank took control of the Agricultural Machinery Central, the cotton gin, a power plant, water wells and other parts of the agricultural productive process. This was the first important economic attack on the Central Union, which was followed by the removal of independent leaders from CNC.

Central Union leaders were subsequently removed from three levels of the CNC in 1943: (1) "Leagues of Agrarian Communities," the name which the CNC adopts at the state level; (2) the National Union of Rural Workers, the CNC labor organization; and (3) the Regional Peasant Committees. With this purge, only the leaders most loyal to the new and conservative administration remained in the official CNC. This organization then became the political arm of the state apparatus in the countryside to subserve the electoral needs of the state while providing limited and weak lobbying services to direct producers through its corrupt, opportunistic leaders.

The crucial blow to the Central Union, however, occurred in 1947 with the creation of a parallel "Central Union" by the CNC, this one with official approval and support. But this union was never legally constituted, for such a measure would have required approval by the majorities of the general assemblies of every *ejido*. Nevertheless, this "Central Union (CNC)" managed to boycott every economic activity initiated by the original union. None of those destructive attacks were followed by positive alternative programs. The CNC waged a purely destructive boycott (Landsberger and Hewitt 1970, 41).

In 1950 the CNC seized control of the last stronghold of the Central Union: the *Mutualidad Comarcana de Seguros Agrícolas,* the insurance company thus far owned and administered by the *ejidatarios'* organization. There were three moves which led to this takeover by CNC. First, when elections were about to be held in the *Mutualidad* buildings in Torreón, *ejidatarios* found the installations surrounded by state police. Second, once they could finally hold the elections, only half of the electors arrived to vote for Central Union incumbents; five days later the CNC held a secret meeting where supposedly the other members elected CNC candidates for the executive committee of the *Mutualidad.* The third and final move was the physical taking over of the administrative building and having the Central Union leader, J. Cruz Sifuentes, sentenced to six months in jail (Landsberger and Hewitt 1970, 43).

Once more and more components of the Central Union were taken over by the CNC people, their resources were subordinated to the political and personal purposes of the leaders. This process of expropriating the class organizations from direct producers also involved the creation of a social group of CNC cadres (*líderes*) who became the contact point, the brokers, between the state and the masses. These cadres developed patron-client relations with their constituency, and they personified what Roger Bartra (1975b, 1978, 1993) has called the "structures of mediation" of the Mexican state. These appointed cadres (rather than elected leaders) usually became corrupt and established their own agricultural enterprises, often under the disguise of an *ejido*. Although these cadres played a fundamental role in boycotting the Central Union, they became a problem for the state by the late 1970s, when the state was trying to combat the agricultural crisis by adding productivist measures to political control.

In the midst of continual economic and political attacks, the Central Union underwent an oppositional political realignment at the national level in 1948. Arturo Orona, its secretary general, and Jacinto López, formed a coalition of opposition groups around the new Popular Party (PP, eventually renamed Popular Socialist Party) of Vicente Lombardo Toledano. López had just broken with the labor CTM, where he had been head of peasant affairs. In 1949 Orona and López formed the UGOCM (*Unión General de Obreros y Campsesinos de México,* or General Union of Mexican Workers and Peasants).

Despite the fact that the Central Union lost its majority influence among La Laguna *ejidatarios,* representing less than 10 percent of them by the mid-1950s, it nevertheless still enjoys much greater respect than CNC today. The "40–69," as it is now called for short, is a democratic and independent organization with clear and effective communication patterns between directorate and the rank and file. Even though the Communist Party had been active in the organization in the 1940s, it is now the least politically active of all regional organizations in La Laguna. It concentrates on the economic problems of its constituency, although its leaders as individuals remained active in the Communist Party until 1969.

The basic goal of "40–69" remains the creation of a strong cooperative system in La Laguna, one that controls both inputs and outputs in the production process. The organization has always demanded the expropriation of all private agricultural land in La Laguna to solve the problem of overpopulation. Similarly, it demands that all irrigation water be granted to the *ejido* sector.

Although the organization has not been successful in many of these demands, it has maintained some economic independence from the bank. The "40–69" has been very successful in marketing, for instance. It has usually achieved the highest cotton prices for its credit societies. This fact is "widely recognized among peasants of all political affiliations in La Laguna . . ." (Landsberger and Hewitt 1970, 85). In 1967 the union got private funding to purchase a cotton gin for its affiliates, and it managed to overcome the bank's opposition. Moreover, there has been a tactical alliance with the private sector in matters such as credit, opposing taxes on cotton, higher electricity rates for pumping water, and so on. In other words, many of the Union's tactics are not dictated by "rigid adherence to ideology but by the needs of their organization" (Landsberger and Hewitt 1970, 86). In fact, Landsberger and Hewitt conclude that the Union is "better equipped to function effectively *within* the existing political system than any of the official peasant committees." (Landsberger and Hewitt 1970, 87).

In contrast, the CNC almost entirely lacks any semblance of democratic mechanisms in its internal life; communication between representatives and rank and file is kept to a minimum, except at election time. "No informant interviewed, whether leader or member of a Regional Committee, could remember, for example, the last time his organization held a general assembly." (Landsberger and Hewitt 1970, 78)

> After 1942 CNC increasingly became part of the political machinery of the official party. Its leadership was no longer elected by the peasantry and its primary function was less and less that of articulating peasant demands. Rather the Regional Committees became paid employees of the official political party, dependent upon key politicians at the state level for their appointment and devoted to assuring those politicians (or their candidates) of the political support of the peasantry (Landsberger and Hewitt 1970, 77).

Given the fact that most CNC cadres were on the payroll of the bank or some other government agency, the Regional Committees "have never attempted to promote the economic independence of peasant groups from government agencies through the formation of regional peasant cooperatives. . . " (Landsberger and Hewitt 1970,81). The only things *ejidatarios* get from the CNC is the processing of complaints against government agencies. However, the matter "is always handled as a *petition* . . . not as a *demand*. The committees can threaten no sanction if their requests are not heeded" (Landsberger and Hewitt 1970, 81).

Why, then, do 80 percent of La Laguna *ejidatarios* remain in the CNC? Landsberger and Hewitt suggest that it is mostly because of the patronage system involving all government agencies, an arrangement that holds out the promise of upward mobility to the most loyal members of CNC (Landsberger and Hewitt 1970, 82).

State Control and the Reemergence of Postcapitalist Struggles

Luis Echeverría's administration (1970–76) began in the midst of a crisis of legitimacy for the Mexican state. The Secretary of Interior in the previous administration, Echeverría was personally identified as the intellectual author and commander of the student massacre on October 2, 1968. Moreover, a popular demonstration in Mexico City again ended in bloodshed and murder at the hands of a paramilitary squad on June 10, 1971. It was also the end of a long period of growth in the

Mexican economy, when the signs of the agricultural crisis had already become apparent (see Chapter 3). Many discontented activists of the 1968 student and popular movement opted for a guerrilla armed strategy to pursue social change, but others concentrated on rural or urban mass organizations.

In confronting the crisis of legitimacy, Echeverría combined a discourse of "democratic opening" with heavy repression of the most radical discontent. By 1973, when land invasions were proliferating in several states of Mexico, Echeverría resorted to agrarianist and populist discourse to appease the movement. Such discourse was imposed on him by the rising discontent of the masses, although Echeverría's administration left its own imprint on the ensuing forms of state intervention. He resurrected the whole idea of collectivism for agriculture, establishing legal mechanisms that would encourage it, but simultaneously guaranteed state control of the new collective *ejidos*.

As an example of this intent, I will briefly describe how the *Empresas Ejidales* (Ejido Enterprises) were conceived of and implemented in La Laguna in 1971. Seven of these enterprises were started as a pilot experiment in this region. Article 6 of the founding statute indicated that the administration board would invariably be headed by the administrative technician, an employee of the bank who would be assisted by an accountant and by those responsible for the several branches being managed. Article 16 describes the tasks of the "administrative technician":

> a) to be responsible for the technical, productive, economic, accounting, organizational, commercial and financial aspects [of the enterprise];
>
> b) to coordinate all activities with the Bank, as well as with the agencies which have a relationship with the enterprise;
>
> c) to listen to the opinion of associate members [i.e., the *ejidatarios*] and *accept those which he considers pertinent* [emphasis added];
>
> d) to comply with the official disposition of his superiors, except those which affect the good functioning of the enterprise;
>
> e) to inform the associate members of all the activities of the enterprise when the Bank so requests and at least once a month;
>
> f) to attend the assemblies of associate members (cited in Aguilar Solís and Araujo 1984, 23).

Quite clearly, the tasks delineated above expected the administrative technician to be a "one-man band" guaranteeing state control. As a bank employee, he had to look after the state's interests.

This ambitious state-control project failed, however. In San Miguel, the enterprises only worked for a few years, and they hardly ever showed a profit. Corruption soon developed among the bank employees, and the *ejidatarios* became disillusioned. By the end of 1985, a mattress enterprise had been closed for about five years, and the cement-blocks factory had been rented out to a bank employee for several months.[3]

Therefore, in 1975 the state implemented a more important initiative to secure state control of the newly encouraged collective *ejidos:* the unification of the three official banks for rural credit to form the new National Bank for Rural Credit (*Banco Nacional de Crédito Rural,* or Banrural). This measure was accompanied by the promulgation of a new General Law for Rural Credit (*Ley General de Crédito Rural,* the central implication of which was to combat the fragmentation of *ejidos:* Only whole *ejidos* were now considered credit-worthy subjects.

Ironically, then, the longstanding tradition of boycotting *ejidos* by splintering them into several "credit societies" was now reversed. It had been an effective policy for dismantling the economic and political power of the Central Union, but it had also created a terribly inefficient and bureaucratic monster. The new policy obviously came into conflict with the CNC cadres, for their clientele was precisely the multiple-credit societies that they had helped to engender. All of these societies were now to be recentralized; they were to deal directly with the bank, not through the mediation of the cadre-brokers.

The new statist and productivist approach met with heavy resistance in La Laguna, both from the local cadres and the state governor of Coahuila, Oscar Flores Tapia. He had established a close alliance with the cadres in order to achieve political control of agrarian unrest. This group's opposition to federal measures was finally resolved through violence. Several high officials of federal agencies were beaten up by the cadre thugs at a party, and the main leaders were eventually incarcerated on charges of fraud. Flores Tapia was accused of "unexplainable enrichment" and removed from his gubernatorial post. Moreover, the bank withdrew all its subsidy for the CNC.

At the same time, in mid-1975, land takeovers proliferated in the region, along with labor disputes in capitalist agricultural enterprises. A new agrarian movement began to emerge in La Laguna. Several capitalist farms faced militant agricultural workers, the majority of them sons of *ejidatarios.* Most of these labor disputes originated in the firing of workers who had financial problems or who wanted to organize into unions to demand a collective bargaining process.

The most significant struggle was that which took place in the property called Batopilas. The owners had failed to pay wages for ten weeks; they wanted to dismiss the workers and then sell the property. But the workers mobilized and started a strike on January 27, 1976 (*El Día* 1985a).

This struggle quickly mushroomed from a labor dispute into an agrarian movement for land and self-managed collective production. The four-month strike grew into a regional conflict. The urban-squatter settlers' movement was at its peak in the cities of Torreón, Francisco I. Madero, and San Pedro de las Colonias, Coahuila. The urban squatter settlers, predominantly of rural background, supported the agricultural workers, sent them food, helped them distribute leaflets, and participated in demonstrations in the urban centers of the region. Many students and *ejidos* also joined the solidarity moves, and in April 1976 the agricultural workers took over the land. As employer resistance stiffened, the struggle escalated into a postcapitalist agrarian movement. In May the governor agreed to proceed with the land expropriation and to support the credit requests by the new *ejidatarios*.

By the end of the 1980s, the Batopilas *ejidatarios* had become exemplary collective producers with a self-managed and democratic organization of production. Moreover, several other *ejidos* followed their route: They wanted to reconstitute the experience of the old Central Union, in which their parents had been activists. They also founded a Coalition of Collective Ejidos of La Laguna (*Coalición de Ejidos Colectivos de La Laguna*) and joined a national organization of independent oppositional organizations: UNORCA (*Unión Nacional de Organizaciones Regionales Campesinas Autónomas*, or the National Union of Autonomous Regional Peasant Organizations), founded on April 6, 1985 (*El Día* 1985b).

Batopilas and the nine other *ejidos* in the coalition are small fraction of La Laguna *ejidos*, however. The vast majority of them are still in disarray or under firm control by the economic apparatuses of the state.

Conclusion

The agricultural workers of La Laguna have most closely resembled the typical idea of proletarians, both in structural as well as in cultural terms, at least in the beginning of the period under study: The class agents were agricultural workers who lived predominantly from wages, and the original objectives of their struggle centered on labor-type demands (wages and collective bargaining). Given their background in capitalist farms, it is not surprising that these class agents got involved in postcapitalist production when they got land grants in the form of collective *ejidos*. Although its benefits accrued privately, the labor process in capitalist farms generally involves cooperation among direct producers. This character contrasts with the more isolated and individually-based peasant labor process. Thus, the new collective *ejidatarios* were ready to pursue a democratic and self-managed productive organization in Time One, as summarized in Table 5.5.

As their economic and political power increased, however, La Laguna collective producers became the target of a major state attack and boycott. Procapitalist state policies in Times Two and Three of this region's social history, however, had the effect of transforming the very structural position of class agents. Their self-managed cooperative production units were severely fragmented, converting direct producers into peasant-workers dependent on the state and its network of corrupt, opportunist cadres. By Time Four, however, the bulk of La Laguna *ejidatarios* had been turned more clearly into a semiproletariat dependent on wages (*anticipos*) from the state.

This form of statist proletarianization certainly did not involve a popular-democratic politics, except in the beginning, when direct producers maintained control of their productive process. The changes in the structural position of class agents provoked by the state also precipitated cultural changes that substantially modified the original objects of struggle. Indeed, the structural changes in La La-

TABLE 5.5   Political Class Trajectory and Objects of Struggle in La Laguna

Moment	Agents	Objects	Outcomes
Time One 1935–47	agricultural workers	wages/collective bargaining	self-management/ collective *ejido*
Time Two 1947–65	noncapitalist collective producers	defense of collective and credit to become peasant-workers	fragmentation, peasantization, subordination to the state
Time Three 1965–75	peasant-workers, somewhat proletarianized	credits and water for viable peasant enterprises	state-controlled, fragmented individual *ejidos,* with cadre brokers
Time Four 1975–90s	semiproletarians under state control	wages, credit, and more land	state-controlled, fragmented *ejidos,* postcapitalist organization in coalition of *ejidos*

SOURCE: Elaborated from analysis in this chapter.

guna entailed a shift from a rather proletarian culture (which might easily take a postcapitalist direction) to a peasant culture focused on individual production. Undoubtedly, this peasant culture was geared more to the market than to subsistence thanks to a generations-old tradition of heavy market involvement. What accounts for this cultural change is the fact that *ejidatarios* have been left with some decision-making capacity on an individual basis, at the level of the immediate production process. Thus, for instance, certain individual productivity differences among *ejidatarios* have clearly emerged and have strengthened individualistic tendencies.

When the Central Union was still strong, it was identified with the policies of the Communist Party of Mexico or the Popular Socialist Party (*Partido Popular Socialista,* or PPS), depending on the time involved. Such identification and the actual links of some *ejiditarios* to these political parties sometimes resulted in the use of the economic organization of *ejidatarios* as a "conveyor belt" for the political purposes of the party. The effects of these practices were quite damaging for the productive organization in La Laguna. First, the productive organization often had to proceed according to a political rather than an economic logic, with negative consequences for productivity. Second, once the identification was clear between collectives and left political parties, the former became an easy target when the state decided to attack the left organizations, even though the collectives had been generally quite productive economic units. Although independent from the state, then, class organizations were not autonomous from the party (either the PCM or the PPS). This distinction between independence and autonomy has been rightly stressed in recent Mexican literature on the agrarian movements (Moguel, Botey, and Hernández 1992; Grammont 1996).

As anticipated in Chapters 1 and 2, the Mexican state did not hesitate to be inconsistent in implementing its agrarian policies in a given region to accomplish its political goals. During *Cardenismo* policies were generally noncapitalist in regions like La Laguna, where there was a strong and militant movement. Peons were organized into labor unions, and they acquired tremendous power, enough to stop agricultural and (with the solidarity of urban workers) industrial production. It was the real power of direct producers in La Laguna, therefore, that accounted for the predominantly noncapitalist character of initial state intervention there. As we will see in the following chapter, however, where the regional correlation of forces favored an agroindustrial bourgeoisie, the same *Cardenista* state did not hesitate to side with the powerful against the agricultural direct producers.

Notes

1. These authors take a fairly broad definition of the Comarca Lagunera, in which they include 15 municipalities, rather than only 9, as most other authors do. In their case, 10 municipalities are from Durango and 5 from Coahuila; whereas in the narrower definition it is only 4 from Durango and 5 from Coahuila. With the broad definition, according to the preliminary 1991 Agricultural and Livestock Census, "there are 41,842 rural producers, of whom 38,555 are ejidatarios, 2,872 are private producers, and 415 are mixed producers" (Salinas de Gortari and Solís González, 1994:12).

2. Personal interview by the author with Enrique Vázquez, former general manager of the Banco Agropecuario de La Laguna (one of three goverment banks for rural credit that had been merged into Banrural in 1975), 10/29/85.

3. Personal interviews by the author with Luis Ortega, 10/30/85, who was the first "administrative technician" in the San Miguel Ejidal Enterprises from September 1971 to August 1972; and with Jesús Ortíz Morales, who was one of the founding ejidatarios in San Miguel, 11/1/85.

6

Atencingo: Peasant-Entrepreneurs and Social Differentiation

Agrarian reform in Mexico, as we saw Chapter 3, was one of the central results of the first major revolution in the twentieth century (1910–17), apparently recreating a peasantry (Wolf 1969). In the sugar industry, as well as in other agroindustries, however, the state was more interested in securing tight control of agricultural production for industrial processing (e.g., tobacco and barley) than in creating a peasantry. The social result of agrarian reform in such sectors was the preponderant proletarianization of direct producers.

Paradoxically, the embrace of economic liberalism by the Mexican state after the mid–1980s (called neoliberalism in Mexico) has fostered a counteragrarian reform that has nevertheless conduced to setting up the conditions for a peculiar type of peasantry to prosper. The new Agrarian Law of 1992 reversed the main features of the legendary agrarian reform that had crested in the 1930s. This law, which resulted from revising Article 27 of the Mexican Constitution, formally ended the state's responsibility for land redistribution. It also allowed for the possibility of selling and privatizing formerly inalienable *ejido* land and promoted associations between private capitalists and *ejido* farmers (Barry 1995; Cornelius 1992; DeWalt, Rees, and Murphy 1994; Gates 1996; and Chapter 3 in this volume).

Simply put, the historical paradox is that while the legendary agrarian reform actually proletarianized large masses of agricultural direct producers, the current counterreform has created the conditions for the peasantization of at least a minority of them. In fact, if such a peasantry does develop in sugarcane production, it will still be subordinated to the needs and interests of corporate sugar-mill

I have greatly benefited from the generous and thoughtful comments provided by Marilyn Gates, Peter Singelmann, and four anonymous reviewers for *Rural Sociology* before publication of Otero (1998a), parts of which are used in this chapter. Horacio Mackinlay, Jaime Moises Bailón, and David Myhre made useful comments to Otero (1998b), parts of which are also used in this chapter.

owners. Given the market-driven nature of current reforms, direct producers are now being forced to take on much greater responsibility for the productive process than in previous decades; they run the risk of being thrown out of the market of commodity producers if they do not comply (Singelmann and Otero 1995). Moreover, the conditions for obtaining and selling individual land certificates, and thus for land reconcentration, have been established by the new Agrarian Law.

This chapter explores the process of political class formation of sugarcane growers in the region of Atencingo, in the southwestern part of the state of Puebla; it is next to Emiliano Zapata's state of Morelos, in the warm and fertile valley of Izúcar de Matamoros. My account is based on the few published sources on the region, field observations, archival research done since 1988, and a survey questionnaire distributed in 1995. My field work was conducted in a series of one-month visits: July 1988, June 1992, June 1994, and June-July 1995. Strategic interviews were conducted with mill executives and field staffers, peasant leaders, *ejidatarios*, private landowners, local authorities, mill workers and union leaders. Archival research was conducted at the Puebla Office of the Secretariat of Agrarian Reform. All files pertaining to the *ejidos* of Atencingo and its annexes were consulted. The nine former annexes eventually became *ejidos* in their own right, one for each of the following villages: Atencingo, Colón, Jaltepec, La Galarza, Lagunillas, Raboso, Rijo, San José Teruel, and San Nicolas Tolentino. Archival research was facilitated by the able assistance of Francisco Javier Gómez Carpinteiro of the Autonomous University of Puebla.

The survey questionnaire was applied to a randomly selected sample of 250 sugarcane growers in the months of June and July of 1995 by Gómez Carpinteiro and four of his best social anthropology students. I trained the team in the intricacies of the survey questions and sugarcane production; Francisco had already conducted field research in San José Teruel for his M.A. thesis (Gómez Carpinteiro 1995).

From thirty-nine *ejidos* or communities that currently supply sugarcane to the Atencingo mill, we sampled twenty. Nine of these were the original communities making up the "*Ejido* of Atencingo and its Annexes" from 1938 to 1971. All nine were included in the sample, considering that the struggles against *ejido* collectivism, centered as they were in these *ejidos*, might have resulted in some differences in cultural orientation or political preferences. The other eleven *ejidos* were chosen at random. Once the twenty communities were selected, random samples of *ejidatarios* were drawn from each, using the latest list of all sugarcane producers in the village, which we obtained from the Mexican Institute for Social Security (*Instituto Mexicano del Seguro Social*, or IMSS). Numbers drawn from each community were proportional to their representation in the total of cane growers in the entire zone, which is close to 5,000. The sample size was 250 to obtain an error below three standard deviations. Each interview took about one hour, with questions ranging from the organization of household production to cultural and political opinions. The vast majority of growers were eager to participate in the survey and offer their views. Questions and closed responses were read out by interviewers, who then wrote down the answers.

The Agrarian History and Cultural Setting

At the turn of the twentieth century, the Atencingo region had lushly fertile valleys and genetically diverse vegetation particularly well suited for sugarcane production (Palacios 1917). Although genetic diversity has declined considerably because of monocrop production, the region remains one of the most productive in sugarcane. The rest of the state of Puebla dedicates a large proportion of land to the cultivation of corn, the typical peasant crop in Mexico. In the central plateau of Puebla alone, about 50,000 peasant households produce corn on approximately 95,000 hectares of land. Thus, cornfields account for as much as 80 percent of cultivated land in the state. Of this production, fewer than 40 percent of the direct producers were selling any corn outside their own villages by 1970, which indicates a low degree of commodification (Felstehausen and Díaz-Cisneros 1985, 286). Some 87 percent of the state's arable land is cultivated through rainfall agriculture, and the rest is irrigated. The ownership of arable land is concentrated in a small number of proprietors: 25 percent of the land is concentrated in only 1 percent of the production units; whereas 37 percent is distributed among thousands of *ejidatarios* with holdings with a mean surface of three hectares each (Cortés Sánchez 1981, 50–51).

This is the larger context of the region of Atencingo. The *ejidos* in the region developed in relation to a capitalist sugar mill located in the town of Atencingo. William Jenkins, a former U.S. Consul in Puebla, who had gained considerable wealth and political influence in his official post by means of nonagricultural business investments, started an economic complex in the valley in 1921, when he purchased the mill and lands of the *hacienda* of Atencingo. This was followed, during the early 1920s, by his purchasing, little by little, of all the neighboring *haciendas*. This expansion was made possible by the financial weakness of the original owners and their fear of the agrarian reform pressures that grew out of the revolution. As he began to reconstruct the Atencingo mill, the other mills attached to the former *haciendas* were stripped and their equipment removed to Atencingo. He then appointed Manuel Pérez, a Spaniard who was reputed to be Mexico's best cane agronomist, as manager of the industrial complex. Pérez remained in this post until his death some twenty years later. The sugar mill eventually expanded to assume great importance in the national economy.

During the 1920s and 1930s, popular pressures for land reform mounted; the land-hungry villagers also constituted a reserve army of labor power for Jenkins. When the resident labor force was insufficient, the mill employees were dispatched to the villages to recruit temporary work gangs. "Owing to a labor surplus in the region, Pérez could readily recruit temporary outside laborers, locate replacements for unsatisfactory ones, and subject those already employed to working conditions they might otherwise have objected to" (Ronfeldt 1973, 16).

Political Class Formation in Atencingo

The main social groups and classes involved in sugar production are sugarcane growers, cane cutters, mill workers, and industrialists. Growers might be *ejidatarios,* private farmers, or mill owners who have integrated industrial and agricultural production. *Ejidatarios* account for about 70 percent of sugarcane production in Mexico (71 percent in Atencingo), a fact that highlights the relevance of the new land tenure legislation.

Until 1988 cane growers had been one of the favored groups of land cultivators who had benefited from agrarian reform. Because sugar has been a key element in popular diets, the state played a central role in controlling the production of sugarcane and its industrial transformation into sugar. The relationship between sugarcane growers and the state became a dependent but reciprocal one: The state received political loyalty from this group of cultivators, and the latter received low but secure incomes (Singelmann 1993). Neoliberal legal and policy changes since the mid–1980s have basically eliminated this reciprocal relationship, fundamentally throwing into question both the political loyalty to the state and the formerly secure incomes of cane growers and other peasant groups (Barry 1995; Gates 1993; 1996; Singelmann 1995; Singelmann and Otero 1995).

Cane growers have undergone several structural changes in the past few decades, moving from a highly proletarianized position, heavily dependent on wage income from the sugar mill and with nearly no autonomy in the production process, to their current fragmentation as a semiproletarianized class of producers, with 25 to 35 percent having succeeded in becoming peasant entrepreneurs. There were two middle phases: an ephemeral experience with self-managed and cooperative production resulting in confrontations between agricultural producers and the mill's administration (1947–52) and a state-controlled phase in which the government appointed the agricultural cooperative manager (1952–61).

Creation of an Agricultural Proletariat in the Broad Sense

In 1937, when President Lázaro Cárdenas was preparing a sweeping national land reform program, impatience, militancy, and strength were growing in the several thousand landless village peasants who remained in the Atencingo region. Because most of these landless peasants lived in villages that had already been granted *ejidos,* the local *ejido* authorities were petitioning for the enlargement of existing *ejidos* or the formation of new ones to accommodate them.

The best lands in the Atencingo region were owned by William Jenkins. Just as the villagers were about to succeed in their demand for these lands, however, Jenkins teamed up with his friend the state governor and intervened to convince

President Cárdenas that the resident laborers of the Atencingo complex should have first claim to the property. His goal was to control cane production through the mill, even if he had to forego land ownership. Conveniently enough, not only for Jenkins but also for many other owners of industrialized *haciendas* and plantations in Mexico, on August 9, 1937, Cárdenas promulgated new laws confirming and clarifying the rights of resident peons over the lands they worked, which had originally passed provisionally in 1936 to address the case of La Laguna. Before this law, only neighboring villagers had been eligible to receive land, while resident peons had been excluded from the benefits of the agrarian reform (Ronfeldt 1973).

Furthermore, in order to make the deal more attractive, Jenkins offered to bestow the lands to his peons and workers and to forego compensation for his property. Hence, 8,268 hectares were allocated to 2,043 of the eligible resident peons living in the area of Atencingo and eight other villages. The expropriation excluded the maximum private-property holding that Jenkins was legally allowed to retain, some 150 hectares in Atencingo. It also excluded some 2,585 hectares that were occupied by buildings or that were deemed unfit for cultivation. The new legislation contained a number of regulations that guaranteed a continuous supply of raw material for Jenkins's sugar mill. All lands were to be worked collectively, and only sugarcane would be planted, rotated with rice every three years. A new cooperative society was to manage the giant *ejido's* financial and agricultural affairs. While this cooperative was supposed to be managed by the *ejido* and only *ejidatarios* were admitted as associate members, the manager of the industrial mill was given considerable power over its operation. He was empowered, for instance, to select and appoint the manager of the *ejidatarios'* cooperative (Ronfeldt 1973).

Thus, while many of the fervently *Zapatista* villagers of this region fought for the revolution and the return of the lands they formerly owned, they lost the decisive battle to Jenkins. Thanks to his political dealings, the least revolutionary, least mobilized workers in the valley were granted the best lands. All leadership posts in the cooperative, whether elective or appointive, were filled by people loyal to the mill administration. In practice, therefore, the Atencingo *ejidatarios* remained the mill's peons. As before, they were hired according to the mill's needs, and they had no practical rights over the new collective *Ejido* of Atencingo and its Annexes. They lived only from their wages, since no profits were distributed between 1938 and 1947. Any grievance could be settled with repression, and no significant organization could emerge for most of this period. Because such direct producers were *ejidatarios* and thus had formal access to land, they fit Luisa Paré's definition of a "proletariat in the broad sense" (1977). In other words, cane growers at this point were proletarians in a peasant disguise whose labor process was controlled by the capitalist sugar mill. In this initial period (1938–47), state intervention succeeded in producing a bourgeois-hegemonic outcome with regard to sugarcane growers. As de Grammont put it, "After the creation of the collective ejido and, at least until 1945, the mill had a better situation than in previous years since the state had practically eliminated its principal enemy: the Zapatistas" (1979, 206).

Self-Management and Democratic Production: An Ephemeral Alternative

By 1945, however, the *ejidatarios* began to make the following demands: The collective *ejido* was to be divided into nine separate ones (i.e., one for each village), a new *ejidatario*-controlled cooperative was to be created with internal assignment of individual plots, and the *ejidatarios* were to have freedom to cultivate crops other than sugarcane and rice. Clearly, these demands were meant to create an independent peasant economy in opposition to the domination by industrial capital. It did not matter that the economic class position of direct producers was that of a rural proletariat. Their demands bore an obvious peasant character.

Thus, until 1945 the main cleavage was between *ejidatarios* and their so-called representatives in the cooperative society, who, in fact, represented the interests of the industrial mill. In 1947, when they were replaced by leaders who actually represented the *ejidatarios,* a new cleavage emerged—between the *ejidatarios'* cooperative and the mill administration. At this point, the *ejidatarios* assumed the character of cooperative direct producers and tried to defend themselves from industrial capital. They were no longer wage earners but cooperative commodity producers (Paré 1979b).

This situation engendered new internal rifts among the *ejidatarios.* Once they were able to control the administrative apparatus of the cooperative, the leaders realized that parceling could rupture the class solidarity of the cooperative against the mill if the latter were to bargain individually with each of over 2,000 *ejidatarios.*

Several approaches thus arose among the *ejidatarios* and their leaders that were closely linked to prevailing cultural orientations in the region. One approach was to oppose the division of the *ejido* in order to maintain a strong position in its struggle against the mill. Another group of leaders had a similar approach, but they were motivated by the possibility of becoming political strongmen (*caciques*) through control of the cooperative. Porfirio Jaramillo, who was democratically elected as cooperative manager in 1947, had an ambiguous policy reflecting the other approaches in his constituency: He proposed to maintain one single *ejido* divided into individual plots but working collectively for sugarcane and individually for other crops. A different group, which benefited from the relationship with the mill, systematically opposed Jaramillo. Others were convinced of the need to parcel the *ejido* and began to oppose the Jaramillo administration they had elected.

Thus, far from staying united in their struggle against the mill, multiple cleavages among the *ejidatarios* postponed the confrontation with their main antagonist while severely weakening their organizational class capacity. All of this, of course, had much to do with most of the *ejidatarios'* cultural preference for becoming small, independent, peasant-family producers rather than being members of a cooperative or a collective *ejido*. Lacking a strong democratic tradition, they felt the *ejido*, rather than providing a secure basis for unified struggle, might prove to be an organizational trap that would facilitate control by the mill or a strongman (Gómez Carpinteiro 1997).

Some important events reinforced the cane growers' peasant cultural orientation during Jaramillo's administration. After the 1946–1947 harvest, profits were distributed to *ejidatarios* for the first time in the *ejido's* nine-year history. From 1946 to 1952, important investments were made in mechanization so as to free the *ejido* from the mill. Previously, the mill's power was reinforced by the *ejido's* need to rent most of the means of transportation from it. A government bank replaced the mill as the only source for *ejido* credit in 1948.

Another crucial event of the *Jaramillista* period (1947–52) was the assignment of "economic parcels" to *ejidatarios:* Each member received a one-hectare plot so that the family could produce crops other than sugarcane. This event was both cause and effect of the peasant orientation of Atencingo's rural proletariat (economically defined). It pushed direct producers into a semiproletarian status, torn between wage income from cane production for the mill and the income from the small plots of land they now controlled. The main crops planted in these plots, corn and beans, were primarily consumed at home, thus complementing wage incomes. Occasionally tomatoes and other vegetables were planted and any surpluses were sold in the local market. The conversion of this proletariat into a relatively prosperous semiproletariat with a strong peasant orientation influenced future struggles in the Atencingo region. Thenceforth, direct producers always focused on resisting proletarianization and attempting to achieve the status of small, independent commodity producers, or peasant entrepreneurs.

Hobbled by the contradictory goals of the cooperative administration and its social base, the experience of self-managed and democratic production came to an end after only five years in 1952. Despite all the efforts by the cooperative's democratic management, its financial and production policies for sugarcane failed. Such failure was due mainly to a systematic boycott waged by the mill, which aggravated internal divisions in the *ejido*. One example of the effects of this boycott was that the mill left sugarcane unprocessed and failed to pay for it as provided by a legal decree of 1943. This decree required the sugar mills to pay for all sugarcane contracted for, whether it had processed it or not. The result of the boycott was a drastic decrease in sugarcane production by *ejidatarios*, who, after 1949, favored other crops instead. By 1951–52, harvested sugarcane had decreased by 50 percent (Ronfeldt 1973).

This critical situation ultimately led the state to plan direct intervention to ensure a continuous supply of raw material to the sugar mill. On January 29, 1952, the president of Mexico issued a decree creating a reorganizing committee to supervise the administration of Atencingo and its Annexes. The main mandate of this commission, led by the state governor, was to appoint a manager for the *ejido* cooperative. The mill thus received state support in order to return *ejidatarios* to their position of de facto wage workers and to stimulate industrial profits. Nevertheless, as Ronfeldt wrote, during this period "the government commission replaced the mill administration as the primary target of a new opposition struggle for power and reform" (1973, 105).

One crucial point left out by Ronfeldt (1973) in his otherwise exceptional political history of Atencingo is the presence of the Mexican Communist Party (*Partido Comunista Mexicano,* or PCM) up until Jaramillo's ousting by the state. Porfirio Jaramillo, a member of the PCM, was actually recruited from the neighboring state of Morelos to lead the *ejidatarios* in this region.[1] During Jaramillo's service as the cooperative manager (1947–52), many Atencingo *ejidatarios* became members of the PCM, as had occurred in La Laguna and other regions with a predominantly capitalist agriculture (Carr 1986). In the midst of President Miguel Alemán's Cold War administration (1946–52), Jaramillo's approach, which promoted a popular-democratic alternative, could have hardly lasted very long. Alemán's administration systematically boycotted collective *ejidos* with socialist or Communist leaderships that proliferated during the Cárdenas administration (Carr 1986; Hewitt de Alcántara 1978).

An *ejidatario* from the ex-annex of Lagunillas remembers, however, that at that time "there were many cells [the basic organizational unit of a party of cadres] of the party [the PCM]. I still have that book on the *Problems of Leninism* with which they indoctrinated us," he commented. This *ejidatario,* having been a Communist, was in the 1970s and 1980s one of the main leaders of individual as opposed to collective agriculture. In fact, he claims to have been the promoter of the first individual group against the collective in Lagunillas, one of the nine original villages. Moreover, by 1988 he had already defended the idea of privatizing the *ejido.*

Much of the explanation for this change in him and most other *ejidatarios* lies in the peculiar forms of collectivism that they endured before and after the *Jaramillista* experience; first the collective was a virtual appendage of the mill, and then it became a quasi-state enterprise. Both forms are a far cry from self-managed and democratic production in which direct producers gain control of the production process. The outcome was, in any case, a mismatch between Jaramillo's drive toward this type of cooperative production and the cultural aspiration of a majority of cane growers to become independent peasant producers. Because the popular-democratic alternative was more the leadership's project than its constituency's aspiration at the time, it could not be consolidated. When this mismatch was combined with the repressive response of the state, the result was firm state control for nearly a decade.

From State Control to Strongman Rule

The state's response to Jaramillo's administration was strong, authoritarian, and repressive. It imposed two cooperative managers who would, in turn, control most agricultural and political affairs of the region from 1952 to 1961. While the increasing profits were distributed among *ejidatarios* during the first administration, it systematically discriminated against opposition *ejidatarios* and favored collaborationists through a patronage system established by the first state-appointed manager, who also introduced gunmen as a form of social control. Porfirio Jaramillo and other leaders of the opposition movement were assassinated during this administration. The mill was generally favored insofar as a steadily increasing cane supply was secured. Expressing their disagreement with the state, however, *ejidatarios* joined the opposition National Zapatista Front (*Frente Nacional Zapatista*). Thus, a negative state intervention against cane growers eventually resulted in their assuming an oppositional political stance.

After the two state-controlled periods came to an end through pressure from below, an elected *ejidatario* took over management but eventually became entrenched as a strongman. Atencingo's history in this period (1961–70) was one of increased factionalism, corruption, renewed intimidation through violence, and erratic economic achievements in cane production. The main protagonist of this history was the neo-*Jaramillista* leader Guadalupe Ramírez, who became the new manager of the cooperative. For the *ejidatarios,* his reaching this post was initially supposed to symbolize the movement's triumph against state control. Ramírez's promises during his campaign for office centered on the division and parceling of the *ejido* and on revoking the 1952 presidential decree, which imposed state control. The latter was achieved immediately as a precondition for *ejidatarios* to elect their cooperative manager, but the most fundamental demands were quickly put aside because of multiple legal and bureaucratic obstacles.

Ramírez soon broke ties with the independent National Zapatista Front, joining the new National Sugarcane Producers' Association affiliated to the National Peasant Confederation (*Confederación Nacional Campesina,* CNC), an affiliate of the ruling PRI.[2] Thus, the Ramírez regime continued to serve state and industrial interests while reaping the benefits of administrative power and control over the patronage system. A positive state intervention combined with corrupt leadership resulted in bourgeois hegemony.

The triumph of *ejidatarios* in electing one of their own to the management position was more apparent than real, since actual control over their work process and livelihood still eluded them. There arose a new dichotomy between the objectives of the leadership and those of the *ejidatarios,* but unlike the Jaramillo period, this time the leader was subservient to the mill's administration and the state. This outcome highlights the need to further explore the role of leadership in political class formation. Depending on the type of leadership, agency might sometimes be more important than structure.

New Peasant Entrepreneurs, Proletarians, and the Semiproletariat

Guadalupe Ramírez's reign came to an end in 1970 with mounting pressure from cane growers for division of the *ejido* and parceling of land. Government authorization of the division of the giant *ejido,* along with Ramírez's ouster from the cooperative's administration, represented a peasant triumph. It would take years, however, before peasants were able not only to parcel out the *ejidos* but also to get individual credit for sugarcane production and finally obtain individual certificates for the lands they worked on. Formal and legal division of the *ejido* into nine *ejidos,* one for each of the villages making up "Atencingo and its Annexes," took place between the end of 1973 and early 1974. But pressures to parcel each *ejido* among individual members bore fruit early on. This struggle was marked by increasing factionalism within each *ejido,* a development that further contributed to the transformation of the *ejido* from an organizational class capacity to an instrument of state control. Such class capacity had been at least latent (and at times overt) in the possibility of a united struggle based on the single large *ejido.* In the *ejidatarios'* eyes, though, the collective *ejido* had functioned primarily as an instrument of the state to implement control over them rather than as an instrument to advance their own interests (Gómez Carpinteiro 1997).

The first archival record of the implementation of land parceling along "areas of individual responsibility" within the collective production system came from a group of peasants from the ex-annex of San José Teruel on June 11, 1972. It addressed the state official of agrarian reform, accusing Guadalupe Ramírez and other former leaders of directing the works of several engineers who were dividing up the land, even though the law required them to work collectively. By May, 10, 1974, however, there was a formal petition from several *ejidatarios* from Lagunillas to form a group separate from the collective *ejido* in order to work along the lines of "individual responsibility." While organizing production along individual lines was permitted by law, government officials made it clear that this policy did not amount to granting individual title to the land or making credit available to individual *ejidatarios*. Therefore, farm management remained collective. It was not until 1983 that individual credit was allowed by areas of individual responsibility (Gómez Carpinteiro 1995). While such areas had been allotted individually since 1974–75, the only money *ejidatarios* ever saw from the farming process was in the form of wages. They were paid as peons and complained that there were many deductions for items such as celebrations, sports courts, bridges, canals, and so on.

With new demands centering on individual production and credit, the political protest and turmoil of previous decades devolved into small-group politicking. The only important regional struggle after division and parceling happened in 1983, when every *ejidatario* had to comply with the 1979 sugarcane decree requiring sugarcane growers to affiliate with either one of the two PRI organizations that formally represented their economic interests. With this provision, which has been renewed in later sugarcane decrees up to the latest, in 1991, each cane grower was forced to choose between the CNC or the CNPP (both part of the PRI) for political-economic affiliation. Therefore, growers have been legally prevented from forming oppositional organizations for struggle.[3] For those not declaring an affiliation, each sugar mill discounts the membership fee anyway and then disburses it between the two PRI organizations in proportion to its total regional membership.

The CNC had obtained a loan for the collective operation of agricultural machinery in 1982 but, given the *ejidatarios'* phobia toward collectivism, more than 70 percent of sugarcane growers in Atencingo chose to affiliate with the National Confederation of Small-Property Owners (*Confederación Nacional de Pequeños Propietarios*, CNPP), renamed the National Confederation of Rural Producers (*Confederación Nacional de Productores Rurales*, or CNPR) in 1993. Ironically, the CNPP's affiliates have been private-property owners (as its name indicates), whereas peasants have typically identified with the CNC (National Peasant Confederation). The CNPP operates not so much as a political organization but as an economic trade union in which the leadership keeps a distance from the official politics and policies of the PRI and is less politicized than the CNC or the Workers' Confederation of Mexico (*Confederación de Trabajadores de México*, CTM). But it remains a corporatist organization affiliated to the ruling PRI.

Such political-economic affiliation of Atencingo cane growers reflects the fact that the aspirations of many are to become peasant entrepreneurs rather than remaining subsistence peasants or semiproletarians torn between wage labor and subsistence agriculture. Given the dual production of sugarcane and vegetables, Atencingo peasant entrepreneurs have come to find themselves in a rather complex economic class situation. They do not truly constitute an agrarian bourgeoisie. As sugarcane producers they usually hire wage labor from three sources: *Libres* (freemen) living inside the *ejido* villages, literally a free labor force with no access to land except to produce for an employer in exchange for a wage; sons of *ejidatarios,* the eldest of whom expect to inherit the *ejido* titles; and migrant workers from the valley and highland peasant communities (Lara 1979). As small commodity producers, however, growers continue to confront industrial capital as their main antagonist in cane production. Furthermore, with vegetable production in the economic parcels, *ejidatarios* confront neither wage workers nor monopoly capital. Rather, the character of this part of their production is typically that of small commodity producers in a competitive market. This real stratification, which involves the development of a middle stratum between the industrial mill and the landless proletariat, prevents an alliance between the small producers and the proletariat against the capitalist mill. Moreover, the *ejidatarios* clearly benefit from the exploitation of wage workers.

Having succeeded in dividing the *ejido* and parceling the land, cane growers effectively deprived themselves of the possibility of constructing class organizations based on the structural capacities of the *ejido*. State manipulation of the *ejidos* during the time of collectivism spawned a deep-seated aversion to anything that smacks of this form of organization, even in the face of clear and certain indications that cooperative production is economically superior to individual production.

That the collective organization of production was best for *ejidatarios* economically is demonstrated in Tables 6.1 and 6.2. These tables are based on eight of the nine *ejidos.* By 1988, only San José Teruel continued to work collectively as a single group. La Galarza, Raboso, Colón, and Rijo each had two groups, one collective and the other individual; but Atencingo, Jaltepec, and Lagunillas fragmented more drastically, into six to seven groups each. The tables, which depict average gross monthly income and average productivity by *ejidatario,* make two points quite clear: (1) that those *ejidos* in which there were two groups, with one of them individual and the other collective, the latter group invariably had a higher productivity (Table 6.1); and (2) that productivity decreased further as more groups proliferated within each *ejido* (Table 6.2).

TABLE 6.1   Atencingo Region: Monthly Gross Income per Sugarcane Producer, by Form of Organization, 1987–88 Harvest[a]

EJIDO	*Average Surface (hectares)*	*Number of Members*	*Gross Monthly Income (current pesos, 1988)*	*Productivity Index*[b]
Teruel	4.0	144	738,725	33.56
La Galarza				
Collective	2.5	127	801,939	44.99
Individual	2.5	154	710,005	28.37
Raboso				
Collective	2.5	140	629,428	13.80
Individual	2.5	99	567,139	2.54
Colón				
Collective	4.0	107	664,646	20.17
Individual	4.0	30	462,339	−16.41
Rijo				
Collective	n/a[c]	53	1,020,887	84.58
Individual	n/a[c]	58	731,315	32.23
Atencingo[d]	2.2	332	483,476	−12.58
Jaltepec[d]	2.9	309	513,189	−7.21
Lagunillas[d]	2.8	441	418,362	−24.36

[a] The minimum wage in 1988 was 240,000 pesos per month.

[b] This index is simply the percentage difference between the weighted gross monthly income of all producers in the nine Atencingo ex-annexes and the average within each *ejido* group, by form of organization. The general average is 553,072 pesos per month.

[c] n/a = not available.

[d] Atencingo, Jaltepec, and Lagunillas have been fragmented into five to six groups each.

SOURCE: elaborated from various internal documents of the Atencingo sugar mill, provided by members of its managerial personnel: "Padrón de Productores del Ingenio de Atencingo, S.A.", "Resumen General Diario de Caña Recibida en Báscula, Zafra 1987–88." The figures for average surface were provided by the chief of field operations.

TABLE 6.2   Atencingo, Jaltepec, and Lagunillas: Monthly Gross Income per Sugarcane Producer, by *Ejido* Group, 1987–1988 Harvest[a]

EJIDO	Average Surface (hectares)	Ejidatario Members	Gross Monthly Income (current pesos, 1988)	Productivity Index(%)[b]
Atencingo				
Group #	2.2	332	483,476	−12.58
No. 1		129	444,520	−19.63
No. 1A		54	520,571	−5.88
No. 2		93	543,886	−1.66
No. 2 Collective		4	443,690	−19.78
No. 3		42	425,460	−23.07
Jaltepec				
Group #	2.9	309	513,189	−7.21
No. 1		137	548,940	−0.74
No. 1A		99	506,387	−8.44
No. 2		23	453,859	−17.94
No. 3		27	455,401	−17.66
No. 4		15	407,806	−26.27
No. 5		8	199,338	−66.96
Lagunillas				
Group #	2.8	441	418,362	−24.36
No. 1		173	441,097	−20.25
No. 1A		92	406,769	−26.45
No. 1B		80	474,252	−14.25
No. 2		66	361,925	−34.56
No. 2A		25	293,730	−46.89
No. 3		5	318,942	−42.33

[a] The minimum wage in 1988 was 240,000 pesos per month.

[b] This index is simply the percentage difference between the weighted gross monthly income of all producers in the nine Atencingo ex-annexes and the average within each *ejido* group, by form of organization. The general average is 553,072 pesos per month.

SOURCE: Same as for Table 6.1.

Even though average surface held by each *ejidatario* varies from one *ejido* to the next, this variation also reflects differences in the relative qualities of land; San José Teruel, for instance, with the highest land surface per individual, has the lowest quality of land. Therefore, variations in the productivity index are due to a number of variables, including the different stages of cane fields. In my view, however (confirmed by the mill's filed engineers and many cane growers themselves), such productivity differences are due mainly to the form of productive organization. From an economic point of view, then, the data in these tables provide a strong argument in favor of cooperative production. Yet because of internal political fragmentation, 1988 was the last time there were any collective groups in the Atencingo region.

While the state now presents fewer obstacles to individual producers seeking to control their production processes, the traditional context has substantially shifted since the mid-1980s, particularly since the privatization of sugar mills that started in 1988. In fact, the new context involves a major change in one of the variables that have been used to explain the character of political class organizations: state intervention. To be sure, the state remains a factor, but mostly as an enforcer of the rules of neoliberal reform: a market-centered dynamic.

Privatization and Restructuring of the Sugar Industry

Because most of the sugar mills in Mexico were on the brink of bankruptcy in the mid–1970s, the state began a process of nationalizations, taking over fifty-four of the sixty-four mills by 1982. This measure was an attempt to save jobs and establish tighter control of sugar production and distribution. After the debt crisis that erupted in 1982, however, President Miguel de la Madrid (1982–88) launched a profound restructuring of Mexico's economy and its role in world capitalism. Shifting from a strategy of state intervention, import substitution, industrialization, subsidies, and protectionism, Mexico moved to a neoliberal policy of emphasizing exports, downsizing the state, privatizing state firms, and opening the doors to foreign competition and investment to promote efficiency and productivity (Otero 1996a).

The decision to privatize the sugar industry was not made by the de la Madrid administration alone; it was also a condition imposed by the International Monetary Fund as part of its 1986 structural adjustment package to restructure Mexico's foreign debt (Singelmann 1993). Another reason was the dramatic increase in internal demand for sugar, both by direct consumers and secondary industries (producers of sweet bread, candy, soft drinks, and so on).

This restructuring in the sugar industry signaled a major change in previous forms of state intervention (Singelmann and Otero 1995). Since 1953 *Financiera Nacional Azucarera, S.A.*, a state institution, financed all sugar production in Mexico to maintain low prices for the sweetener. "Sugar prices were fixed from 1958 to 1969, and they were the lowest in the world" (Igartúa 1987, 25).

Aside from this subsidy to consumers and secondary industries, production costs also increased because of the great inefficiency and lack of incentives for industrialists to renew their equipment. A study conducted by *Nacional Financiera* on the adequacy of industrial equipment in sugar mills concluded that, as of 1969, only 25 percent of all sugar mills operated with modern equipment, 45 percent with semiobsolete equipment, and 30 percent with completely obsolete equipment (Igartúa 1987, 27). This industrial inefficiency soon took its toll on sugarcane growers, whose income depended partly on how much sugar the industrial mills extracted from their sugarcane.

By the mid-1980s, sugarcane growers were already facing unfavorable terms of trade with respect to industrial products (García Chavez 1992). They were being doubly squeezed by increasing costs and declining relative prices of their crop. At the same time, the industry, by now largely in government hands, was being managed according to political rather than economic criteria. The government's dilemma was huge: It had to promote capital accumulation in the sugar industry while meeting sugarcane growers' demands for higher crop prices, offer sweeteners to domestic consumers at politically acceptable prices, and subsidize costs of raw materials in secondary industries (Singelmann 1993). The industry, moreover, suffered from corruption and winked at overstaffing to maintain employment levels. As a net result, sugar processing was a losing business for the state (Flora and Otero 1995).

Therefore, in an effort to increase competitiveness and efficiency, the Mexican government began to privatize sugar mills in 1988. The state's newly reduced role in the economy has involved, among other things, the elimination of most price supports for sugarcane and subsidies for agricultural inputs. As a result, the long-standing alliance between cane growers and the state is being redefined. The low but secure incomes that cane growers took for granted in exchange of political loyalty to the state and the ruling party are no longer assured. This novel context poses tremendous challenges to cane growers as producers and to the corporatist organizations of the PRI that had been "representing" them since the early 1980s. Because they can no longer guarantee any special concessions from the state, grower organizations are scrambling to devise new political relationships with their constituency. At the same time, after nearly a decade since reprivatization of sugar mills, the industry has become highly concentrated in a few large corporations. These are perceived by most sugarcane growers as a new threat to their incomes.

The Atencingo mill was one of the first to be sold, partly because its sugarcane suppliers are endowed with some of the very best lands in the country. The industrial plant was beset with problems of overstaffing and corruption, but a new plant had just been installed before its sale. This investment alone may largely explain the heavy losses that the Atencingo mill was showing in the years prior to its privatization in 1988. Installation of the new plant was plagued with multiple technical problems and delays, requiring a total of eight years instead of the initial estimate of two.[4]

The sale of the Atencingo mill can be seen as a bargain for the new owners; the government wanted to give them an incentive to engage in industrial restructuring. The mill's book value was $65.22 million in 1988, but it was sold for only $20.65 million. Moreover, the purchase was arranged with a down payment of only 10 percent of this amount, with the rest payable in ten years. The new owners, however, would need to be very able administrators to cope with the challenging political task of industrial restructuring in a highly combative sector.

Grupo Escorpión, the new corporate owner of the Atencingo mill, was the second-largest producer of bottled soft drinks in Mexico in 1988. It encompassed eight bottling companies from central and southern Mexico, including *Embotel-ladora Metropolitana,* which produces Pepsi-Cola for Mexico City. Since this in-dustry is a major consumer of sugar, *Grupo Escorpión* decided to control its im-portant raw material by integrating backward.

During the first meeting between representatives of the new owners and na-tional and local representatives of CNPP, which I witnessed in July of 1988, the former made a number of promises that may help to give a picture of their man-agerial approach. They said, for instance, that 90 percent of the yields from the 102 hectares of the *Campo de Abajo* (a field used for experimentation with new sugarcane varieties) were to be devoted to social investments in the community, such as schools, sports facilities, and so on. They also said that local managers would have total autonomy in decision-making, with minimal supervision from the corporate headquarters. They hoped to increase processed sugarcane by 50 percent and to introduce new technology in order to produce liquid sugar di-rectly, rather than producing refined sugar first and then melting it for use in soft-drink production. Furthermore, a computerized accounting system would be introduced to give clear figures to each grower. Employment opportunities would be expanded, but the mill itself could not be the main employer of surplus workers. The overall goal was to convert the industrial part of the operation into the most efficient in Mexico.

Seven years after that first meeting, two key promises, unfulfilled as of 1995, were those regarding new technology and investments in community social pro-jects from yields of the *Campo de Abajo.* In fact, there had been few investments in new production technology, although the computerized accounting system was already in place. Moreover, fifty hectares from the *Campo de Abajo* were con-verted for the expansion of housing for mill workers, but sugarcane growers had not gained anything from it.

By the time privatization of the sugar industry had been completed in 1993, much industrial concentration had occurred. Only fifty mills out of sixty-four in 1988 remained in operation, and it was expected that these would further consol-idate into about twenty-five (Aguilar 1993). *Grupo Escorpión* now owns nine mills and controls upwards of 30 percent of sugar production in Mexico, which has come to be dictated by the corporate needs of the Pepsi-Cola bottling conglom-erate and its drive to gain market share from its arch-rival, Coca-Cola. It seems to be succeeding, too. *Grupo Gemex,* Escorpión's corporate parent (whose stocks are publicly traded in New York), is now the largest Pepsico franchise in the world in terms of sales volume and territorial coverage (Varela and Villegas 1993). It gen-erates $100 million in yearly sales in the Mexico City metropolitan area alone (Olguín 1993). Coca-Cola de México removed its chief executive officer in 1994, partly due to his "failure to snap-up a few sugar mills when that industry was pri-vatized. . . . The company is now forced to buy sugar from Pepsi distributors that had more foresight" (*El Financiero Internacional* 1994).

For cane growers, industrial restructuring has involved significant operational changes. From a situation in which they had a number of social guarantees from a paternalistic state, they now have to fend for themselves with no subsidies while facing a large and powerful buyer of their crop that is interested only in maximizing profits. While the state and previous mill owners were also large and powerful, state policy proceeded from political criteria designed to insure minimum social guarantees to cane growers.

The new situation confronts growers with both economic challenges and opportunities. Some will be successful by pursuing a peasant-entrepreneurial approach and meeting the new efficiency requirements. Data from the survey I conducted in 1995 suggest that the category of peasant entrepreneurs will include between 25 to 35 percent of growers in the Atencingo region (likely fewer in other regions). The majority, however, will either fall back into subsistence farming or choose to sell their land to their more entrepreneurial neighbors and join the wage-labor market. The following analysis presents data from some of the main frequency distribution results of questions regarding growers' views of the mill and their relationship to it, their expectations in the new market-oriented environment, and their cultural orientation.

Questions that address the issue of relationships between cane growers and mill administration clearly reveal a mistrust on the part of cane growers. Missing cases (i.e., growers who did not respond to a question) on these questions range from a low of 1.2 percent (three respondents) to 2.4 percent. With regard to timeliness of payments made by the mill, 57.6 percent of growers said that payments were usually late. The amount received in loans was insufficient, according to 68.0 percent, while these were disbursed later than required, according to 78 percent. The final liquidation or payment was late, according to 87.2 percent. The objective truth about the latter is that the payment was indeed late: It was made after a legal grace period of thirty days after the official end of the sugarcane harvest. The fact that not all respondents said that the payment was late probably reflects that a few, less than 10 percent, have a good feeling about the mill, that they are basically used to getting their final payments late, or that they are unaware of the mill's legal obligation for timely payments.

To the general question, "Do you trust the new mill administration?" 47.6 percent responded "less than before," and fully 90.8 percent think that the sugarcane is not accurately weighed upon delivery to the mill. Despite such lack of trust toward the mill, sugarcane producers continue to grow this crop, mainly because it provides the greatest security and only with sugarcane can growers avail themselves of some loans for cultivation. Indeed, these two reasons account for 78.6 percent of responses as to why growers stick to sugarcane (43.6 percent going to "more secure income," and 25.6 percent saying that they "may obtain loans").

Cane growers' are overwhelmingly pessimistic about the mill's privatization and the new sugar decree of 1991 requiring greater productivity and efficiency from both the industrial and the agricultural parts. To the question of whether these changes benefit growers, 85.6 percent responded "no", 6 percent said "yes", and 8.4 percent did not respond to this question. A different question on the same issue elicited a very similar response. The question was, "From the positive and the negative repercussions of recent changes (previously described), which will prevail the most?" 83.6 percent said "the negative ones," while only 12 percent said "the positive ones," with 4.4 percent not responding.

When asked whether the new situation might present new opportunities, responses were not as pessimistic. Several questions on this topic were phrased differently but offered growers the same alternative responses. These are summarized in Table 6.3. While these results tend to be split, at least a substantial proportion of respondents sees that opportunities will also be there, notwithstanding new difficulties and risks. Slightly more than half of cane growers see no risks of losing their land, but more than a third think that there is such a threat (those answering "yes" or "maybe").

Another question on opportunities and risks had a slightly different set of possible responses, with very similar results. For the question, "Is the new government program that hopes to turn peasants into entrepreneurial producers a realistic one?" responses are shown in Table 6.4, below.

Personal identity is an important indicator of cultural orientation and is related to the productive strategies likely to be followed by cane growers. A direct question on personal identity was asked, and respondents were given a number of choices to pick from. They also could give their own words to capture their sense of identity. The results were as follows: 55.6 percent consider themselves plainly "peasants," 16.8 percent "workers," 6.4 percent "peasant-entrepreneurs," 2.4 percent "renters," and 17.6 percent mentioned "other" categories, including "*ejidatario*," "producer," "proprietor," and "cultivator." Missing cases represented only 1.2 percent (or 3 respondents).

A related identity question was, "Who will have the greatest opportunities for success within the new environment?" Responses are given in Table 6.5, where it is clear that a substantial proportion of Atencingo cane growers, 39.2 percent, regard investing one's own capital as critical in exploiting new opportunities. Fol-

TABLE 6.3   Growers' Opinions on New Threats and Opportunities

Question or Issue	No	Yes	Maybe	Don't Know	Missing Values
Are there new opportunities?	45.6	32.4	7.6	7.2	7.2
Are there new difficulties?	22.0	62.0	2.4	3.2	10.4
Are there new risks?	37.6	36.8	2.4	7.2	15.6
Are there risks of losing land?	50.8	26.0	8.0	8.8	6.4

SOURCE: *1995 Survey of Sugarcane Growers in the Atencingo Region*

TABLE 6.4   Realistic for Government to Expect Entrepreneurial Peasants?

Response	Number	Percent
No	113	45.2
Maybe	75	30.0
Yes	27	10.8
Don't know	17	6.8
Yes, with government help	13	5.2
Missing values	5	2.0
TOTALS	250	100.0

SOURCE: *1995 Survey of Sugarcane Growers in the Atencingo Region*

lowing closely with 34.4 percent is a very related aspect: hiring labor. Both of these items (73.6 percent) are crucial ingredients in producing a peasant-entre-preneurial class. An indication that few in the Atencingo region will turn to subsistence production (by choice) is that only 6 percent responded that "those who use their crops for self-consumption" will succeed.

The question shown in Table 6.6 takes the converse entry point to the same issue: What approach to cultivation is most likely to force growers to abandon sugarcane? It is quite obvious that reducing family labor investment is considered by most as a sure way to fail in this business, which highlights the household character of the operation. Curiously, relying on loans is also regarded by more than a fourth as a danger which may end up in abandoning sugarcane cultivation. I say "curiously," because 100 percent of *ejidatario* cane growers currently depend on financing by the mill.

Politically, cane growers are still trapped by having only one legal option—joining the corporatist PRI organizations. These organizations, however, are in turn facing unprecedented challenges to the control of their constituencies in the face of neoliberal state policies that prevent them from giving growers much

TABLE 6.5   Type of Producer with Greatest Opportunities to Succeed

Type of Grower	Number	Percent
Those who invest more capital	98	39.2
Those who hire more workers	86	34.4
Those who invest more with loans	48	19.2
Those who use their crops for self-consumption	15	6.0
Those who sell their land	1	0.4
Missing values	2	0.8
TOTALS	250	100.0

SOURCE: *1995 Survey of Sugarcane Growers in the Atencingo Region*

TABLE 6.6   Type of Producer Most Likely to Leave Sugarcane Cultivation

Type of Grower	Number	Percent
Those who invest least family labor	113	45.2
Those who resort most to loans	68	27.2
Those who focus on crops for self-consumption	39	15.6
Those who hire more workers	24	9.6
Those who invest more capital	5	2.0
Missing values	1	0.4
TOTALS	250	100.0

SOURCE: *1995 Survey of Sugarcane Growers in the Atencingo Region*

support in exchange for their affiliation. This is particularly true of the CNPR, whose members have always been primarily interested in economic performance rather than political favors from the state. Therefore, the continued imposition of neoliberal reforms will result in an increasing inability of corporatist organizations to control their constituencies. Hence new oppositional and popular-democratic struggles are sure to emerge in Mexico's countryside.

If this prospect is true for the sugar industry, it is even truer for most other subsectors of agriculture, which have had a less intimate and favored relationship with the state than sugarcane growers. This increased militancy is being demonstrated by the emergence, in 1993, of "*El Barzón*" (the Yoke), a rural debtors movement comprised of small- and medium-size cultivators. This social movement of nearly one million members has expanded its membership by half by including urban debtors (Rodríguez Gómez and Torres 1994; *La Jornada* 1995). The Chiapas uprising in January 1994 has as yet been but the most radical of such new struggles to emerge in Mexico's countryside since the advent of neoliberal reforms (Collier 1994; Harvey 1996; Nash 1995).

Theoretical Recapitulation

The purpose of this section is to theoretically summarize the material presented in this chapter by contrasting the theory offered in this book with established *campesinista* and *proletarista* positions. This discussion centers on the main elements of political class formation: objects of struggle and organizational outcomes. For the case of Atencingo, as well as for other regions, we can divide the historical period studied into five moments, each of which presents a different combination of elements in relation to the main agents involved, i.e., the original agricultural workers who became recipients of *ejido* land grants in the 1930s. Table 6.7 presents a summary of these combinations.

The most striking thing about this table, from a *proletarista* perspective, is that no matter how proletarianized, agricultural workers never posed proletarian demands

TABLE 6.7   Political Class Trajectory and Objects of Struggle in Atencingo

Moment	Agents	Objects	Outcomes
Time One 1938–1947	Agricultural workers	Land, individual production for subsistence	Collective *ejido* shell, private control; bourgeois-hegemonic
Time Two 1947–65	Same as above, with "economic parcels"	Land, individual production for market	From brief self-management to state control; oppositional
Time Three 1965–75	More proletarianized, with reduced economic parcels	Land, indiv., for market	Division and parceling of collective *ejido* individual subor dination of producers to state; bourgeois-hegemonic
Time Four 1975–88	Peasant-entrepreneur social differentiation	Credit for viable farming, higher prices	State control of individual producers; bourgeois-hegemonic
Time Five 1988–97	Peasant-entrepreneur, increasing social differentiation	State subsidies, fair prices from sugar mill, good leaders	Private control by corporation with transnational capital (Pepsico); bourgeois-hegemonic, but could become oppositional, at least electorally

SOURCE: Elaborated from the analysis in this chapter.

in their struggle. On the contrary, when they were more highly proletarianized, in Time Three, the struggle for division and parceling out of the state-controlled collective *ejido* was fiercest. And it was at this time (1971) that the social agents finally achieved their goal of producing on individually allocated plots.

Paradoxically, this event took place in the context of Luis Echeverría's administration, during which collectives faced tightened control by the state. Later on,

Echeverría tried to restore state control with the creation of the National Sugarcane Commission and by declaring sugarcane a crop of "public interest" in October of 1975 (Pérez Arce 1979, 33–36).

The intent of this new state agency was to restore a collectivized production while maintaining individual bargaining with each *ejidatario* on the basis of sugarcane quality. At this point, the recently formed peasant-entrepreneurs organized themselves into the National Union of Sugarcane Producers, affiliated to the CNC. Their struggle now centered on obtaining credits for a viable farming operation and for getting increases in guaranteed prices for sugar cane. These struggles always remained within corporatist structures and did not present a threat to bourgeois hegemony.

The apparent mismatch between the position of class agents in production and their objects of struggle (from a *proletarista* perspective) stems from a deeply ingrained peasant culture. Although such a culture was certainly modified by the advancement of capitalism and commercialization, the social agents managed to maintain a great interest in individual control of production. This interest was intensified after their democratically elected leader, Porfirio Jaramillo, was able to allow that each *ejidatario* be assigned a one-hectare plot for subsistence crops.

Contrary to what radical *campesinistas* may have expected, on the other hand, the peasant character of demands in Atencingo did not in themselves result in oppositional struggles: They were always integrated into a hegemonic discourse and politics. Even in the most combative periods (especially 1947–52), the oppositional factions of Atencingo sought the favor of state officials to advance their political positions. Therefore, these factions were oppositional only in relation to the internal politics of the *ejido,* not in relation to the state. Most of the time, Atencingo *ejidatarios* were careful to maintain their distance from truly oppositional organizations for fear of upsetting their potential allies in the state bureaucracy.

The history of Atencingo, therefore, provides us with at least three theoretical lessons. First, merely ascertaining the class position of agents is not sufficient to predict the object of struggles or the character of organizations created for struggle. This is the most general lesson.

Second, once a struggle takes on a peasant character, even if it is waged by agricultural workers, it does not necessarily bear a revolutionary character, as radical *campesinistas* might hold. In fact, reformist *campesinistas* might be right on this count: If you consolidate the peasant economy, you might actually increase production, although not necessarily productivity. For increases in peasant production are usually labor-intensive. Thus, peasants might produce greater yields per hectare, but with greater expenditures of labor. The ultimate peasant triumph, which involved dismantling cooperative production, actually resulted in a decreased productivity, as shown in Tables 6.1 and 6.2.

The political outcomes are consistent with what *proletaristas* expect of peasant struggles. The problem for *proletaristas,* though, is that in Atencingo the social agents were not peasants but agricultural workers (economically defined). Furthermore, a peasant economy can coexist with a capitalist developmental dynamic, but not without problems. Indeed, as soon as the Atencingo workers got their individual plots of land, the process of social differentiation accelerated considerably.

Given the imminent tendency to social differentiation within capitalism, however, I do not see any fundamental reason why the new peasant-entrepreneurs could not become politically articulated into a popular-democratic struggle that might lead to a new hegemony. The crucial point is the following: Peasants or peasant-entrepreneurs are neither intrinsically revolutionary (the *campesinista* fantasy) nor inherently conservative (the *proletarista* fantasy): They merely want to be left alone to produce according to their own logic. Whether they adopt a bourgeois-hegemonic or a popular-democratic discourse will depend on the context in which peasants or peasant-entrepreneurs develop. In my view they have much better chances of surviving in a popular-democratic global context than in a bourgeois-hegemonic one, but the condition is that such a society actually be democratic and not one in which the state imposes the form of production that its bureaucrats decide is best for direct producers. Statist socialism has plainly had grievous problems in dealing with agricultural producers (Szélenyi 1987).

The third theoretical lesson is that, given the regional balance of class forces in Atencingo, the *Cardenista* state was willing to be inconsistent with its own global agrarian policy regarding collective ejidos. The Atencingo land distribution was the most recent of our three case studies and there, in contrast to the other two regions, the state favored the instrumentalization of the collective *ejido* by the capitalist sugar mill. By contrast, in both La Laguna and El Yaqui the state interventions were decidedly noncapitalist, favoring direct producers who had become collective *ejidatarios*. Vast support was given to them in credits and organizational efforts from the state during *Cardenismo*. In Atencingo, *ejidatarios* were forced by law to produce only sugarcane and to look to the industrial mill as their only source of credit. Their *ejido* was thus just a fig leaf for what was actually an organization controlled by the capitalist mill. Similar inconsistencies in state policy, but of an opposite nature, emerged later, especially during Luis Echeverría's administration.

Conclusion

Given the vast heterogeneity of the structural class positions in rural Puebla, the agrarian struggles in the Atencingo region have been clearly dominated by the demands of the most homogeneous group: the *ejidatarios*. Their struggles since the 1930s centered on resisting proletarianization and attaining peasant status. They finally succeeded in 1971. From then on the question for direct producers became what kind of peasants they would become, subsistence or entrepreneurial. A neoliberal alternative is, of course, selling the land and relying entirely on wage incomes.

The *ejido* organization provided its members with a structural capacity for a coherent and unified struggle. It offered them a legal and organizational framework in which to pose their demands. This structural capacity, however, did not predetermine the class character of their politics. Rather, each of the two critical aspects in this process was shaped by factors other than structural class positions or structural capacities, i.e., the prevailing or shifting cultural orientations, which fostered a market-oriented, peasant-entrepreneurial struggle for land and autonomy in production. The resulting class organizations, in turn, depended rather closely on the character of state interventions and the nature of the ejidatarios' leadership. State intervention determined whether the organizational outcomes were bourgeois-hegemonic, oppositional, or popular-democratic. Leadership hinged on factors such as the organization's degree of autonomy from the state and/or the ruling class and the character of alliances or affiliations with other organizations. Leadership is a variable that requires further exploration, and it will likely assume more salience as Mexico evolves toward a genuinely democratic electoral system. The growth of citizenship and democratic leadership will further shake the foundations of corporatism.

While the outcome of the early phase of the *ejido* struggles (1947–52) was popular-democratic, the predominant outcome throughout was bourgeois-hegemonic. Ironically, as peasant demands advanced amid this rural proletariat (economically defined), its structural capacities for unified struggles weakened. With the emergence of the state's neoliberal reform, even the former corporatist organizations of the PRI are having to change: They will either become more effective economic organizations or they will further erode their political influence among cane growers. Neither these organizations nor the state they represent are capable of offering cane growers the low but secure incomes of yesteryear. Thus, the codependency of the past has been ruptured. Future structural and political developments will largely depend on the new cultural orientations of cane growers, their productive strategies as they confront market forces, and the types of leadership that develop. The leaders will have an impact on the character of the alliances established with other organizations in civil society and the autonomy (or lack thereof) of class organizations.

While the state will continue to provide the general context in which rural struggles take place, it is no longer capable of responding to pressures from rural social actors that involve major state subsidies or other forms of disbursements, apart from social assistance programs. As regards cane growers the state might, however, continue to require that they join either of the two PRI organizations for political representation. To the extent that cane growers become increasingly disenchanted with imposed representation that cannot restore the social guarantees of yesteryears, they might begin to seek other organizational options, perhaps parallel to those they are forced to join under the law.

From the various regional cultures prevailing among sugarcane producers, only two of them focus on trying to maximize profits: One is, of course, that of capitalist farmers; and the other is that of peasant-entrepreneurs. The main difference between these two cultures is how each type of producer tries to achieve his or her goal of profit maximization: While the capitalist grower does it on the basis of typical capitalistic mechanisms of exploiting wage labor and comparative advantages, the peasant-entrepreneur is still based on the logic of a peasant household. The latter focuses on maximizing the use of family labor as its most abundant resource and faces greater restrictions in other resource endowments. The option of seeking to maximize comparative advantages in other crops is simply not there for the peasant-entrepreneur because of insufficient resources and limited financial alternatives. Financial dependence on the sugar mill is taken as a given.

This mix of cultural orientations and peasant (or capitalist) productive strategies pose a serious antinomy for neoliberal reform in the Mexican sugar industry: The problem of productive scale will persist at least in the short-to-middle term, as most cane growers intend to hold on to their land and will remain small farmers. Similarly, the peasant subsistence culture will not necessarily adapt to neoliberal expectations for a greater rationalization in the use of land, machinery, and so on. On the other hand, while capitalist growers could resolve the problem of productive scale and the "rational" use of technological resources (according to the profit motive), there is clearly a declining interest in maintaining sugarcane as their main product: Neoliberalism has opened an array of more attractive and previously unavailable options.

These antinomies lead to a logical conclusion. As capitalist cane growers consolidate a market-driven and profit-oriented culture, they will be less interested in supplying a dominant capitalist sugar mill and more inclined to seek better financial alternatives in export crops. One alternative is that the mill itself will have to take full responsibility for sugarcane production, as is happening already in the northwestern states of Nayarit and Sinaloa in a renewed form of corporate plantation agriculture wherein the mill rents and operates between 80 and 90 percent of *ejido* lands (field notes from Los Mochis, Sinaloa, 1996).

In Atencingo, however, the trend is to strengthen the growth of a new type of producer: a peasant-entrepreneur who is oriented to the market, yes, but working under a basically family-based logic. Considering that a peasant-entrepreneurial culture has emerged in the region since the 1950s, what has been regarded as a counteragrarian reform will result in a historical paradox. This reform will finally establish the conditions for a small but vigorous peasant-entrepreneurial class to thrive. Conversely, a majority of cane growers will probably be forced into traditional subsistence farming or even out of farming altogether and into the urban labor markets of Mexico, the United States, or Canada. As internal social differentiation accelerates within the *ejidos*, sugarcane *ejidatarios* will no longer fall into the relatively homogeneous social category of previous decades. The *ejido*'s fate is steeped in uncertainty: Will it assume a new meaning as a class organizational force in the neoliberal context, and which internal group of *ejidatarios*, if any, might it come to favor politically?

Notes

1. This information comes from various founding ejidatarios interviewed several times since 1988 (their names could be made available to other researchers). Ronfeldt (1973) recounted that Jaramillo's administration was sabotaged during its last two years, but he did not mention the important role played by the *Jaramillista* Communist affiliation.

2. The CNC is one of the corporatist pillars of the ruling PRI, along with the CTM, its labor counterpart, and the *Confederación Nacional de Organizaciones Populares* (CNOP, National Confederation of Popular Organizations). The latter, which includes teachers, government bureaucrats, and a host of other urban groups, also includes "small" property owners in the CNPP (National Confederation of Small Property Owners). In contrast to the CNC, the CNPP is supposed to articulate non-ejidatario agricultural producers, which include the whole spectrum from small peasant proprietors to the agrarian bourgeoisie. The latter, however, tends to be organized in other lobbying organizations (de Gramont 1990, 1996b; Mares 1987). In 1993 CNOP changed its name to FNOC (*Frente Nacional de Organizaciones y Ciudadanos*, or National Front of Organizations and Citizens) and CNPP became CNPR or National Confederation of Rural Producers (*Confederación Nacional de Productores Rurales*), which, in line with the 1992 Agrarian Law, tends to erase the former distinction between ejidatarios and small property owners.

3. This did not prevent an important number of growers to affiliate with a Neo-Cardenista organization in the region after the tainted national elections of 1988. For the most part, though, growers retain their forced membership in one of the official organizations, and use them more as economic than political tools.

4. During my first visit to Atencingo, a few days after its sale had been announced, its management personnel was unusually helpful. I had access to financial statements, industrial personnel, payroll, retirements, and agricultural data for several years with virtually no restriction. Such openness progressively diminished in subsequent visits, and disappeared by 1995, when more adversarial relationships had developed with cane growers.

7

El Yaqui Valley: Toward Self-Managed, Democratic Production

Northwestern Mexico is usually regarded as the region where capitalism has developed most thoroughly in agriculture. This chapter focuses on southern Sonora, specifically the Yaqui Valley. We will follow a complex set of class trajectories for both the subordinate as well as the ruling classes. A central concern will be with the formation of a ferocious agrarian bourgeoisie that violently separated direct producers from their means of production. This process, initiated at the turn of the twentieth century, involved moving the Mexican frontier farther northwest, toward the United States, and crushing the Yaqui and the Mayo Indians who were in the way. Many of these Indians were converted from peasant producers into an agricultural semiproletariat. Although some land was distributed through agrarian reform during the Cárdenas administration (1934–40), the land-hungry bourgeoisie did not hesitate to run roughshod over the *ejido* to expand its agricultural production in one of the most fertile valleys of the country.

Located in the southern part of Sonora, the Yaqui Valley is adjacent to the Mayo Valley. These two valleys are named after the Indian tribes that used to inhabit the region and the two main rivers that irrigate their lands. Both the Mayos and Yaquis valiantly combated every attempt by the central government of Mexico to dispossess the Indians of their land throughout much of the nineteenth century. The histories of these two tribes diverged significantly in the 1880s, however, in the midst of the Porfirian expansion toward the Northwest.

By the mid-1880s, the Mayos were finally "pacified." They accepted the military, political, economic, and, eventually, cultural victory of the rising capitalism in Mexican society. Indeed, the Mayos entered a quick process of acculturation that dovetailed with their proletarianization. As workers, they were an extremely valued labor force. The Yaquis were regarded equally highly, except that their

I greatly benefited from thoughtful critiques and suggestions from David Barkin, Roger Bartra, Barry Carr, and Nora Hamilton, who were reviewers of a previous article (Otero 1989b) on which this chapter is based.

stubborn concern for autonomy led them to resist colonization much more tenaciously than did the Mayos. They were to carry out a war of resistance for decades at a very high cost. They were massacred—almost exterminated—and deported to distant regions of Mexico (Oaxaca and Yucatán). Some flew to Arizona (Hu-DeHart 1984; Spicer 1969a, 1969b, 1980). Eventually many of these exiles went back to their land in the mid-1920s to establish Yaqui communities and rebuild their culture. The Yaquis also benefited from agrarian reform in 1937, during the Cárdenas administration.

As was the case in La Laguna, by the 1970s the bulk of agricultural direct producers were heavily, though not completely, proletarianized. The seasonal character of agricultural production made it impossible for most of them to get permanent wage labor; therefore, they had to complement their income with commercial activities or with marginal odd jobs. The structural position that predominated here was thus proletarian or semiproletarian for close to 75 percent of the agricultural labor force (Hewitt de Alcántara 1978, 228). Given the long experience of capitalist cooperation in agricultural labor processes of this region, the agrarian struggles of the 1970s were postcapitalist in character (see Chapter 1).

Although the central demand in Sonora was precisely land, it was accompanied by demands for machinery, installations, and, more importantly, control of the production process. The demand for land thus shed its peasant skin in evolving toward a postcapitalist character.

State interventions have been dominated by the disproportionate strength of the agrarian bourgeoisie in southern Sonora. Therefore, the class organizations that arose had an oppositional character, although from the late 1940s to the early 1970s they were heavily repressed and largely dismantled. It was not until the mid-1970s that the agricultural semiproletariat was able to organize itself to confront the state and the powerful agrarian bourgeoisie.

As this chapter shows, the resulting Coalition of Collective Ejidos of the Yaqui and Mayo Valleys (*Coalición de Ejidos Colectivos de los Valles del Yaqui y El Mayo*) today offers exemplary organizational lessons, both political (democratic and independent) and economic (productive), for the agrarian movement in Mexico and elsewhere. Although its model may not have been precisely reproduced elsewhere, other regional movements in Mexico have turned to the coalition not only to provide enthusiastic solidarity but also to learn the lessons of its experience. Clearly, the coalition itself has built on the previous lessons of the Mexican postrevolutionary agrarian movement. What follows is a more detailed account of its political class formation centered on the structural, political, and cultural changes in the Yaqui region of southern Sonora.

The Agrarian History and Cultural Setting

Before the rule of Porfirio Díaz (1876–1910), the distant geographical position of Sonora allowed the Yaquis, Pápagos, Seris, and Mayos to be cut off from the republic for must of the nineteenth century. But the stakes changed as capitalism sought to expand into the fertile lands of Mex 's northwest. Moreover, the Indians became a potential labor force.

Of the five principal rivers in Sonora (Magdalena, Sonora, Metape, Yaqui, and Mayo), only the Yaqui flowed year-round (Aguilar Camín 1977). This fact might explain the dramatic, recurrent struggle to control the Yaqui valley's lands and water. And it may also explain some of the cultural differences between Yaquis and Mayos. In contrast to the Mayos, the Yaquis were able to sustain an independent economy for a longer period of time after the first contacts with Mexican society. Conversely, the Mayos, owing to their weaker material basis for social reproduction, began to sell their labor power before the 1850s in mining concerns at Alamos, one of the first white urban settlements in the Mayo area (Hu-DeHart 1981, 1984).

The pacification of the Mayos laid the foundation for the proverbial Sonoran industriousness (Aguilar Camín 1977), providing the emerging bourgeoisie with the hardest working and most hardiest labor force in the state. After their pacification, a few Mayos were granted small plots of land by the federal government, although the majority worked for wages in ranches, mines, and haciendas. This small favor (land and jobs), along with the relentless repression they had endured previously, turned the Mayos into a relatively docile labor force.

This process of primitive accumulation separates the direct producers from their means of production. Once this process is complete, direct producers have no way to sustain themselves except by selling their labor power (Marx 1967). In North America such a process is intimately related to the expansion of U.S. capitalism toward its southwest (Mexico's northwest). In 1900 U.S. settlement companies began to enter Sonora under the auspices of the government and the mediation of influential local politicians who had close family ties with the rising agrarian bourgeoisie. The Sonoran bourgeoisie was interested in inviting foreign companies in order to promote the immigration of industrious capitalists who would stimulate the state's economy. Immigration was accompanied by heavy penetration of investment, technology, and the entrepreneurial culture that characterized the U.S. southwest. The central concern was for profits, which were pursued with a voracious single-mindedness (Aguilar Camín 1977, 55–59).

By the time of the Mexican civil war (1912–20), the vast majority of the Yaqui Indians had been either killed, deported, or forced into exile by the army of Porfirio Díaz. Those who stayed were eventually recruited by the revolutionary army of Alvaro Obregón with the promise of restoring their land. It was not until the early 1920s that the deported Yaquis were allowed to return to their tribal territory. Obregón was forced to live up to his promise during his presidency (1920–24). The powerful capitalist interests, however, were stronger than Obregón's willingness to fulfill his promise. After their return from exile or deportation, the members of the tribe were reduced to the northern bank of the Yaqui river, i.e., outside the fertile valley lands. When they went to Obregón in protest, the Mexican army immediately occupied the Yaqui townships.

After more than two decades of massacre, deportation, and wage labor, however, the returned Yaquis restored a peasant economy centered on subsistence crops such as corn, beans and squash. Besides the Yaqui land grants, some *ejidos* were formed prior to the *Cardenista* period (1934–40), but they were mostly symbolic. The thirty-eight *ejidos* that existed held 188,055 hectares of marginal land, which was farmed by 4,071 *ejidatarios* and their families. Because of the poor quality of these lands, many Yaquis and other mestizo workers had to sell their labor power in the region to supplement their income.

By 1935 conditions had worsened for direct producers. Farm workers were paid only Mex$1.56 daily, compared to Mex$2.33 in 1929. The polarization of land-tenure distribution was profound. Of 10,409 plots registered by the first agricultural census in 1930, 5,577 (or 53.6 percent) were under ten hectares each, and they controlled a mere 0.3 percent of the land! There were only thirty-eight *ejidos* of fifty hectares or more, controlling 0.4 percent of the land. Finally, the latifundia sector (with more than 1,000 hectares per plot) controlled 89 percent of the land and represented only 8.8 percent of the private holdings (Sanderson 1981, 91–93). This sector would soon be shocked by the *Cardenista* agrarian reform in Sonora.

Cardenismo: the End of Agrarian-Bourgeois Hegemony?

In 1937 17,000 hectares of irrigated land were distributed among 2,160 landless workers. The remaining 27,638 hectares of irrigated land were divided among 840 landowners, in compliance with the legal maximum surface of one hundred hectares permitted by *Cardenista* legislation. Another 36,000 hectares of arid lands were also distributed to *ejidos* in 1937, and a similar amount was given to landowners in compensation for the 17,000 irrigated hectares that were distributed to *ejidatarios*. The proportion of land held in *ejidos*, however, declined sharply in the following decade to 17 percent because of an unprecedented expansion of the agricultural frontier through the development of irrigation infrastructure by the state (Siles-Alvarado 1968).

With the *Cardenista ejidos* land distribution, the organization for production in most of the irrigated land was collective, and the Ejido Bank became a major presence in credit and technical assistance. Created by Cárdenas to financially and technically support the new collective *ejidos*, the Ejido Bank was crucial in the early years of agrarian reform in attaining good productivity levels. In the first few years (1938–43), the average yields from collective ejidos were higher than the regional average for all farms (Sanderson 1981, 146).

At this time (1937) the Yaquis were not only struggling for land in a typical peasant fashion; they were also struggling for their nationality. Nevertheless, when the state distributed land to them, they had to accept the state's rules of the game, which included the heavy involvement of its economic apparatuses in organizing agricultural production. Therefore, the Yaquis' newly reconstructed peasant economy was now converted into collective farms closely supervised by the Ejido Bank. This development left the new *ejidatarios* in quite a vulnerable position, in relation to both the state and the agrarian bourgeoisie.

Indeed, for the Yaquis at least, the successful struggle for land resulted in a definitive defeat in their national struggle. Henceforth they had to submit to the Mexican national state under its own terms; the state gained the initiative in the future of agrarian development in the region. The conditions were thus established for a full integration of the Yaquis into national life—namely, an integration into the process of capitalist development. This was also the condition for a gradual transformation of Indian-peasant struggles into popular-democratic and postcapitalist struggles. Yet it took more than three decades for this type of struggle to emerge.

End of Agrarian Reform and Attack on Collective *Ejidos*

The end of Cárdenas's agrarian reform dates from 1938, when productivism set in at the end of his administration. Overall state policy was geared toward stimulating the industrialization process, and agriculture became subordinated to this goal. After World War II the ideology of the Cold War came to dominate the Mexican government. The CNC and CTM were converted into powerful political arms of the state to control peasants and workers. As in La Laguna (Chapter 5), the collective *ejidos* were major targets, not only because they had become strongholds of opposition and socialist organizations, but also because they were seen by private capitalist firms as an ideological threat, an example that might spread. The productivist drive in economic policy was thus combined with a commitment to individualistic ideology that clashed with the collective *ejidos.*

In fact, this individualism and individual title went along with bourgeois pressure for the government to extend *certificados de inafectabilidad* (certificates of immunity), which constitute a warranty that holders of such certificates are not subject to land expropriation for twenty-five years. This guarantee was touted as an incentive for agricultural entrepreneurialism to develop fully. Between 1938 and 1950 the landowners in Sonora were granted forty-one certificates of immunity covering 598,460 hectares (Sanderson 1981, 147). Although most of this land was initially earmarked for grazing, it was eventually made arable through large government investments in irrigation infrastructure, and the certificates of immunity would still hold.

The new Credit Law bolstered the individualistic thrust by reducing collective exploitation to a mere alternative under the law rather than the officially preferred mode of agrarian organization and

> by dropping the requirement that *ejidos* use medium- and long-term infrastructure credit communally [or collectively]. Later, in 1947, ejidal credit organizations were subsumed under the control of the Ejidal [sic] Bank , which assumed full authority

for the capitalization, development, marketing and credit functions of the ejido, at the expense of local societies (Sanderson 1981, 144–145).

At this point the Ejido Bank became the actual employer of the *ejidatarios* by turning them, in effect, into state workers in a peasant disguise and appropriating their production process. Although the legal tools and political atmosphere for dismantling the collectives were established by the end of 1942, government agencies began a tenacious campaign against them only at the start of Miguel Aleman's administration in 1946. State policies had thus shifted clearly in favor of the agrarian bourgeoisie and against the *ejidatarios*.

In response to adverse state policies, *ejidatarios* began to form oppositional organizations. Many joined the General Union of Workers and Peasants (*Unión General de Obreros y Campesinos de México*, or UGOCM), referred to in Chapter 5. This mass organization was linked to the newly formed *Partido Popular* (PP, eventually called Popular Socialist Party, *Partido Popular Socialista*, or PPS), led by Vicente Lombardo Toledano, the former secretary-general of the CTM during *Cardenismo*.

During the Cárdenas administration, the members of collective *ejidos* were affiliated with the official *Confederación Nacional Campesina*, CNC, and the CTM (Carr 1986). The state had established a popular alliance with peasants and workers, and their leaders could even be active in the Communist Party and still hold executive posts (to which they were democratically elected) in the CNC or CTM.

When Miguel Alemán came to power, along with the Cold War and anticommunist ideology, such allegiances were no longer possible. Communist leaders were quickly purged from the CNC and CTM. Both of these organizations began to assume an entirely different character: From being actual representatives of their constituency, they became corporatist state apparatuses for the political control of workers and peasants. Sensing these global changes, "the CNC took an increasingly individualistic position toward land tenure and exploitation during the 1940s, even joining with private property owners in some states to pressure the regime for stabilization of land tenure" (Sanderson 1981, 138).

The Ejido Bank also became a major state weapon against collective *ejidos*. It granted them credit only under absolute certainty of recovery. This in itself did not have too adverse an effect. But by 1949 those who wanted to retain a collective organization of their *ejidos* faced great difficulty in obtaining credit at all, and midterm loans were completely suspended for them, thereby hindering their ability to keep pace with mechanization and other technological advances. Conversely, the bank showed a strong disposition to help *ejidatarios* realize profits if they were in turn willing to fragment their collective *ejidos* into individual plots. But this helpful attitude of the bank toward the individualists only lasted through 1950. By then most collective *ejidos* had been dismantled (Sanderson 1981, 175–78).

Steven E. Sanderson quotes a revealing statement from an editorial of *El Imparcial*, a daily newspaper of Sonora, which appeared on June 21, 1950; the piece stated that the federal government had decided to attack the strongholds of the PP with a "powerful weapon: economics." The editorial then goes on to explain the political logic of such attack:

> The Ejidal[sic] Bank entered the game to reorganize not only the ejidal Union, but the credit societies that depend on it, liquidating once and for all everything that smells of the Partido Popular in order to give entry . . . to the flag of the CNC, an adherent . . . of the PRI (cited in Sanderson 1981, 141).

The history of the relationship between the bank and collectives in El Yaqui and El Mayo Valleys is astonishingly similar to that in La Laguna (see Chapter 5). The bank clearly appropriated the *ejidos'* productive processes and precipitated their economic failure, thereby accomplishing the state's goal of weakening the power base of UGOCM and PPS, the oppositional organizations that timidly challenged PRI hegemony.

As regards the operation of *ejidos,* Charles J. Erasmus provides a description as of 1959. He says that the sole source of credit for collectives is the Ejido Bank. And in all cases it is the Bank

> which determines the crops to be planted, oversees the work, and sells the harvests. The Bank may buy farm machinery for a collective or pay contractors to clear, plow, plant, and harvest. In this area it seldom finances anything but mechanized operations. To maintain members of collectives between harvests, the Bank advances them a daily wage later deducted from the harvest profits (Erasmus 1961, 214–15).

Inaugurated in 1939, the Central Union, the economic organization created by direct producers for the self-management of their collective farms and other agricultural activities, remained under their control until 1953, as was the case with its counterpart in La Laguna. It managed a machinery center, a shop for the sale of machinery parts and tires, a gas station, a commercialization department for crops and inputs, and even a suburban bus line. Moreover, the Union gave its member *ejidos* a leading edge in bargaining their crops at higher prices than those obtained by private entrepreneurs (Hewitt de Alcántara 1978, 181–82).

Like its counterpart in La Laguna, the Central Union in El Yaqui maintained political links with what eventually became UGOCM and the PPS. The local leadership had also been part of CNC or CTM until it became clear, under *Alemanismo* (1946–52), that these organizations offered no possibilities of carrying on the Cardenista plan for collective *ejido* development. Maximiliano R. López, who led the agrarian struggle in the 1930s, was director of the Central Union in the 1940s, as was Arturo Orona in La Laguna. López remained with CTM up to 1947. But once the *Alemanista* counterreforms began, he allied himself with several other regional peasant leaders—Jacinto López, Ramón Danzós Palomino, Bernabé Arana, and Arturo Orona—to form UGOCM. This mass organization eventually established links with Lombardo's PPS. UGOCM was set up as an alternative to oppose CNC and CTM, while the PPS combated the PRI itself.

The state rewards to those *ejidatarios* who deserted collectivism, however, also meant reducing the membership of the Central Union. By 1953, the government attack on this economic organization included stealing machinery from the union-run enterprises. When Maximiliano López went to Mexico City to file a protest, he was assassinated. This was the last blow to the Central Union. After his murder the regional organizations that made up the Central Union were not much more than paper organizations.

According to Cynthia Hewitt de Alcántara, the state of economic, political, and cultural disarray in which the *ejidos* were left after the official boycott is exemplified by the village of Benito Juárez, typical of the Yaqui and Mayo valleys in the early 1970s. Life had been highly secularized and monetized, and hardly any community life remained. Organized participation in community affairs was limited to a meeting of students' parents once or twice a year, called by the only teacher in the village school. The members of the *ejido* as such had not met in years to talk about their common problems. This was of course understandable since the four credit societies there were dominated by a single rich man who rented land from his colleagues. There was not even a yearly celebration to commemorate the anniversary of agrarian reform in the Yaqui Valley. In the Benito Juárez village,

> once collectivist, there is no community spirit. On the contrary, intrigues and mistrust abound, like in the whole valley after the terrible decade of the fifties. . . . It is the logical extreme which has resulted from a long and systematic campaign to disorganize the valley ejidos. Not even religion has been useful to cure the wounds of this society: As one of the inhabitants of Benito Juárez said, . . . "in this place there is no more God than [money] bills." One Catholic priest appeared two or three times in the village but never came back because nobody would attend his services (Hewitt de Alcántara 1978, 226).

The process of acculturation has been widespread among both the Yaqui and Mayo Indians, but through different processes. The Mayos are more integrated with whites and mestizos even though 50 percent of the population in the Mayo region is Indian. In contrast, the Yaquis (about 12,000 in 1959) live mostly isolated from non-Indians except at Vicam station, where there are more whites (Erasmus 1961, 191). This difference might be due to the many conflicts between the Yaquis and the larger white and mestizo society throughout Mexican history, which has led the Yaquis to maintain greater solidarity and cultural identification than the Mayos have (Hu-DeHart 1981, 1984).

By the 1960s the agrarian bourgeoisie had consolidated its economic and political power to the extent that the *ejidos* established during *Cardenismo* succumbed to its insatiable drive for capitalist penetration in Sonoran agriculture. The legal impediments to capitalist penetration were not enough to keep the Sonoran bourgeoisie out of the fertile lands that were granted to *ejidatarios,* whether Indian or mestizo. By the mid–1960s, 80 percent of *ejido* land was rented out to capitalist cultivators, and the holders of *ejido* titles often worked for a wage on their own plots (Hewitt de Alcántara 1978, 193).

The systematic economic boycott against collective *ejidos* was coupled with a policy of divide and conquer by which the state rewarded some *ejidatarios* in order to integrate them into the mass organizations it controlled. The UGOCM and the PPS were tremendously weakened or never really achieved significant strength. At the same time, the extension of capitalist relations of production resulted in a significant deterioration of Mayo and Yaqui cultures. With the ebbing of a strong ethnic identity, many Indians opted for acculturation as an individual strategy to try to adapt more effectively to the new rules of the market. Unfortunately for the agrarian bourgeoisie, this deterioration of Indian-peasant culture was wedded to a new culture emerging from the very capitalistic production process to which direct producers were increasingly exposed as wage workers. This combination had an important effect on future agrarian struggles in which demands for land were accompanied by demands for other means of production and democratic control of the production process.

The New Agrarian Movement: Toward Self-Managed and Democratic Production

The boycott against collective *ejidos* in the period from 1947 to 1954 period was followed by a tremendous expansion of the agricultural frontier in Sonora. This process greatly strengthened the agrarian bourgeoisie and provided plenty of employment opportunities for the expanding labor force. In fact, the irrigated surface in the state increased from 150,000 hectares in 1940 to 552,000 (368 percent) in 1960. Even though agriculture in Sonora became increasingly mechanized, the expansion of the frontier allowed for the growth in employment opportunities until the early 1970s. The economically active population in agriculture grew from 61,500 in 1940 to 133,700 (217 percent) in 1960, a much slower growth rate than that of the of irrigated surface. By 1970 just over 100,000 people were employed on roughly 700,000 hectares of irrigated surface (Ferra Martínez 1987, 4–5).

Sonoran agriculture began to experience the effects of the capitalist crisis by the early 1970s (described in Chapter 4). The formerly highly successful credit unions run by the agrarian bourgeoisie entered a phase of heavy losses in the 1971–74 period (Quintero 1982). Declining prices in cotton led many entrepreneurs in the Yaqui valley to shift a large portion of land to wheat, which is an intensely mechanized crop. About 96 days/men are required for each hectare of the cotton crop, in contrast to roughly 7.5 for wheat. In Sonora a reduction of 108,436 hectares of cotton caused unemployment for 36,166 day laborers in 1975 (Canabal Cristiani 1984, 219). Between 1974 and 1975, the number of day laborers displaced from agriculture nationwide reached 7,233,366.

In 1970, 73 percent of the economically active population in Sonora's agriculture was made up of rural workers, while 1 percent of that population owned 42 percent of the arable land. Meanwhile, the capital-intensiveness of agricultural operations had been accelerating. According to some estimates, while in 1940 investment in machinery constituted one-third of the investment in wages, twenty years later investment in machinery exceeded payrolls by 50 percent (Jiménez Ricárdez 1976). These changes have created a reserve labor pool that reduced wages and thus further increased capitalist profits until the overproduction crisis set in.

Thus, by the mid-1970s three factors had influenced the emergence of a combative social mobilization for land and the control of the production process: (1) increasing unemployment and deterioration of the material condition of the masses, (2) a general process of radicalization in the nationwide class struggle as a result of the deepening of capitalist and peasant agricultural crises, and (3) interbourgeois infighting over the 1976 presidential succession.

By 1975 the agricultural proletariat and semiproletariat were largely unorganized or were affiliated with the official CNC, the Independent Peasant Central (*Central Campesina Independiente,* or CCI), or UGOCM-Jacinto López, all of which had signed the *Pacto de Ocampo,* a deal with President Luis Echevarría by which those organizations agreed to maintain social peace in the countryside. UGOCM had suffered severe repression and several splinters by this time. Two of them kept the same name and could be distinguished only by their last name. Thus, UGOCM-Jacinto López fell under bourgeois-hegemonic sway and state control by joining the *Pacto de Ocampo.* The Agrarianist Mexican Council (*Consejo Agrarista Mexicano,* or CAM), also signed the pact (Ferra Martínez 1982; Sanderson 1981).

The left faction of the UGOCM, however, initially became UGOCM-PPS, linked to the *Partido Popular Socialista.* But this organization later became UGOCM-PPM, reflecting a splinter in the PPS itself. Whereas the PPS had become almost a left appendage of the official PRI, the PPM represented a return to its traditionally *Lombardista* positions. The UGOCM-PPM thus belonged to this nationalist left tradition, with a Stalinist background.

Moreover, the CCI also had some influence in Sonora, but this organization had undergone division by 1975 as well. The CCI-Garzón joined the progovernment *Pacto de Ocampo,* while the CCI-Danzós became the Independent Central of Agricultural Workers and Peasants (*Central Independiente de Obreros Agrícolas y Campesinos,* or CIOAC) in 1975. The name CIOAC reflected new debates within the Communist Party (PCM) in which *proletarista* authors such as Roger Bartra and Sergio de la Peña were having an important influence in characterizing the changes in the Mexican agrarian structure. As we saw in Chapter 2, these analyses tended to see great promise for socialism with the increasing presence of an agricultural proletariat. Consequently, the CIOAC began to favor a struggle for unionization over the traditional struggle for land in the countryside. CIOAC was led by members of the PCM, which continued to espouse a Leninist, *proletarista* strategy until 1982.[1]

In the early 1970s, though, under organizational conditions dominated by *proletarista* conceptions on the left and official control of most mass organizations, the struggle for land actually lost momentum in Sonora. Both official and oppositional organizations dedicated their greatest efforts to unionize day laborers (Ferra Martínez 1982). But this narrowly economistic leadership was soon challenged from below, by the masses themselves. They would pose a new objective for the struggle: the demand for land, yes, but accompanied by the demand for the rest of the means of production and the democratic control of the production process.

1975 Land Takeovers

On October 19, 1975, land petitioners (groups of people formally organized to demand land and registered at the Ministry of Agrarian Reform, as provided by Article 27 of the Mexican Constitution until 1992) affiliated with the CAM and CCI-Garzón occupied three plots close to the village of San Ignacio Río Muerto in Sonora. Most of them were residents of this village. The local and national media gave widespread publicity to the incident, while the organizations of landowners demanded energetic action from the governor of Sonora, Carlos Biebrich, accusing him of weakness.

On October 23 Biebrich sent the Judicial Police backed by army troops to evict "the invaders." The occupants were evicted "peacefully" from two of the plots, but their eviction from the one owned by the Dengel family was quite violent: Seven occupants were killed, thirty were wounded, and many more were arrested, despite the fact they had already agreed to leave the land. As a result of this bloody measure, Biebrich was forced to resign his gubernatorial post on October 25 and was replaced by an old politician, Alejandro Carrillo Marcor (Oswald, Rodríguez, and Flores 1986).

The October 1975 land occupations took place in the context of interbureaucratic and interbourgeois conflict over the presidential succession of 1976. Biebrich had been an important figure within the PRI promoting the candidacy of Mario Moya Palencia, then secretary of the interior and a favorite of Mexican bourgeoisie. By the time of the land takeovers, though, a different official candidate was announced: José López Portillo. Thus, the events in Sonora were exploited for revenge among different PRI factions. But this fact alone certainly does not explain the rise of agrarianist mobilization in Sonora. The agricultural semiproletariat acted because of the economic crisis in Mexico and because they had struggled for land through official channels for so many years with so little result. Because the state constantly refused to intervene in its favor, this semiproletariat generated an oppositional movement.

From Spontaneous Mobilizations to an Alliance of
Oppositional Organizations

After the October massacre, direct producers began to carry out other land takeovers outside the framework of official organizations. Even independent organizations such as the UGOCM-PPM and the CIOAC were left behind, for they, too, initially believed the October events had resulted merely from bureaucratic infighting, and they resolved to remain neutral.

Toward the end of 1975, regional leaders of land-petitioning groups, most of whom had been affiliated with the CNC, the CCI, or the UGOCM-Jacinto López, began to hold secret meetings to decide upon the future tactics of their struggle. Most of these leaders had already broken with the official organizations of the *Pacto de Ocampo;* the masses were no longer willing to go along with the government's collaborationist pact.

On April 3, 1976, at daybreak, about eight hundred land petitioners took over block 407 (each "block" consisting of about four hundred hectares of land), a property called San Pedro that belonged to the Bórquez Esquer family. Located in the heart of the Yaqui Valley, about ten kilometers from Ciudad Obregón, San Pedro had several buildings densely surrounded by trees that formed a natural protective barrier against armed repression by the state (Sanderson 1981, 191). The land occupiers took several precautions. They dug ditches in the two access roads, leaving room only for their own vehicles to cross over, and they set explosives in strategic places in case these entrances had to be suddenly blocked. Also, they had powerful lights to illuminate the two access roads at night, and they prepared armed groups for self-defense (Ferra Martínez 1982, 15–16).

The Bórquez family was one of the most prominent landowning families in the region, and its influence with the government was considerable. Its members had followed the usual methods for avoiding legal constraints on private land tenure in the agrarian reform legislation, registering four hundred hectares under the names of the four Bórquez brothers. With each new birth in the family, they would buy more property and register it under the new child's name. "By 1975, the Bórquez family, counting 97 members, had amassed nearly 27,000 hectares of land" (Benjamin and Buell 1985).

A few hours after the land takeover, the army surrounded block 407. On April 6 the government sent two representatives from the Ministry of Agrarian Reform to negotiate. Although the land occupants decided to accept mediation, they also took the representatives hostage until the government withdrew its forces from the vicinity of block 407.

With the army present, the land occupants received broad support and solidarity from other groups of land solicitors, relatives, Yaqui Indians, and students. Many of these supporters camped outside the military site in a show of solidarity.

In the meantime, the land petitioners established a formal organization to represent their interests known as the Independent Peasant Front (*Frente Campesino*

Independiente, or FCI). Despite the language of its demands, they were clearly more proletarian and postcapitalist than peasant in nature:

- handing the latifundia to collectively organized peasants, giving first priority to the agricultural workers of the expropriated plot
- expropriation of *latifundia* without compensation
- nationalizing of private banks
- reduction of the maximum allowance for private property [from 150] to 20 hectares
- peasant control of crop commercialization and natural resources
- right to unionization and to strike for agricultural workers
- derogation of the right to *amparo agrario* [the right to stop implementation of agrarain reform by the state] for *latifundistas* [large landowners]
- formation of peasant brigades and self-defense groups
- annulment of all "certificates of immunity" protecting agricultural and grazing land
- democratic representation of the peasants
- cheap credit and provision of machinery for poor peasants (FCI document, cited in Ferra Martínez 1982, 22)

Clearly, this program calls for reforms that go well beyond a "peasant" view of how land should be administered. Nevertheless, many left observers call the agents of this struggles peasants because land remains a central demand. My argument in this regard is that the demand for land takes on a qualitatively different character once it is posed alongside the other demands specified above. The overall character of such demands lead toward the construction of an alternative hegemonic project with a popular-democratic content, one in which production units would assume a postcapitalist character.

Peasants, Proletarians, or Semiproletarians?

Ferra Martínez (1982), Quintero (1982), and Canabal Cristiani (1984) document the fact that up to 80 percent of the land solicitors were temporary or permanent wage earners in agriculture or agroindustries and that some of them were sons of *ejidatarios* or landless day laborers living in *ejido* villages. In his conclusions Ferra Martínez maintains that the struggles for land and unionization were becoming increasingly complementary. Nevertheless, he does not distinguish between different contents in the struggle for land itself. Clearly, the FCI program (quoted above) contains a profoundly popular-democratic and postcapitalist character in its global demands. Amazingly, even Roger Bartra (1982) talks about the Sonoran "peasantry."

The actors in these struggles should be properly considered agricultural semi-proletarians, not peasants, in their production and reproduction relations. They occupy several "class positions" during the year, like Michael Kearney's (1996) "polybians," but quite likely most of their income comes from wage employment. Given the temporary nature of wage employment, however, struggling for unionization is probably not the best strategy for this semiproletariat. Their job experience tells them that salaried jobs are not very stable in agriculture and are rather hard to come by in industry. Neither provides them with much economic security. From this point of view, then, struggle for land may offer a longer-term payoff in employment and security.

Economically, the struggle of the semiproletarians of northwest Mexico has a postcapitalist content. As wage workers, they have been immersed in relations of capitalist cooperation for several generations, a fact that naturally gives them a preference for organizing production cooperatively. Because commodification has taken hold in most spheres of life in the region, the preferred orientation of production is toward the market. They struggle not only for land, but also for the other means of production, for a cooperative organization, and for democratic control of the production process. Their struggle resembles that of a factory takeover by industrial proletarians (in a restricted sense). Such a struggle is postcapitalist in the sense that agents are resisting proletarianization as a permanent or temporary way of life: They actually want to transcend a proletarian condition by gaining full control of the overall production process. This struggle establishes the conditions for the appearance of a popular-democratic project.

In sum, land as an object of struggle does not in itself determine the economic or political character of struggles in the countryside. Aside from the demand for access to land and other means of production, other elements of the political class character of struggles include (1) the method of organizing production (household or cooperative), (2) the character of class organizations vis-à-vis the state and the bourgeoisie (oppositional or collaborationist), and (3) the degree of autonomy of the organization and the alliances it establishes with other left or popular (or right) organizations. As shown below, the Sonoran struggles resulted in a progressive postcapitalist and popular-democratic struggle on all of these counts.

The Land Expropriation

A few days before Echeverría's presidential term came to an end, on November 19, 1976, nearly 100,000 hectares of land were expropriated in the Yaqui and Mayo Valleys. Close to 37,131 hectares were irrigated land, and the remainder were for grazing. Three-fourths of the irrigated land belonged to twenty-one families, several with close kinship relationships among them. Almost 75 percent of the grazing land was held by only four persons, one of them Faustino Felix, ex-governor of Sonora. Some 40 percent of the privately held irrigated land in the Yaqui Valley was affected (Benjamin and Buell, 1985). The lands of seventy-two families were expropriated; many of these families also represented industrial and commercial interests. This measure was taken immediately following the second devaluation of the peso that year (after twenty-two years of a stable exchange rate), when capital flight, fears, and rumors were at their peak. One of the rumors suggested the imminence of a military takeover led by Echeverría himself.

Once the FCI and the other opposition organizations forced the state to expropriate lands of the most productive agrarian bourgeoisie, the state struck back at the FCI by including only a small percentage of its members in the new *ejidos*. In these cases, members of the same group of land petitioners were split up and assigned to different *ejidos*. Then the *Pacto de Ocampo* organizations immediately moved in to reap the benefits of the struggle and to try to control the situation politically because most of the beneficiaries were members of the group (Ferra Martínez 1982; Castellanos and Terrazas 1982).

But this time, however, the constituency of those organizations had learned an important lesson from the FCI. They realized that their having received land was not due to the intervention of the CNC, CCI, CAM, or UGOCM-Jacinto López but the result of their own independent mobilizations. Thus, most of them soon withdrew from those corrupt and corporatist organizations (Canabal Cristiani 1984, 174).

Sonora's agricultural semiproletariat had been immersed in the climate of oppositional struggle waged by the FCI. Although most of its individual members were not given land grants, their consciousness had already transcended their individuality and subjectivity to become the collective consciousness of the semiproletariat in the region. The lessons of combativity, solidarity, and independence from the state had been learned, and the collaborationist role of the *Pacto de Ocampo* organizations had finally been uncovered. These organizations would no longer be able to hide their true character: Political apparatuses of the state, acting mostly to control the masses and usually stepping on their interests to favor bourgeois hegemony.

In the process of land redistribution, Echeverría violated his own Agrarian Code of 1972 on two counts. First, the land distributed allowed for only five hectares of irrigated land for each new *ejidatario,* when the law specified a minimum of ten. This allotment severely limited the employment capacity of the land for each *ejidatario*. Second, the dam in the Yaqui valley already stood at capacity. Thus, Echeverría proposed to "extend a water district already plagued by drought and perennial water-storage shortages." (Sanderson 1981 194)

In spite of the material problems involved in these violations of the law, the new *ejidatarios* confronted the situation successfully. In fact, they have surprised all sectors of Mexican society with their exemplary work in economic (productivity) and political (democratic) terms.

Appraisals of the Coalition of Collective *Ejidos*

Before, the government told us what we could and could not do. Now, we tell them what to do for us.

—A farmer of the Coalition of Collective Ejidos of the Yaqui and Mayo Valleys
(quoted in Benjamin and Buell 1985)

All of the evaluations of the experience of the *Coalición de Ejidos Colectivos de los Valles del Yaqui y El Mayo* suggest that it has been highly successful for direct producers and even for the nation. An investigative reporter from *Unomasuno,* a Mexico City daily, specifically highlighted the achievements in both productivity and political independence after eight years of the land takeovers (Coo 1984a, 1984b). He interviewed the local president of the right-of-center National Action Party (*Partido Acción Nacional,* or PAN) and even he had to concede, "Those friends have attained a *very interesting* productivity and besides working the land very well, they have invested their profits in equipment and agroindustries, which gives their work a *very interesting* dimension [emphasis in original]." (Quoted in Coo 1984a).

Another aspect discussed in the *Unomasuno* article is the direct producers' substantial degrees of independence from the state and the bourgeoisie in constructing their own organization (Coo 1984b, 7). This successful story is an outgrowth of the adverse state interventions that direct producers had to confront. If the state eventually intervened in their favor, it was because the politically organized agricultural workers imposed those policies on the state, just as they imposed land redistribution. This might be called the "subjective moment" in political class dynamics, in which a subordinate class, once politically formed, is able to successfully determine the direction of certain state policies in its favor while maintaining its political independence from the state.

In the summer of 1985, the Institute for Food and Development Policy of San Francisco, California, sent a reporter to the Yaqui valley. A brief account of her visit was published in the institute's monthly newsletter *Food First News* (1985). The reporter describes the coalition experience as exemplary, providing many positive lessons for other popular struggles in Third World agriculture. The institute's full report appears in Benjamin and Buell (1985).

Because favorable state interventions resulted directly from the initiative and political strength of direct producers, such interventions did not coopt their organizations. On the contrary, the workers were the collective actors, the subject of the process, so that new successes resulted in further strengthening their class organizations. In this "subjective moment" the subordinate classes had the upper hand; hence the epigraph of this section: "Before, the government told us what we could and could not do. Now we tell them what do for us." This new position involved, of course, gaining greater degrees of autonomy from the economic apparatuses of the state, namely from the Ejido Bank and a democratic leadership (Gordillo 1985a, 1985b, 1988). (This bank was renamed the *Banco Nacional de Crédito Rural,* or simply Banrural, in 1975.)

The Coalition's Program and Performance

Besides struggling to obtain the full ten hectares that the *ejidatarios* were entitled to by law, the coalition's program also included (1) the struggle against merchant capital for better marketing conditions, (2) the self-financing of *ejidos* and the independence form the bank through a credit union, (3) establishing other productive activities such as dairy operations and textile enterprises from their cotton crop, and (4) constructing urban units to provide adequate housing to *ejidatarios* close to their work sites and to foster closer relationships in the community. Many of these activities were designed to provide more employment opportunities to *ejidatarios* and their sons and daughters, while also strengthening their organization economically and politically (Canabal Cristiani 1984, 215).

Table 7.1 shows yields per hectare in the coalition *ejidos* for wheat, soybeans, and corn as compared with the *ejido*-sector and private-sector average yields and the Yaqui valley's average yield. Only the three most important crops for the coalition were chosen for comparison. Wheat is the most important crop, with over 50 percent of coalition land surface usually dedicated to it. The other crops occupy from 2.5 to 30 percent of arable land. This pattern of land use is similar in the *ejido* and the private sector as well (Oswald, Rodríguez, and Flores 1986, 282).

Except for 1980–81 and 1985–86 in wheat and 1982 and 1985 in soybeans, the coalition crop yields were always higher than the regional average. They followed the productivity of the private sector very closely and usually had higher yields in corn production. The coalition has not had yields equal to or higher than those of the private sector for all crops because it has an explicit policy of cost savings based on eliminating agrochemicals. In fact, coalition technicians have determined that the cost of high-priced agrochemicals is not sufficiently offset by increased yields. Therefore, the minimum yield differentials between the coalition *ejidos* and the private-sector farms involve reduced costs for the coalition and practices that are less damaging to the regional environment, especially reduced dependence on agrochemicals.[2]

As a formal organization, the coalition was inaugurated in May 1978 after the successful struggle against Banrural's retention of *ejido* profits to pay affected landowners. This was the first victorious battle that the new *ejidatarios* waged against unfavorable state intervention. The lesson learned was that they would need to consolidate their class organization not only to defend themselves against the state's impositions but also to propose concrete alternatives for productive organization. The technical department of the coalition was established immediately after this struggle (Castaños 1982).

The next major battle was waged to gain financial independence from Banrural, when the *ejidatarios* decided that they did not want to pay the insurance fees to the government-run *Aseguradora Nacional Agrícola y Ganadera, S.A.* (Anagsa). Anagsa only protected the bank's credits and failed to make an allowance for lost profits by the producer. As an alternative, the coalition created its own common fund with the fees formerly paid to Anagsa, and it provided broader coverage than Anagsa did: 100 percent of crop losses instead of Anagsa's 70 percent. Banrural immediately opposed this initiative, threatening to withhold credit for the coalition if it did not insure with Anagsa. Through the combative mobilization of direct producers, the battle was won by the coalition. Although the common fund was started with no capital (except the funds provided by the Bank's loans for agricul-

TABLE 7.1   Yield per Hectare of the Principal Crops of the Yaqui Valley by Type of Productive Organization, 1980–1986 (in metric tons)

| | | Wheat | | |
Agricultural Cycle	Coalition	Ejido Sector	Private Sector	Regional Average
1980–81	4.351	4.579	4.613	4.403
1981–82	5.314	5.215	5.465	5.190
1982–83	5.008	4.864	5.106	4.941
1983–84	5.243	4.988	5.312	5.121
1984–85	4.876	4.744	5.009	4.861
1985–86	4.543	4.408	4.837	4.595

| | | Soybeans | | |
Agricultural Cycle	Coalition	Ejido Sector	Private Sector	Regional Average
1982	2.009	2.054	2.188	2.108
1983	1.826	1.646	1.838	1.710
1984	1.644	1.545	1.689	1.608
1985	1.978	2.013	2.180	2.092
1986	2.154	2.114	2.127	2.119

| | | Corn [a] | | |
Agricultural Cycle	Coalition	Ejido Sector	Private Sector	Regional Average
1981–82	3.944	4.033	4.341	4.136
1982–83	4.163	3.801	4.044	3.914
1983–84	4.153	3.908	3.900	3.905
1984–85	4.244	4.069	4.236	4.113
1985–86	4.714	3.896	4.078	3.958

[a] Data for the coalition are for the summer cycle in each year; those for the other sectors are for the winter cycle. Therefore, some of the yield variations may be due to differences in the agricultural cycle.

SOURCES: Based on data from the *Departamento de Asistencia Técnica, Coalición de Ejidos Colectivos de los Valles del Yaqui y El Mayo* (supplied by Israel Gaxiola, Coordinator), for Coalition yields; and on data from the *Departamento de Estadística Agrícola, Distrito de Riego 148*, Cajeme, Sonora, *Secretaría de Agricultura y Recursos Hidráulicos* (information on District 41, Yaqui Valley), for *ejido*, private sector, and regional average yields.

tural insurance), by 1982 it had a capitalization of Mex$41,876,787 ($1,820,730 at the current exchange rate). With Anagsa, the *ejidatarios* never knew the destination of their payments.

The struggle for independence from the Banrural, however, had to go further. The coalition decided to create its own credit union, along with a marketing department, for thus far the bank had been in charge of marketing its crops. The credit union began operations in 1979. By 1982 there were forty-three member *ejidos*, organized in three *ejido* unions; others joined later.

News of the coalition's credit union spread through the state of Durango and all the way to Chiapas in Southeastern Mexico. A peasant group in Durango requested membership and in 1981 started operations with very satisfactory results. The Union of Ejido Unions in Chiapas requested a concession to form their own credit union from the Ministry of Finance in 1981 (Coalición 1982).

In addition to gaining the marketing advantages through the department of marketing, this department has been instrumental in purchasing farm inputs. For instance, under a contract with Fertimex, a state-run company, fertilizers have been purchased at bulk prices.

The initial bottom-up, democratic organizing drive of the FCI has been carried over to the coalition. Its internal organization allows and encourages the direct participation of all its members. Of the seventy-six *ejidos* that were constituted after the 1976 expropriation, fifty of them now form part of the coalition. There are monthly assembly meetings of each *ejido*, with 70 to 90 percent of their members attending. Each *ejido* elects new leaders to the *comisariado ejidal* (*ejido* commissariat): a president, a secretary, and a treasurer, every three years. Election for consecutive terms is prohibited in order to prevent the entrenchment of personal power (Benjamin and Buell 1985).

The tendency of most agrarian movements in Mexico to elect the most charismatic personalities has shifted to favor those *ejidatarios* with the best executive abilities. An intermediate steering committee, made up of the representatives from each *ejido* (presidents of the *comisariado ejidal*) meets monthly, and there is a president of the coalition as a whole. In addition, various other departments are dedicated to special functions, such as the technical department and the department of marketing.

The coalition has hired a large technical staff, but the farmers have been very careful that these professionals do not make decisions for them. They are only supposed to provide *ejidatarios* with the information to make decisions for themselves, within their democratic organization.

Because the initial land grants did not include land for housing facilities, most *ejidatarios* have widely dispersed living arrangements, usually some distance from their work sites. The coalition thus had to struggle to acquire additional land for an *ejido* urbanization project. It finally received support from the governor of Sonora, Samuel Ocaña, and obtained 410 hectares for urban zones throughout the Yaqui and Mayo Valleys: "By 1985, the ejidos had built 12 urban zones. With 5,600 homes, as well as local schools, daycare centers and recreation facilities, it is the largest peasant housing project in all of Mexico" (Benjamin and Buell 1985, 9). The project seeks to bring the *ejidatarios* closer together into urban communities, closer to the agricultural work sites; reduce unemployment; and, of course, provide housing for families. The last aspect is highly regarded by *ejidatarios*, most of whom did not own a house before the urbanization project. Given the very hot temperatures of the Yaqui region, all the *ejido* houses were provided with air conditioning units in at least one room. This feature is unthinkable for peasant- or working-class housing in other hot regions of Mexico.

The cultural traits that have developed in the coalition's experience place a great emphasis on a strong work ethic, efficiency, collective work, solidarity with other members of subordinate groups and classes, and independence from the state. In a survey conducted in 1981 with a sample of 5 percent of the membership of each *ejido*, 76.5 percent responded that they preferred the collective over the individual or household form of organization. This is a very high percentage, considering the extent to which individualist ideology was promoted in the 1950s and 1960s. Even though 32 percent gave qualified support (e.g., "as long as we maintain a good organization and no divisions arise," or "as long as we all share the work equally," and so on), a large majority supports the collective organization. As regards participation, 64 percent of the respondents said they assisted in determining what crops, seeds, fertilizes, and other inputs should be used by their *ejido*, and 51 percent said they participate in establishing the internal rules of their *ejido* (Camarena Castellanos and Encinas Terrazas 1982, 124–38).

Some of the new cultural traits, which favor collectivism, solidarity, and participation, are evident in the following description of what the coalition considers to be two of its central commitments:

> We want to make it quite clear: the Coalition of Collective Ejidos has a double commitment: with itself, that all the collective ejidos which constitute it develop economically, but that they must struggle for betterment in all other aspects; that they have a greater participation in the solution to their problems; that the ejido general assembly in each ejido constitutes a force which prevents the entry of reaction; that they do not seek to solve their problems through personal solutions or by sectoralizing or dividing the ejidos but, instead, that they analyze and propose the best solutions as a single unity, putting the collective interest forward, over personal interest and prestige. With regard to all the struggling peasant and working-class organizations of the country: we owe what we have achieved to the fact that we are not alone. We form part of a unity of peasants, workers, and committed professionals. . . . We want to seal this commitment: we put what we have at the disposition of the Mexican workers' struggle. Our experience, as in the case of Chiapas, for the constitution of a Credit Union; our association, as in the case of Durango, to be open for the entry of new members. With these we strengthen our political and economic unity (Coalición 1982, 21–22).

This declaration was made at the 1982 annual meeting in support for the Sonoran collective *ejidos,* a gathering sponsored by the coalition along with dozens of other organizations of workers, peasants, and professionals. These yearly meetings have been part of the demonstrations of solidarity that vast sectors of the

Mexican left and democratic organizations have offered to the coalition, having made the coalition's struggle part of their own struggle.

Epilogue

The past two decades have been marked by recurrent economic crisis in Mexico and currency devaluations, which have made imports almost prohibitive in a context where most of the industrial enterprises and modern agricultural operations depend heavily on the import of machinery and raw materials. The *ejidos* of the coalition are no exception. Mexico's economic problems are severely affecting the coalition, which relies greatly on the imports of machinery from the United States, specifically from International Harvester, Ford International, and Allis Chalmers (Benjamin and Buell 1985, 10).

At a meeting of scholars and agrarian leaders in Culiacán, Sinaloa, in 1987, Juan Leyva Mendivil, former president of the Coalition, presented a paper as a representative of the Northwestern Peasant Alliance (*Alianza Campesina del Noroeste*, or ACN), which includes *ejidos* from Sonora and Sinaloa. The paper is dedicated to an economic analysis of the effects of the debt crisis of the 1980s on agricultural production in their *ejidos*. Such an analysis is still relevant at the end of the crisis-ridden 1990s.

Production costs, for instance, far exceeded wheat prices. From 1980 to 1986, prices increased by 1,633 percent compared with cost increases of 2,528 percent. In terms of kilograms of wheat, in 1980 it took 2,110 kilograms to cover costs per hectare; in 1986 *ejidatarios* had to produce 3,270 kilograms for the same purpose. Conversely, in 1980 profits were 2,390 kilograms per hectare, in contrast to only 1,230 kilograms in 1986. The difficulties of keeping up with technical change and replacing machinery are evident in the following figures. In 1982 the *ejidos* needed 306 metric tons of wheat to purchase a thresher; by 1986 they needed 965 metric tons to replace it (Leyva Mendivil 1987).

Given the relatively small amount of land per *ejidatario* received in 1976 (5 hectares), the producers are still obliged to seek external employment. In a study conducted in 1982 by a group from the National Agricultural University, Chapingo, among 5 percent of the *ejidatarios,* 60 percent of current income came from *ejido* employment, and 40 percent from selling labor power outside the ejido (Quintero 1982).

One of the problems for the coalition has been that not all of its agroindustrial enterprises have functioned properly. The most dramatic example of a poor economic decision was the purchase of a cotton gin from Anderson Clayton in the mid–1980s. This purchase took place in the context of decreasing attention to cotton cultivation in the region and when the gin was in virtual bankruptcy. As a result, the coalition was facing great economic difficulties in paying for the gin by the late 1980s and required a loan of $214,600 to sustain its overall operation.

In 1987, in the midst of such difficulties and the impending presidential elections in Mexico, Governor Rodolfo Felix Valdéz and his functionaries strongly pressured the coalition to formally join the CNC of the PRI. Despite the fact that the coalition president, Juan Díaz Leal, seemed to be willing to proceed in exchange for economic help, the masses prevented him from taking such a step. They were not willing to compromise their strategic political autonomy for conjunctural help. Later on, forty-four presidents of *comisariados ejidales* met with the governor to explain the coalition's statutory position to remain autonomous from *all* political organizations. Nevertheless, one of the three *ejido* unions that make up the coalition, the Nineteenth of November, which is the most active and best organized, formally joined the CNC in early November 1987.

It was rather curious to observe during field work that although most of the coalition leaders have personally rejoined the CNC and the PRI, all of those I interviewed in November 1987 thought that the coalition as such should *not* join the official corporatist organizations. It was probably strategically fortunate for the coalition that it has developed democratic mechanisms to prevent such a possibility, even when its president may have been willing to give up the fight for political autonomy. For the coalition, the economic future depends largely on its own political strength and mobilization.

El Yaqui: Theoretical Recapitulation

It is hard to see how either *campesinistas* or *proletaristas* would have predicted the surprising outcome of agrarian struggles in Sonora. As a matter of fact, the outcome of these struggles was somewhat of a disillusionment for *proletaristas*. Roger Bartra (1982), for example, interpreted this agrarian movement as a last resort of "technocratic populism" seeking to forestall agrarian unrest. In contrast, Arturo Warman (1980) celebrated the fact that even agricultural workers were fighting for supposedly "peasant" demands.

In his article on the problem of the agricultural proletariat, Warman, after noting that workers in Sonora had been separated from their means of production for three or four generations, states, "This proletarian group has recently organized around strictly agrarian demands and not [around demands] of a working class character, with all their implications" (1980, 172). There are two fallacies in Warman's treatment of the problem. First, he identifies the demand for land as a "strictly agrarian," i.e., peasant, demand. As I have argued in this and other chapters, one must look at the totality of demands in order to assess the character of agrarian struggles. Furthermore, the analysis of the objects of struggle must be supplemented with the analysis of class organizations. Only with these two criteria in mind can we adequately determine the political class character of a social movement.

Second, when Warman deals with "permanent agricultural proletarians," he says that they usually ally with rural capitalists. I wonder whether Warman is ac-

TABLE 7.2   Political Class Trajectory and Objects of Struggle in El Yaqui Valley

Moment	Agents	Objects	Outcomes
Time One 1938–47	Noncapitalist cooperative producers	Land, nationality	Self-managed collective *ejido;* popular-democratic
Time Two 1947–65	Same as above, but breaking down into individual production	Maintaining self-managed production (e.g., credit)	Fragmentation of collective *ejido* peasantization formal subordination to state; bourgeois-hegemonic
Time Three 1965–75	Semiproletarians, more proletarianized than in La Laguna	Credit and water for viable peasant production	Renting out of *ejido* land further fragmentation of collectives; bourgeois-hegemonic
Time Four 1975–76	Semiproletarians, more proletarianized than in La Laguna	Land, collective production, self-management	Self-managed democratic and cooperative production; popular-democratic
Time Five 1976–97	Postcapitalist producers	Fair prices for inputs and crops, trying to withdraw from petrochemical dependency and imported inputs	Self-managed democratic and cooperative production; popular-democratic, with trend toward new corporatism by some leaders

SOURCE: Elaborated from the analysis in this chapter.

tually talking about proletarians or wage workers who occupy what Erik Olin Wright has called "contradictory class locations" between capital and labor (1978, 1979). At least for Sonora, it is quite likely that permanent workers have supervisory positions, i.e., contradictory class locations. Hence it is not so surprising that they should ally with their employers rather than with other wage workers.

Bartra's interpretation is also flawed for at least two reasons. First, he labels the class agents as "peasants," attending merely to their demand for land (like Warman), when they were actually a semiproletariat highly dependent on wages (if we retain a production-based, structural concept of economic class). Second, he assumes that the initiative for land redistribution came from the state (as did Sanderson in 1981), when it was actually the opposite: Given the regional correlation of class forces, the movement imposed on the state the policy of land redistribution. (see Table 7.2 for an Historical Summary)

Capitalist development in the Mexican countryside has resulted in a process of "depeasantization without full proletarianization" (Chapter 4). Strictly speaking, then, the new economic subjects that emerge are semiproletarians: They cannot rely solely on wages to fulfill their reproduction needs. Therefore, the rest of the social relations into which they enter to attain economic reproduction might be conducive to the preservation or formation of noncapitalist cultural elements, even if many of these develop within a market context. Given the structural heterogeneity of countries like Mexico, we must go beyond an economic class-reductionist analysis in the study of political class formation. I have suggested the importance of three other determinants: regional cultures, state intervention, and leadership types.

Notes

1. At this time, the PCM began a series of transformations, reflecting both changes in the Communist camp as well as a greater influence from Eurocommunism. The latter favored an electoral route to socialism, rather than the traditional Leninist-inspired revolutionary route. The PCM first turned into the Unified Socialist Party of Mexico (*Partido Socialista Unificado de Mexico*, or PSUM) in 1982, and in 1987 it became the Mexican Socialist Party (*Partido Mexicano Socialista*, or PMS). In the 1988 elections the PMS supported a broad coalition's presidential candidate, Cuahutemoc Cárdenas, the son of former President Lázaro Cárdenas. He was widely believed to have won the 1988 elections, but the PRI still imposed its candidate, Carlos Salinas. The PMS was in turn dissolved in 1989 to form the new Party of the Democratic Revolution (*Partido de la Revolución Democrática*, or PRD), which still exists today representing a broad coalition of former communists, Maoists, Trotskyists, former PRI members, and other nationalists.

2. Personal interview with Israel Gaxiola, Coordinator of the Technical Department of the Coalition, Ciudad Obregón, Sonora, 11/23/87.

8

Conclusion: Farewell to the Peasantry?

The purpose of this concluding chapter is threefold. The first section synthesizes this book's main argument. In the second section I recapitulate the chief issues in the Mexican debate on the agrarian question and point out some research and political problems that remain to be solved. Drawing on a review of recent literature, the last section discusses the political implications of neoliberalism in rural Mexico.

Concepts and History

I have argued that in rural Mexico the process of political class formation has been mediated by the prevailing forms of regional cultures, state intervention, and leadership types; I have also argued for a causal link with the position of class agents in production relations. In addition, I have placed the semiproletariat, rather than the proletariat or the peasantry, at the center of agrarian struggles in contemporary Mexico.

Political class formation is a complex and overdetermined process that is impossible to gauge by looking at production relations alone. I have proposed that this process is constituted by two fundamental elements: (1) object(s) of struggle and class organizations and (2) their relative degree of independence from the state and the ruling class. Regional culture and state intervention, while undoubtedly linked causally to production relations, are more useful in predicting political class formation: Prevailing regional culture generally defines the object(s) of struggle; state intervention shapes the character of class organizations. Furthermore, leadership types help to determine the extent to which class organizations remain independent from the state and autonomous from other political organizations.

Thus, in order to understand political class formation, one must examine the interactions of its components. When studying the object(s) of struggle, we must also inquire into the forms of productive organization that arise after successful struggles for land: whether the organization centers on individual or cooperative production, and whether it is nonmarket- (subsistence) or market-oriented (cash

149

crop). With regard to class organizations, one must ask whether they are oppositional, bourgeois-hegemonic, or popular-democratic. This aspect is determined by the kinds of alliances established with other class and political organizations.

Economically, it is not as important whether productive organizations are cooperative or individually based, as long as class agents have some degree of autonomy in constituting the political character of their organization as popular-democratic. Politically, the expansion of popular-democratic class organizations represents a strengthening of civil society against the state. Such organizations gain the power to shape state interventions in their favor.

In our case studies, the Sonoran Coalition established alliances and solidarity relations with the most democratic and progressive forces in Mexico. Throughout the three regions under study, we also saw several instances of agrarian struggles that assumed a postcapitalist character in production and were politically popular-democratic . Even Atencingo was the scene of the embryonic formation, however ephemeral, of a semiproletariat waging a postcapitalist struggle. This was the case during Porfirio Jaramillo's popular administration of the cooperative (1947–52). Its short duration was due to the fact that the direct producers' object of struggle was actually different from that of their own leaders: Rather than producing cooperatively, however democratic their leadership was, they chose to struggle for the individual parceling of land. The prevailing peasant culture in the region was a major determinant of this outcome.

On the other hand, except for Jaramillo's administration, it was always the case that class organization in Atencingo ended up being integrated into bourgeois-hegemonic discourse and politics: All winning factions remained loyal to their corporatist affiliation. Oppositional factions were coopted as soon as they gained administrative control of the *ejido*'s affairs, or somehow were favored by state intervention. The step toward a "subjective moment" in political class formation was not taken. Such a subjective moment requires that favorable state interventions emerge bottom-up from the very initiative of direct producers rather than from the state.

The initial phase of collectivization in both La Laguna and El Yaqui also represented instances of a political class formation with a postcapitalist and popular-democratic character. In both cases nonmarket peasant cultures had been severely undermined for two to three generations, but the agricultural proletariat and semiproletariat nevertheless participated in a noncapitalist culture: They were democratically assuming control of a postcapitalist production process. What prevented this economic and political formation from consolidating was not a clash between leadership and constituency over demands, but the overwhelming attack and boycott by the state.

Although initially favoring the postcapitalist organization of direct producers, the *Cardenista* agrarian reform actually set the institutional conditions for a shift in the character of state interventions that affected future struggles. After land redistribution and the formation of collective *ejidos,* the new *ejidatarios* had to submit to the rules of the game imposed by the Mexican state. In particular, they had to submit to the state's most forceful economic apparatus for dealing with the *ejido:* the Ejido Bank. Although the bank underwent a democratic phase in the beginning, promoting the self-sustaining economic independence of collective *ejidos,* it was eventually used to destroy this mode of organization. Indeed, the state appropriated, so to speak, the organization of Yaqui Valley and La Laguna *ejidatarios* by controlling their production process. In the Yaqui Valley the effect was an accelerated process of deterioration of the *ejido* economy with a simultaneous strengthening of private capitalist agriculture. In La Laguna there emerged a proletarianization process in which the state became the new employer. In both cases wage labor became widespread, although it was unable to account for the full reproduction of direct producers.

Strictly speaking, then, the new economic subjects who emerged from these processes were structurally semiproletarians: They could not rely solely on wage labor to fulfill their reproduction needs. Their need to engage in other relations of *re*production has been conducive to the preservation or formation of noncapitalist cultural elements. In the context of increasing commercialization and the deepening of capitalist production relations, the semiproletarian condition presupposes two interrelated ways of life: (1) collective work within the labor process of capitalist agriculture, which involves cooperation; and (2) reliance on social relations of reciprocity, kinship, and solidarity to achieve reproduction during times of unemployment. These social relations and their associated values might be conducive to shaping a noncapitalist or even a postcapitalist object of struggle as in Sonora (and Batopilas in Coahuila, both in the 1970s): cooperative, self-managed, and democratic production.

One of the crucial findings in this study deals with the subjective moment of political class formation. Although I have, for the most part, posited political class formation as a dependent variable, once certain classes become politically formed, they also become independent variables that have an effect on the very process of their future formation and/or consolidation as an economic and political class. That is to say, once classes build and/or gain control of their organizations of struggle, they can wrest state interventions favorable to their interests, even as their practices reinforce the cultural values that shaped their struggles in the first place. In this book, we saw embryonic cases of this subjective moment in the three regions during the late 1930s and early 1940s. But the clearest example of this finding emerged from the case of the Coalition of Collective Ejidos in Sonora (Chapter 7).

The political class trajectories described in Chapters 5 through 7 addressed, among other things, one crucial puzzle that I have attempted to solve in this book: Why have class agents that started out in the same structural position in the 1930s, that of agricultural workers, followed different political class trajectories and ended up at diverse destinations in each of the case studies? My analysis of Mexican regions lead to the conclusion that class position by itself is not a sufficient predictor of class destination in the process of political class formation—regional cultures, state intervention, and leadership types play a critical mediating role as well. A schematic representation of my model of political class formation appears in Chart 8.1.

Peasant entrepreneurs, subsistence peasants, proletarians and postcapitalist producers are all equally likely to develop along either coopted, bourgeois-hegemonic, oppositional, or popular-democratic lines. No single political orientation inheres in structural class position and processes. One must allow for the complicating influences of regional cultures, the character of state intervention, and the leadership in shaping political outcomes.

I in no way entirely discount the impact of class structure and processes on political outcomes. In fact, the alternative model of causality I propose in Chapter 2 makes it clear that class structural processes themselves are causally linked to regional cultures, state intervention, and leadership types. But social structure is not the whole story, only part of it. Each realm of society has its own relative autonomy, even when influenced by others (Archer, 1996). Because the temporal qualities of class structure, regional culture, state interventions, and leadership are usually quite different, one must allow for complex causal interactions, not unidirectional economic schemata, in analyzing the complexities of political class formation.

Another distinguishing feature of this study is that I have given more importance to class structural *processes* than to class *positions* per se. The latter are encompassed by the former. Yet class structural processes also include the social relations of *reproduction*. And it is precisely this sphere that I consider most crucial here in shaping regional culture. Without a doubt, class position also enters the picture, to the extent that reproduction is largely determined by class position. But, at least analytically, it is necessary to separate the two spheres of class structural processes: relations of production and relations of reproduction. In exploitative relations, production refers predominantly to the relations between exploiters and exploited; reproduction, in contrast, refers predominantly to the social relations among the exploited. This distinction between the two realms of structural processes has important and lasting effects on regional cultures.

Transcending the Mexican Debate

In this section I will first restate the main positions in debate about the agrarian question in Mexico. I will then point out the main tenets that have been challenged in this analysis and outline some of the problems that remain to be solved by future research and political practice.

It will be remembered from Chapter 2 that both *campesinista* and *proletarista* scholars usually draw political conclusions from the economic analysis of class structure. This is one crucial feature of this polemic. Another one is that most authors have generalized their propositions for the entire country, usually on the

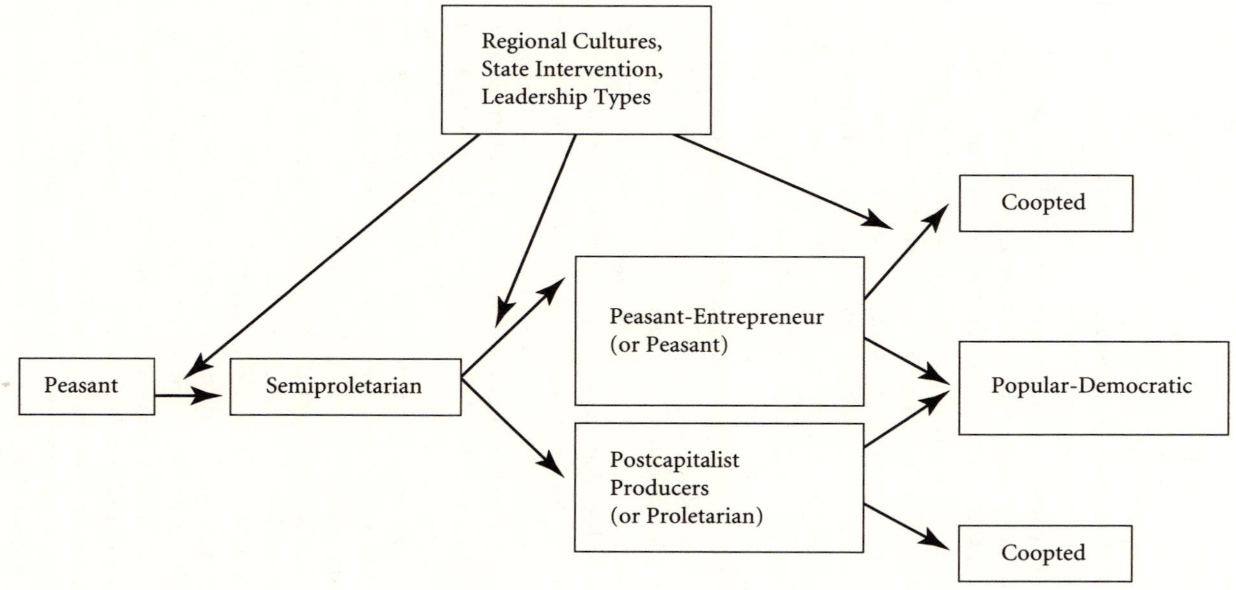

CHART 8.1   Multidirectionality of Political Class Trajectories in a Nonreductionist Model

basis of field work in one particular region, as Cynthia Hewitt de Alcántara has pointed out (1984, 178). Both of these features have resulted in inadequate formulations of political programs. Neither the struggle for unionization (stressed by *proletaristas*) or the struggle for land (stressed by *campesinistas*), therefore, can be seen as adequate policies for all of rural Mexico. In order to devise better policies for the subordinate groups and classes of rural Mexico, one must pay attention to all the constitutive elements of political class formation.

The formal ending of agrarian reform in 1992 has created greater obstacles on the struggle for land; semiproletarianized producers with continued access to land are obliged to struggle for the improvement of institutional assistance to peasant production since, as we saw in Chapter 3, neoliberal reform has largely dismantled most of the state institutions that used to provide such assistance. In some ways, given the extent of bureaucracy and corruption in state agencies, this trend can be seen as a positive development for rural Mexico. But new institutions with a new logic must be created. Organizations of subordinate groups and classes in the countryside could play a vital role in determining the nature and course of such institutions from the bottom up (Fox and Aranda 1997).

This study concentrated on those regions where agrarian reform resulted in the organization of collective *ejidos*, which represent about 12 percent of the *ejidos* created after the revolution. This focus corresponds to a methodological choice: It is an explicit attempt to focus on the most capitalistic operations before the reform, for it is there that one might expect to find the most proletarianized agricultural direct producers. Such a methodological choice maximizes the possibility of falsifying the *proletarista* theses with which I sympathized before starting my research. And in fact, the case of Atencingo demonstrates how, despite a profound proletarianization of direct producers, their central demands revolved around peasant concerns. If such was the case under proletarianization—within peasant cultural surroundings, to be sure—what can we expect from struggles of direct producers who are in merely semiproletarian or peasant positions? Class reductionism, therefore, is clearly inadequate.

Regions with more peasant or semiproletarian class structures, then, will likely focus their struggles on production-related matters and the individual organization of production. Whether such producers will be basically oriented toward subsistence or the market will depend on the degree of commodification and capitalist development and the prevailing regional cultures. A related issue is the extent to which these kinds of direct producers can construct and sustain oppositional class organizations. Will their organizations inevitably veer in a bourgeois-hegemonic direction, or can they establish alliances with other oppositional and left organizations to forge an alternative popular-democratic project?

Peasant struggles have been tremendously important in Mexico's postrevolutionary history throughout the twentieth century. But it was usually the state apparatus that capitalized on this reality: In fact, the stability of the Mexican political system can be largely explained by the capacity of the state to integrate peasant struggles into its "mediation structures" (R. Bartra 1978). Of course, this state-peasantry alliance has evolved in contradictory ways, combining favorable reproductive interventions with repressive measures. But the essence of Mexican reformism has consisted of articulating democratic demands that were absorbed and partially satisfied by the state apparatus while avoiding the constitution of a popular-democratic pole that would antagonize the bourgeois power bloc (R. Bartra 1978).

Therefore, two crucial facts should be highlighted. On the one hand, after the *Cardenista* agrarian reform, the peasant economy and capitalism were able to live together and grow. This fact is fatal to the radical *campesinista* thesis that peasant demands are intrinsically revolutionary. On the other hand, the severe deterioration of the peasant economy since the mid-1960s confirms the real cleavages and contradictions of its development within a capitalistic context. The deterioration of the peasant economy led to semiproletarian land seizures and demands for land (A. Bartra 1979a; 1979b). But we have seen that the character of the struggle for land varied with the articulation of associated demands and the kinds of class organizations that emerged.

Most *proletarista* authors consider wage payments as a sure sign of proletarianization. Given the long history of wage labor in the Mexican countryside, these scholars have not hesitated to prescribe unionization as the central tactic of struggle. Because they view the process of differentiation as extremely advanced, *proletaristas* generally discard the possibility that struggles for land have any revolutionary potential; any struggle for land is characterized as "peasant" and therefore "petit bourgeois" and conservative in content (Posadas and García 1986, 182). Moreover, no distinctions are made among the proletarianized producers of different cultural regions. Their unionization prescription might not be adequate for all regions, given their vast diversity.

In fact, while some advancements have been achieved through unionization—shortening the working day and the payment of minimum wages—the experiences of labor struggles in rural Mexico have often been disastrous. Even when those short-term demands were achieved, the cost was severe repression against the leadership (Posadas and García 1986). The battle for unionization has met with a rather simple response: When workers threaten to strike, the agrarian bourgeoisie resorts to one or more of the following: repressing the leadership, hiring new workers from the nearly unlimited supply of agricultural labor power, or increasing mechanization (de Grammont 1986).

The Mexican state has most often refused to grant legal recognition to the unions sponsored by independent organizations (such as the CIOAC). Therefore, workers have no protection from labor legislation. Even the CTM and the CNC, which also have labor organizations, have had problems in getting their coopted unions legally registered. And wage laborers who have chosen to join these coopted unions have generally been condemned to submission to the corrupt cadres doing the state's bidding.

I am not suggesting that unionization, and labor-type struggles generally, should be ruled out in rural Mexico, especially now that the agrarian reform is legally over. There are a few cases where rural workers actually succeeded in signing collective bargaining agreements with agricultural enterprises, but they have generally been affiliated with official organizations (de Grammont,1986). The adverse conditions for implementing a unionization tactic, therefore, should be very clear: a nearly limitless pool of agricultural workers to serve as strikebreakers; the typically repressive response of the state and employers to unionization; and the seasonal character of most wage-employment positions, which undermines organizational efforts that must cope with continual changes in employers and fellow workers (Salazar and Paré 1986). Therefore, labor struggles are viable in a rather limited and localized number of situations, mostly in northern and northwestern Mexico.

Class Organizations, Civil Society, and Neoliberalism

Some of the emergent political issues brought about by neoliberalism in Mexico's countryside are addressed by three articles in Randall's *Reforming Mexico's Agrarian Reform* (1996). These may be summarized as follows: First, the uprising in Chiapas, discussed by Neil Harvey (1996b), highlights the vast heterogeneity of Mexico's agrarian structure. In Chiapas the law and public institutions largely represent the interests of the ruling classes. Introducing democracy in this context, therefore, requires a structural reform of significant proportions. These themes are further elaborated in Harvey (1998a).

Second, Armando Bartra argues that the state's role in economic production is declining significantly in rural Mexico, even as it grows more direct, paternalistic, and client-efficient in electoral terms (1996, 174). In other words, traditional corporatism, channeled through organizations such as the National Peasant Confederation (*Confederación Nacional Campesina*, CNC) is being replaced or supplemented by a neocorporatism represented by Pronasol and Procampo. The money distributed by these agencies in 1994 had a clearly electoral goal for the PRI government, with about 3.5 million rural families receiving money. This means that about "10 million or 15 million voters went to the polls duly rewarded and with reason to thank the official party" (A. Bartra 1996, 183).

Finally, Jonathan Fox's contribution to Randall's collection supplements these analyses with a discussion of electoral information from the 1994 presidential contest, using the Federal Electoral Institute (*Instituto Federal Electoral*, or IFE) and *Alianza Cívica* as the main sources. The focus is on whether voters can exercise the right to a secret ballot or whether they face pressure; it also examines the presence of opposition political parties in rural areas. Fox first confirms some of the information provided by A. Bartra regarding the distribution of Procampo funds. More than 2.8 million checks were distributed within two weeks of the 1994 elections (in violation of the government's promise to stop check distribution two weeks before the elections). He then notes that it is impossible to measure the degree to which access to the state's new rural development programs' funds was conditioned on electoral support. But looking at the degree to which ballot secrecy was violated is an indicator of "the pool of voters who were vulnerable to efforts to condition access to the reform programs" (Fox 1996b, 190). Other background information presented in this study is that Mexico's rural vote is clearly tilted toward the ruling PRI: "In 'very urban' areas [Zedillo] reportedly won only 34 percent, but in 'very rural' areas he received 77 percent of the votes counted" (Fox 1996b, 191).

Violations of ballot secrecy in the 1994 presidential elections varied considerably: not having screens, having someone watching the voting, voters showing their ballot to other people. Such violations responded to a clear pattern consistent with *Alianza Cívica*'s assertion that "the 1994 presidential elections involved two distinct election-day processes, one 'modern' and relatively clean, the other filled with irregularities, including widespread violation of ballot secrecy and direct pressures by local bosses on voters." (Fox 1996b, 205) These irregularities were clearly more rampant in places where opposition parties could not be part of the executive committee administering the balloting place. Because the opposition parties were least capable of sending representatives to the most indigenous municipalities, these were the least likely to have guaranteed access to a secret ballot.

Fox and Aranda's book *Decentralization and Rural Development in Mexico* (1996) is an important pioneer study of the new World Bank policy that is supposed to address poverty alleviation, environmental issues, gender, and the concerns of indigenous peoples. The authors raise the right questions about how to increase both the government's and the bank's accountability for their development decisions. Some key conditions for reducing the gap between policy targets and practice are increasing community-based participation and access to information *before* implementing projects, and creating adequate institutional channels for investigating complaints by affected "stake holders."

According to Fox and Aranda, neoliberalism has brought about two policy trends related to decentralization. One is to move away from traditional clientelism and toward combinations of community participation, job creation, community implementation, and oversight of projects. The second trend is a decreased bias against the poorest municipalities in disbursing transfer funds. Several municipal reforms since 1983 have given municipalities an increased responsibility for service delivery, and town councils have been created to decentralize municipal administration. Where these policy trends converge, as in the case-study location of Oaxaca, the result is an increase in the municipal government's capacity to respond to development needs with greater efficiency and accountability. Alternatively, if decentralization is countered by persistent authoritarianism, then accountability is doomed to failure. The key message of this book is, therefore, that a bottom-up and democratic approach in designing and implementing development projects is the most promising for rural communities.

Finally, Hubert Cartón de Grammont, in his *Neoliberalismo y organización social en el campo mexicano* (1996a), has put together another fine collection of essays that analyzes the new challenges for rural social organizations. He has been one of the most active producers and promoters of rural studies in Mexico in the past two decades (1986, 1990, 1995; de Grammont and Tejera Gaona 1996). In fact, he was the key organizer of the first meeting of the "Red de Estudios Rurales" in Taxco, Guerrero in 1994, and then its second meeting in Querétaro in February 1998. In this second meeting the network became formally organized into the Mexican Association of Rural Studies (*Asociación Mexicana de Estudios Rurales,* or AMER) which will meet periodically as a professional association.[1]

In his introduction, de Grammont argues that there is a new dualism emerging in the countryside: On the one hand, there is a gradually shrinking group of viable producers who can play successfully within the new market-led rules and remain eligible for official and private lending; on the other, there is a growing group of "the poor," at best eligible only to receive help from government-assistance programs, which cannot help much in production.

One of the key contributions of de Grammont's collection is that it implicitly clarifies what civil society is all about in rural Mexico. By addressing the complexity and heterogeneity of rural producers and their organizations, de Gramont and contributors give the reader a much better idea than the rather simplified version of civil society popularized by the EZLN (*Ejercito Zapatista de Liberación Nacional*). The latter seems to imply that civil society is made up primarily of organizations of the subordinate groups and classes. If this were the case, expanding civil society would be tantamount to changing the balance of power between the state and society. De Grammont's own contribution describes the organizations of private cultivators in rural Mexico. As it turns out, even if private-sector organizations are not monolithic, their organizations have been key players in influencing the policy change toward neoliberalism and the promotion of NAFTA.

Now, if some organizations of the private sector, whether big, medium, or small, are becoming more militant, it is because the corporatist channels for exerting pressure on agricultural policy have become very ineffectual. In this new rise of activist citizenship, three types of social actors emerge: individuals, organizations by type of peasant or cultivator, and social movements. Increasingly, social movements are acquiring the character of broad fronts made up of local or regional organizations that take a distance from political parties; they want to preserve their autonomy. They may nevertheless be linked to any of the existing political parties or even to the state apparatus, or they may be independent from the state. While such social movement organizations may be described as "multi-party" because their members may also be militants in several different parties, their loyalty is primarily to their social organization rather than to their party.

While the peasant movements of the 1960s and 1970s centered on the demand for land (A. Bartra 1979a, 1979b), the new focus of rural struggles since the 1980s has shifted toward a number of concerns related to productive organization (de

Grammont 1996b). Moreover, rural social movements have struggled for self-management and democratic production (Otero 1989b), the appropriation of the productive process in general (Gordillo 1988), territorial control and autonomy (Moguel, Botey and Hernández 1992; Rubio 1996), and the struggle for the appropriation of social and political life (Harvey 1996c). With the EZLN uprising, finally, the democratic reform of the state cannot be postponed any longer (Harvey 1996c, 1998b).

The new social movement organizations also engage in new forms of social action and forms of expression. Direct action and intense mobilization and struggle have largely replaced negotiation and political subordination. Therefore, the weakest link of traditional corporatism is that between social organizations and the ruling PRI. This is why new mobilizations are completely overflowing the traditional channels of representation and policy making.

De Grammont's article (1996b) addresses primarily the organization of the private sector, from small cultivators to large agroindustrial corporations, and describes their internal contradictions. While private-sector organizations agree that land should be privatized, there are those who favor a private agrarianism of small cultivators, some state support, and opposition to NAFTA; others, mainly the best-positioned for agroexports, largely support and indeed promote the neoliberal reform. De Grammont profiles the changing relations of private-sector cultivators with the state. The two groups went from a rather cozy relationship to the status quo in the currently belligerent situation. In de Grammont's view, belligerence, even within the private sector, is due to the fact that only the largest and most productive can hope to survive in the neoliberal context.[2]

De Grammont's collection uses primary sources and ethnographic material to provide a wealth of factual information on new organizational processes.

From the new dualism posited by de Grammont, one might anticipate that the wealthiest and most productive cultivators and agroindustrialists will be most successful in exerting pressure on the state. Indeed, they might be creating a new form of more autonomous and effective corporatism for their interests. The middle and poor producers, however, will find such relationships increasingly frustrating, and many will be forced out of agriculture altogether. But before this happens, we are likely to witness a much greater growth of a subordinate but combative part of civil society of the sort so often praised and addressed in EZLN communiqués.

From these texts we can see that progress toward democracy in Mexico is slow, heavily constrained, and largely limited to liberal democracy. Where participation is promoted or allowed, however, as in some development projects, then results can be more encouraging (at least at an economic level). It remains to be seen whether people will be content with achievements of this nature or continue pushing for a more significant form of political transition, one that might allow them to steer the development model itself in a more equitable direction.

Conclusion

In the introduction to this study, I argued that political class formation is related to the emergence of civil society insofar as it refers to the building of voluntary associations of direct producers. To the extent that independent and autonomous class organizations emerge and consolidate, so, too, does civil society. In this sense civil society is also a terrain for democratization. Until 1994 political parties had achieved a minimal advancement in electoral democratization that focused on political society or the state. Thus, the majority of the electoral reforms resulted in changes that left the authoritarianism of Mexico's political system virtually intact. If anything, they accomplished the modernization of authoritarianism, which legitimated the continued domination of the PRI (Otero, 1996a).

An advancement of democracy in political society will be significant only to the extent that it goes hand in hand with a consolidation of subordinate groups and classes in civil society. Only thus can the EZLN's political principle "command by obeying" ("*mandar obedeciendo*") be turned into reality. That is to say, with an invigorated civil society, leaders and popular representatives will actually have to respond to the wishes of the electorate and their constituencies—to command by obeying. In this view of democracy, those officials who are not accountable to the popular will have to abandon their posts through some recall mechanism. This process would lead to a tremendous increase in the development of democratic leadership. To command by obeying, then, presupposes not only the democratization of electoral political processes; it also presupposes the consolidation of an organized civil society that is able to demand clear accountability from its representatives and enhances the development of a democratic culture. The objective of this new popular-democratic paradigm is to advance toward a fair and transparent electoral process, yes, but also toward the organized consolidation of subordinate groups and classes in civil society.

The era of globalization and neoliberalism has blossomed with the demise of state socialism and the Cold War. Accordingly, future struggles by subordinate groups and classes must take on a democratic character. A new hegemonic project, not explicitly socialist but rather geared to popular-democratic struggles, has to seek the reformation of capitalism. The recent movement toward democratic transition in Mexico demands that political parties adopt a new attitude toward the mass organizations of subordinate groups and classes. Rather than trying to coopt them as in the past and turning them into "conveyor belts" of party politics, political parties will have to respect the independence and autonomy of such organizations and to command by obeying them. As Judith Adler Hellman has argued (1994), mass organizations also would do well to give up their traditional mistrust of political parties and establish tactical alliances with them while zealously guarding their independence from the state and their autonomy from political parties. The alliance of popular-democratic parties and class organizations might not overthrow capitalism, but only such an alliance can curb its exploitative excesses and perhaps even push it toward a societal democracy.

Notes

1. AMER's web page may be consulted at http://serpiente.dgsca.unam.mx/piisecam-rer. The electronic discussion network, Scholars for Rural Development (or MRD) also has a web page and is a major internet source with many useful links to sites on rural Mexico: http://anthap.oakland.edu/anthap1/mrindex. htm.

2. Other contributors to de Grammont's volume address the relationship of the corporatist CNC and the new peasant movement (Horacio Mackinlay 1996), the role of independent organizations (Blanca Rubio 1996), rural work and labor organizations (Sara Lara 1996), the new forms of representation brought about by the *Unión Nacional de Organizaciones Regionales Campesinas* (UNORCA) (Neil Harvey 1996c), the indigenous movement for autonomy (Sergio Sarmiento Silva 1996), other forms of productive organization for commercialization (Juan de la Fuente and Joaquín Morales 1996), women's productive groups (Rosa Aurora Espinosa G. 1996), and expressions of resistance against the new Agrarian Law (Adriana López Mojardín 1996).

References

Aguilar Camín, Hector. 1977. *La frontera nomada: Sonora y la revolución mexicana.* Mexico City: Siglo XXI Editores.

Aguilar Camín, Hector. 1982. *Saldos de la revolución.* Mexico City: Nueva Imagen.

Aguilar Solis, Samuel and Hugo Andrés Araujo. 1984. *Estado y campesinado en La Laguna: La lucha campesina por la tierra y el excedente.* Folleto de Divulgación, vol. 1, no. 5. Saltillo: Universidad Autónoma Agraria Antonio Narro.

Alavi, Hamsa. 1973. "Peasant Classes and Primordial Loyalties." *The Journal of Peasant Studies.* 1(1).

Alvarez, Sonia E., Evelina Dagnino, and Arturo Escobar. 1998. *Cultures of Politics, Politics of Cultures: Re-Visioning Latin American Social Movements.* Boulder and Oxford: Westview Press.

Althusser, Louis and Etienne Balibar. 1968. *Para leer El Capital.* Mexico City: Siglo XXI Editores.

Appendini, Kirsten. 1994. "Transforming Food Policy Over a Decade: The Balance for Mexican Corn Farmers in 1993." Pp. 145–160 in Cynthia Hewitt de Alcántara, ed., *Economic Restructuring and Rural Subsistence in Mexico.* La Jolla, CA: Center for U.S.-Mexican Studies, University of California, San Diego.

Appendini, Kirsten A. de and Vania Almeida Salles. 1976. "Agricultura capitalista y agricultura campesina en México: Diferencias regionales en base de datos censales." Pp. 29–68 in Rodolfo Stavenhagen, et al. *Capitalismo y campesinado en México.* Mexico City: SEP-INAH.

Appendini, Kirsten A. de and Vania Almeida Salles. 1980. "Precios de garantía y crisis agrícola." *Nueva Antropología.* Mexico City. Year IV, nos. 13–14, May.

Archer, Margaret. 1996. *Culture and Agency: The Place of Culture in Social Theory.* Revised Edition. New York: Cambridge University Press.

Avila Méndez, Agustín. 1986. "Testimonios de dos huelgas: la Huasteca potosina y la Comarca Lagunera." 219–236 in de Grammont, 1986.

Baitenmann, Helga. 1998. "The Article 27 Reforms and the Promise of Local Democratization in Central Veracruz." 105–123 in Cornelius and Myhre 1998b.

Barkin, David, and Billie R. DeWalt. 1988. "Sorghum and the Mexican Food Crisis." *Latin American Research Review.* 23(3):30–59.

Barkin, David, and Blanca Suárez. 1982. *El fin de la autosuficiencia alimentaria.* Mexico City: Centro de Ecodesarrollo and Nueva Imagen.

Barry, Tom. 1995. *Zapata's Revenge: Free Trade and the Farm Crisis in Mexico:* Boston: South End Press.

Bartra, Armando. 1996. "A Persistent Rural Leviathan." 173–184 in Randall 1996.

Bartra, Armando. 1979a. *La explotación del trabajo campesino por el capital.* Mexico City: Editorial Macehual.

Bartra, Armando. 1979b. *Notas sobre la cuestión campesina (México 1970–76).* Mexico City: Editorial Macehual–ENAH.

Bartra, Roger. 1993. *Agrarian Structure and Political Power in Mexico.* Baltimore: Johns Hopkins University Press.

Bartra, Roger. 1982a. *Campesinado y poder político en México.* Mexico City: Ediciones Era.

Bartra, Roger. 1982b. "Capitalism and the Peasantry in Mexico." *Latin American Perspectives.* Vol. 9, no. 1, issue 32, Winter.

Bartra. Roger. 1978. *El poder despótico burgués.* Mexico City: Ediciones Era.

Bartra, Roger. 1975a. "Sobre la articulación de modos de producción en América Latina." *Historia y sociedad.* Mexico City. Segunda época, no. 5. Spring.

Bartra, Roger. 1975b. "Peasants and Political Power in Mexico: A Theoretical Model." *Latin American Perspectives.* Vol. 5, no. 2, issue 8, Summer.

Bartra, Roger. 1975c. "Campesinado y poder político en México." in Roger Bartra et al., *Caciquismo y poder político en México rural.* Mexico City: Siglo XXI Editores.

Bartra, Roger. 1975d. "Y si los campesinos se extinguen . . ." *Historia y sociedad.* Mexico City. Segunda época, no. 8, invierno.

Bartra, Roger. 1974a. *Estructura agraria y clases sociales en México.* Mexico City: Ediciones Era.

Bartra, Roger. 1974b. *Marxismo y sociedades antiguas.* Mexico City: Grijalbo.

Bartra, Roger and Gerardo Otero, 1987. "Agrarian Crisis and Social Differentiation in Mexico," *Journal of Peasant Studies* (London). 14(3):334–362.

Beals, Ralph L. 1932. *The Comparative Ehnology of Northen Mexico Before 1750.* Berkeley: University of California Press.

Benjamin, Medea and Rebecca Buell. 1985. "Coalition of Ejidos Report: The Coalition of Ejidos of the Valleys of Yaqui and Mayo, Sonora State, Mexico." San Francisco, California: Institute for Food and Development Policy.

Burawoy, Michael. 1979. *Manufacturing Consent.* Chicago and London: University of Chicago Press.

Canabal Cristiani, Beatriz. 1984. *Hoy luchamos por la tierra.* Colección Ensayos. Mexico City: Universidad Autónoma Metropolitana-Xochimilco.

Cancian, Frank. 1992. *The Decline of Community in Zinacantán: Economy, Public Life, and Social Stratification, 1960–1987.* Stanford, Calif.: Stanford University Press.

Cancian, Frank. 1972. *Change and Uncertainty in a Peasant Economy: The Maya Corn Farmers of Zinacantán.* Stanford: Stanford University Press.

Carr, Barry. 1973. "Las peculiaridades del norte mexicano 1880-1928 : Ensayo de interpretacion." Historia Mexicana. 22 (3) : 320–346.

Carr, Barry. 1980. "Recent Regional Studies of the Mexican Revolution." Latin American Research Review. 15 (1) : 3–14.

Carr, Barry. 1986. "The Mexican Communist Party and Agrarian Mobilization in the Laguna 1920-1940," paper presented at the meetings of the Latin American Studies Association, Boston, MA, USA. 22–25 October.

Carr, Barry and Steve Ellner. 1993. *The Latin American Left: From the Fall of Allende to Perestroika:* Boulder: Westview Press.

Carrasco, Pedro. 1969. "Central Mexican Highlands: Introduction." in Vogt, 1969.

Castañeda, Jorge G., 1993. *Utopia Unarmed: The Latin American Left After the Cold War.* New York: Alfred A. Knopf.

CEPAL (Schejtman, Alejandro). 1992. *Economía campesina y agricultura empresarial: Tipología de productores del agro mexicano.* Mexico City: Siglo XXI Editores.

Chayanov, A. V. 1974. *La organización de la unidad económica campesina.* Buenos Aires: Nueva Visión.

Chollett, Donna. 1995. "Restructuring the Mexican Sugar Industry: Campesinos, the State and Private Capital." 23–40 in Singelmann. 1995.

Coalición de Ejidos Colectivos de los Valles del Yaqui y El Mayo. 1982. *En defensa del ejido.* Mexico City: Centro de Estudios Económicos y Sociales del Tercer Mundo.

Coello, Manuel. 1981. "¿Recampesinización en la descampesinización?" *Revista mexicana de sociología.* Year XLIII, no 1.

Coello, Manuel. 1975. "Caracterización de la pequeña producción mercantil." *Historia y sociedad.* Mexico City. Segunda época, no. 8.

Collier, George A., with Elizabeth Lowery Quarantiello. 1994. *Basta! Land and the Zapatista Rebellion in Chiapas.* Oakland, Calif.: Food First.

Contreras, Ariel José. 1977. *México 1940: Industrialización y crisis política.* Mexico City: Siglo XXI Editores.

Coo, Jorge. 1984a. "Probó el ejido colectivo ser más eficiente." *Unomasuno.* Mexico City: December 15.

Coo, Jorge. 1984b. "Libertad para organizarse, base del éxito en el Valle del Yaqui." *Unomasuno.* Mexico City. December 17.

COPARMEX. 1982. *El Día.*

Córdoba, Arnaldo. 1972. *La formación del poder político en México.* Mexico City: Ediciones Era.

Córdoba, Arnaldo. 1974. *La política de masas del cardenismo.* Mexico City: Ediciones Era.

Cornelius, Wayne A., 1992. "The Politics and Economics of Reforming the *Ejido* Sector in Mexico: an Overview and Research Agenda," *LASA Forum,* 23(3):3–10.

Cornelius, Wayne A., Ann L. Craig and Jonathan Fox, eds., 1994. *Transforming State-Society Relations in Mexico: The National Solidarity Strategy.* U.S.-Mexico Contemporary Perspectives Series, 6. San Diego: Center for U.S.-Mexican Studies, University of California, San Diego.

Cornelius, Wayne and David Myhre. 1998a. "Introduction." 1–20 in Cornelius and Myhre 1998b.

Cornelius, Wayne and David Myhre, eds. 1998b. *The Transformation of Rural Mexico: Reforming the Ejido Sector.* La Jolla, CA: Center for U.S.-Mexican Studies, University of California, San Diego (UCSD).

Cortés Sánchez, Sergio. 1981. "Notas sobre la estructura económica de Puebla." *Crítica.* Year III, no. 8–9, January–June.

Covarrubias Patiño, Daniel. 1996. "An Opinion Survey in the Countryside—1994." 107–116 in Laura Randall, ed. *Reforming Mexico's Agrarian Reform.* New York and London: M.E. Sharpe.

Craig, Ann. 1983. *The First Agraristas: An Oral History of a Mexican Agrarian Reform Movement.* Berkeley: University of California Press.

Cumberland, Charles C. 1952. *Mexican Revolution: Genesis under Madero.* Austin and London: University of Texas Press.

Cumberland, Charles C. 1975. *La revolución mexicana: Los años constitucionalistas.* Mexico City: Fondo de Cultura Económica.

Davidson, Alastair. 1984. "Gramsci, the Peasantry and Popular Culture." Journal of Peasant Studies. 1 (4): 139–154.

de Grammont, Hubert C., coord. 1996a. *Neoliberalismo y organización social en el campo mexicano.* Mexico City: Plaza y Valdéz and Instituto de Investigaciones Sociales, Universidad Nacional Autónoma de México.

de Grammont, Hubert C.. 1996b. "La organización gremial de los agricultores frente a los procesos de globalización en la agricultura." 21–67 in de Grammont 1996a.

de Grammont, Hebert C., coord. 1995. *Globalización, deterioro ambiental, y reorganización social en el campo.* Mexico City: Instituto de Investigaciones Sociales, Universidad Autónoma de México and Juan Pablos Editor.

de Grammont, Hubert C. 1990. *Empresarios agrícolas y el Estado: Sinaloa 1893–1984.* Mexico City: Universidad Nacional Autónoma de México (UNAM).

de Grammont, Hubert C., coord. 1986. *Asalariados Agrícolas y sindicalismo en el campo mexicano.* Mexico City: Instituto de Investigaciones Sociales, Universidad Autónoma de México and Juan Pablos Editor.

de Grammont, Hubert C. 1979. "Historia de las luchas sociales en la zona de Atencingo." 185–262 in Paré 1979a.

de Grammont, Hubert C. and Héctor Tejera Gaona, coords. 1996. *Nuevos procesos rurales en México: Teorías, estudios de caso y perspectivas,* four volumes. Mexico City: UNAM, UAM, INAH.

de Janvry, Alain. 1981. *The Agrarian Question and Reformism in Latin America.* Baltimore: Johns Hopkins University.

de Janvry, Alain, Gustavo Gordillo, and Elisabeth Sadoulet. 1997. *Mexico's Second Agrarian Reform: Household and Community Responses.* Transformation of Rural Mexico Series, Number 1. La Jolla, CA: Center for U.S.-Mexican Studies, University of California, San Diego.

de la Fuente Hernández, Juan, and Joaquín Morales Valderrama. 1996. "Crisis rural y respuesta campesina: La comercializadora agropecuaria de occidente." 283–353 in de Grammont 1996a.

del Castillo, Gustavo. 1979. "Desarrollo de la hacienda algodonera." In Leticia Gándara, Gustavo del Castillo, and William K Meyers. *La Comarca Lagunera: Su historia. Parte II: Las haciendas algodoneras.* Cuadernos de la Casa Chata. Mexico City: Centro de Investigaciones Superiores del INAH.

de la Peña, Sergio. 1980. "Las fuerzas proletarias en México." 109–144 in José María Calderón, et al. *Economía y política en el México actual.* Mexico City: Editorial Terra Nova.

de la Peña, Sergio. 1982. *Capitalismo en cuatro comunidades rurales.* Mexico City: Siglo XXI Editores.

DeWalt, Billie R. and Martha W. Rees, with Arthur D. Murphy. 1994. *The End of Agrarian Reform in Mexico: Past Lessons, Future Prospects.* Transformation of Rural Mexico Series, no. 3. Ejido Reform Research Project. La Jolla, CA: Center for U.S.-Mexican Studies, University of California, San Diego.

Diamond, Larry, ed. 1992. "Introduction: Civil Society and the Struggle for Democracy." Pp. 1–27, in *The Democratic Revolution: The Struggles for Freedom and Pluralism in the Developing World.* New York: Freedom House.

Downing, Theodore E. 1988. "A Macro-Organizational Analysis of the Mexican Coffee Industry, 1988–1977," 175–193 in Philip Quarles van Ufford, Dirk Kruijt and Theodore

Downing, eds. *The Hidden Crisis in Development: Development Bureaucracies.* Tokyo and Amsterdam: United Nations University and Free University Press.

Dresser, Denise. 1991. *Neopopulist Solutions to Neoliberal Problems: Mexico's National Solidarity Program.* Current Issue Brief Series, no. 3. La Jolla: Center for U.S.-Mexican Studies, University of California, San Diego.

Dryzek, John S. 1996. *Democracy in Capitalist Times: Ideals, Limits, and Struggles.* New York and Oxford: Oxford University Press.

Eckstein, Sholmo (Salomón). 1966. *El ejido colectivo en México.* Mexico City: Fondo de Cultura Económica.

Eckstein, Shlomo (Salomón). 1970. "Collective Farming in Mexico: The Case of La Laguna." In Rodolfo Stavenhagen, ed. *Agrarian Problems and Peasant Movements in Latin America.* Garden City: Anchor Books.

Edelman, Robert. 1987. *Proletarian Peasants: The Revolution of 1905 in Russia's Southwes.* Ithaca and London: Cornell University Press.

El Día. "UNORCA, unidos venceremos." April 6.

El Día. 1985a. "Lo regional se mueve: Entrevista a ejidatarios de Batopilas, Zacatecas (sic: should say "Coahuila," instead of "Zacatecas.")." June 15.

Encinas R. Alejandro, coord, and Juan de la Fuente, Horacio Mackinlay, and Emilio Romero, comps. 1995. *El campo mexicano en el umbral del siglo XXI.* Mexico City: Espasa Calpe.

Erasmus, Charles J. 1961. *Man Takes Control: Cultural Development and American Aid.* Minneapolis: University of Minnesota Press.

Espinosa G., Rosa Aurora. 1996. "Modernización y organización productiva en grupos de mujeres del sur de Guanajuato." 397–439 in de Grammont 1996a.

Escobar, Arturo, and Sonia E. Alvarez, eds. 1992. *The Making of Social Movements in Latin America: Identity, Strategy, and Democracy.* Series in Political Economy and Economic Development in Latin America. Boulder and Oxford: Westview Press.

Esteva, Gustavo. 1975. "La agricultura de México de 1950 a 1975: El fracaso de una falsa analogía." *Comercio Exterior.* Mexico City. Vol 25, no. 12, December.

Esteva, Gustavo. 1978. "Y si los campesinos existen." *Comercio Exterior.* Mexico City. Vol. 28, no. 6, June.

Esteva, Gustavo. 1980. *La batalla en el México rural.* Mexico City: Siglo XXI Editores.

Esteva, Gustavo. 1983. "Los campesinos existen." *Nexos.* Mexico City: Year VI, vol. 6, no. 71, November.

Falcón, Romana. 1977. *El agrarismo en Veracruz: La etapa radical (1928–1935).* Mexico City: El Colegio de México.

Feltenhausen, Herman and Heliodoro Díaz-Cisneros. 1985. "The Strategy of Rural Development: The Puebla Initiative." *Human Organization.* Vol. 44, no. 4, Winter.

Ferra Martinez, Carlos. 1982. "El movimiento campesino de Sonora: 1975–1976." Paper presented at the Segundo Congreso Nacional sobre Problemas Agrarios. Chilpancingo, Guerrero, Mexico, June 7–11.

Flora, Cornelia Buttler, and Gerardo Otero. 1995. "Sweet Neighbors? The State and the Sugar Industries in the United States and Mexico under NAFTA." 63–74 in Singelmann 1995.

Foley, Michael W. 1989. "Agricultural Policy and Politics: Theory and Practice." *Latin American Research Review.* XXIV(1):233–249.

Food First News. 1985. "Collective Farming: Can It Work?" No. 22, Summer.

Fowler Salamini, Heather. 1979. *Movilización campesina en Veracruz (1920–1938)*. Mexico City: Siglo XXI Editores.

Fox, Jonathan. 1996a. "How Does Civil Society Thicken? The Political Construction of Social Capital in Rural Mexico." *World Development*. 24(6):1089–1103.

Fox, Jonathan. 1996b. "National Electoral Choices in Rural Mexico." 185–209 in Randall 1996.

Fox, Jonathan. 1993. *The Politics of Food in Mexico: State Power and Social Mobilization*. Ithaca: Cornell University Press.

Fox, Jonathan, and Josefina Aranda. 1996. *Decentralization & Rural Development in Mexico: Community Participation in Oaxaca's Municipal Funds Program*. Monograph Series, 42. La Jolla, CA: Center for U.S.-Mexican Studies, University of California, San Diego.

Friedman, Harriet. 1980. "Household Production and the National Economy: Concepts for the Analysis of Agrarian Formations." *The Journal of Peasant Studies*. 7(2)

García Chavez, Luis Ramiro. 1992. *La agroindustria cañera de México frente a la apertura comercial*. Mexico: Universidad Autónoma Chapingo.

García Zamora, Rodolfo. *La agricultura en el laberinto de la modernidad*. Serie Economía, Espacio y Población. Zacatecas: Facultad de Economía, UAZ.

Gates, Marilyn. 1993. *In Default: Peasants, the Debt Crisis, and the Agricultural Challenge in Mexico*. Latin American Perspectives Series, no. 12. Boulder: Westview Press.

Gates, Marilyn. 1996. "The Debt Crisis and Economic Restructuring: Prospects for Mexican Agriculture." 43–62 in Otero 1996b.

Giddens, Anthony. 1984. *The Constitution of Society: Outline of the Theory of Structuration*. Cambridge: Polity Press.

Giddens, Anthony. 1976. *New Rules of Sociological Method: A Positive Critique of Interpretative Sociologies*. London: Hutchinson.

Gilly, Adolfo. 1998. "Chiapas and the Rebellion of the Enchanged World." 261–334 in Nugent 1998.

Gilly, Adolfo. 1974. *La revolución interrumpida*. 4th Edition. Mexico City: Editorial El Caballito.

Gledhill, John. 1995. *Neoliberalism, Transnationalization, and Rural Poverty: A Case Study of Michoacán, Mexico*. Boulder and Oxford: Westview Press.

Gómez-Jara, Francisco A. 1970. *El movimiento campesino en México*. Mexico City: Editorial Campesina.

González Navarro, Moisés. 1968. *La Confederación Nacional Campesina: Un grupo de presión en la reforma agraria mexicana*. Mexico City: B. Costa-Amic Editor.

Gordillo, Gustavo. 1985a. "La otra Sonora: El asalto al cielo de los campesinos." *El Día*. August 11.

Gordillo, Gustavo. 1985b. "El ejido, eje de la producción alimentaria." *El Día*. August 17.

Gordillo, Gustavo. 1988. *Campesinos asalto al cielo: una reforma agraria con autonomía*. Mexico City: Siglo XXI Editores.

Gutelman, Michel. 1974. *Capitalismo y reforma agraria en México*. Mexico City: Editorial Era.

Hamilton, Nora. 1982. *The Limits of State Autonomy: Post-Revolutionary Mexico*. Princeton: Princeton University Press.

Hansen, Roger D. 1974. *La política de desarrollo mexicano*. Mexico City: Siglo XXI Editores.

Harris, Richard L.. 1992. *Marxism, Socialism, and Democracy in Latin America*. Boulder: Westview Press.

Harris, Richard L. 1978. "Marxism and the Agrarian Question in Latin America." *Latin American Perspectives.* 5(4):2–26.

Harvey, Neil. 1998a. *The Chiapas Rebellion: The Struggle for Land and Democracy.* Durham, NC: Duke University Press.

Harvey, Neil. 1996b. "Impact of Reforms to Article 27 on Chiapas: Peasant Resistance in the Neoliberal Public Sphere." 151–171 in Randal 1996.

Harvey, Neil. 1996c. "Nuevas formas de representación en el campo mexicano: La Unión Nacional de Organizaciones Regionales Campesinas Autónomas (UNORCA), 1985–1993." 239–282 in de Grammont 1996a.

Harvey, Neil. 1998b. "Rural Reforms and the Question of Autonomy in Chiapas." 69–89 in Cornelius and Myhre 1998b.

Harvey, Neil. 1996a. "Rural Reforms and the Zapatista Rebellion: Chiapas 1988–95." 187–208 in Otero 1996b.

Heller, Agnes. 1985. *Everyday Life: Rationality of Reason, Rationality of Intellect.* London: Routledge and Keagan Paul.

Hellman, Judith Adler. 1994. "Mexico and Popular Movements, Clientelism, and the process of Democratization." *Latin American Perspectives.* 21(2):124–142.

Hellman, Judith Adler. 1983. *Mexico in Crisis,* 2nd Ed. New York: Holmes & Meir.

Hewitt de Alcántara, Cynthia. 1978. *Modernización de la agricultura mexicana.* Mexico City: Siglo XXI Editores.

Hewitt de Alcántara, Cynthia. 1984. *Anthropological Perspectives on Rural Mexico.* New York: Routledge and Keagan Paul.

Hewitt de Alcantara, Cynthia. 1994. "Introduction: Economic Restructuring and Rural Subsistence in Mexico." 1–24 in Cynthia Hewitt de Alcantara, ed. *Economic Restructuring and Rural Subsistence in Mexico.* Transformation of Rural Mexico, Number 7. La Jolla, CA: Center for U.S.-Mexican Studies. University of California, San Diego.

Hu-DeHart, Evelyn. 1981. *Missionaires, Miners, and Indians: Spanish Contact with the Yaqui Nation of Nortwestern New Spain.* Tucson: University of Arizona Press.

Hu-DeHart, Evelyn. 1984. *Yaqui Resistance and Survival: The Struggle for Land and Autonomy, 1881–1910.* Madison and London: University of Wisconsin Press.

Huizer, Gerrit. 1973. *El potencial revolucionario del campesinado en América Latina.* Mexico City: Siglo XXI Editores.

Ianni, Octavio. 1977. *El Estado capitalista en la época de Cárdenas.* Mexico City: Ediciones Era.

Igartúa, Gabriela. 1987. "La Crisis de la industria azucarera." 19–45 in Paré, 1987.

Jimenez Ricárdez, Ruben. 1976. "Movimiento campesino en Sonora." *Cuadernos Agrarios.* No, 7, January-March.

Katz, Friederich. 1982. *La guerra secreta en México.* 2 vols. Mexico City: Ediciones Era.

Katznelson, Ira and Aristide R. Zolberg, eds. 1986. *Working-Class Formation: Nineteenth-Century Patterns in Western Europe and the United States.* Princeton: Princeton University Press.

Kearney, Michael. 1998. "Mixtec Political Consciousness: From Passive to Active Resistance." 134–146 in Nugent 1998.

Kearney, Michael. 1996. *Reconceptualizing the Peasantry: Anthropology in Global Perspective.* Boulder, CO and Oxford: Westview Press.

Knight, Alan. 1986. *The Mexican Revolution: Porfirians, Liberals and Peasants.* Vol. I. New York: Cambridge University Press.

Laclau, Ernesto. 1977. *Ideology and Politics in Marxist Theory.* London: New Left Books.

Laclau, Ernesto, and Chantal Mouffe. 1985. *Hegemony and Socialist Strategy: Towards a Radical Democratic Politics.* London: Verso.

Laclau, Ernesto, and Chantal Mouffe. 1982. "Interview with Laclau and Mouffe." *Socialist Review.* Vol. 12, no. 6, November–December.

Landsberger, Henry A. N/d. "Political, Social and Economic Determinants of the Success of Mexican Ejidos: A qualitative and Quantitative Study of Rural Organizations." Department of Sociology, University of North Carolina-Chapel Hill. Mimeo.

Landsberger, Henry A., and Cynthia Hewitt de Alcántara. 1970. "Peasant Organizations in La Laguna, Mexico: History, Structure, Member Participation and Effectiveness." Research Papers on Land Tenure and Agrarian Reform, no. 17, Inter-American Committee for Agricultural Development (CIDA-OAS).

Lara Flores, Sara María. 1996. "Mercado de trabajo rural y organización laboral en el campo mexicano." 69–112 in de Grammont 1996a.

Lara, Sara. 1979. "La importancia de la comunidad campesina y las formas de conciencia social de los jornaleros de Atencingo." 115–184 in Paré, 1979a.

Le Bot, Yvon. 1997. *Subcomandante Marcos: El sueño zapatista.* Barcelona: Plaza y Janés Editores, S.A.

Lenin, V.I. 1967. *The Development of Capitalism in Russia.* Moscow: Progress Publishers.

Liga de Agrónomos Socialistas. 1940. *El colectivismo agrario en México: La Comarca Lagunera.* Mexico City. N/P.

López Cámara, Francisco. 1967. *La estructura económica y social de México en la época de la reforma.* Mexico City: Siglo XXI Editores.

López Mojardín, Adriana. 1996. "A contracorriente: Expresiones de resistencia a las reformas de la legislación agraria." 441–478 in de Grammont 1996a.

Loyola Díaz, Rafael. 1980. *La crisis Obregón-Calles y el Estado mexicano.* Mexico City: Siglo XXI Editores.

Mackinlay, Horacio. 1996. "La CNC y el 'nuevo movimiento campesino' (1989–1994)." 165–238 in de Grammont 1996a.

Mackinlay Grohmann, Horacio. 1994. "El fin de la Reforma Agraria Mexicana y la privatización del ejido," *Polis 93: Anuario de Sociologia.* 99–130.

Mares, David. 1987. *Penetrating the International Market: Theoretical Considerations and a Mexican Case Study.* New York: Columbia University Press.

Marx, Karl. 1967. *Capital.* 3 Vols. New York: International Publishers.

Marx, Karl. 1971. *El dieciocho brumario de Luis Bonaparte.* in Carlos Marx and Federico Engels. *Obras escogidas.* Vol. I. Moscow: Editorial Progreso.

Marx, Karl. 1975. *El capital, libro I, capitulo VI (inédito).* 5th edition. Mexico City: Siglo XXI Editores.

Matute, Alvaro. 1980. *La carrera del caudillo.* Vol 8 of *Historia de la revolución mexicana 1918–1924.* Mexico City: El Colegio de México.

Medin, Tzvi. 1972. *Ideología y praxis política de Lázaro Cárdenas.* Mexico City: Siglo XXI Editores.

Medin, Tzvi. 1982. *El minimato presidencial: Historia política del maximato (1928–1935).* Mexico City: Ediciones Era.

Meillassoux, Claude. 1972. "From Reproduction to Production: A Marxist Approach to Economic Anthropology." *Economy and Society.* Vol I, no. 1, February.

Meillassoux, Claude. 1977. *Mujeres, graneros y capitales.* Mexico City: Siglo XXI Editores.

Meiksins Wood, Ellen. 1995. *Democracy Against Capitalism: Renewing Historical Materialism.* New York: Cambridge University Press.

Moguel, Julio, Carlota Botey, and Luis Hernandez, coords. 1992. *Autonomía y nuevos sujetos sociales en el desarrollo rural.* Mexico City: Siglo XXI Editores and CEHAM.

Moore Jr., Barrington. 1966. *Social Origins of Dictatorship and Democracy: Lord and Peasant in the Making of the Modern World.* Boston: Beacon Press.

Myhre, David. 1998. "The Achilles' Heel of the Reforms: The Rural Financial System." 39–65 in Cornelius and Myhre 1998b.

Myhre, David. 1996. "Appropriate Agricultural Credit: A Missing Piece of Agrarian Reform in Mexico." 117–138 in Randall 1996.

Nueva Antropología. 1981. Monographic issue on Sistema Alimentario Mexicano (SAM), Mexico City. Year V, no. 17, May.

Nugent, Daniel, ed. 1998. *Rural Revolt in Mexico: U.S. Intervention and the Domain of Subaltern Politics.* Durham and London: Duke University Press.

Nuijten, Monique. 1998. *In the Name of the Land: Organization, Transnationalism, and the Culture of the State in a Mexican Ejido.* The Hague, The Netherlands: Thesis Landbouw Universiteit Wageningen.

Núñez Madraso, Cristina. 1995. "New Social Actors in the Sugarcane Sector?" 55–62 in Singelmann 1995.

Nutini, Hugo G., Pedro Carrasco and James M. Taggart, eds. 1976. *Essays on Mexican Kinship.* PITT Latin American Series, Pittsburgh: Pittsburgh University Press.

Nutini. Hugo G., and Betty Bell. 1980. *Ritual Kinship: The Structure and Historical Development of the Compadrazgo system in Rural Tlaxcala.* Vol. 1, Princeton: Princeton University Press.

Otero, Gerardo. 1998a. "Atencingo Revisited: Political Class Formation and Economic Restructuring in Mexico's Sugar Industry." *Rural Sociology.* 63(2):272–299.

Otero, Gerardo. 1998b. "Culture and Productive Strategies among Sugarcane Growers in Puebla, Mexico." 91–103 in Cornelius and Myhre 1998b.

Otero, Gerardo. 1996a. "Neoliberal Reform and Politics in Mexico: An Overview." 1–26 in Otero, 1996b.

Otero, Gerardo, ed. 1996b. *Neoliberalism Revisited: Economic Restructuring and Mexico's Political Future.* Boulder: Westview Press.

Otero, Gerardo. 1989a. "Agrarian Reform in Mexico: Capitalism and the State." 276–304 in William Thiesenhusen, ed. *Searching for Agrarian Reform in Latin America.* Boston: Unwin Hyman.

Otero, Gerardo. 1989b. "The New Agrarian Movement: Toward Self-Management and Democratic Production," *Latin American Perspectives,* 16(4):29–59.

Otero, Gerardo. 1983. "Lucha por la tierra y organización clasista del campesinado." *Crítica.* Puebla. No. 14, February.

Otero, Gerardo. 1980. "Lucha de clases, Estado y campesinos." *Revista del México Agrario.* Year XIII, no. 4, October-December.

Otero, Gerardo, Peter Singelmann and Kerry Preibisch. 1995. "La fin de la réforme agraire et les nouvelles politiques agricoles au Mexique." 241–273 in *Le Mexique: De la réforme néo-libérale à la contre-révolution: la présidence de Carlos Salinas de Gortari.* Henri Favre and Marie Lapointe, eds. Paris: l'Harmattan.

Otero San Vicente, Napoleón. 1986. "Geología regional: una llanura aluvial llamada Comarca Lagunera." *Suma.* Torreón, Coahuila. No. 8, April.

Paige, Jeffrey M. 1975. *Agrarian Revolution: Social Movements and Export Agriculture in the Underdeveloped World.* New York: Free Press.

Paré, Luisa. 1977. *El proletariado agrícola en México.* Mexico City: Siglo XXI Editores.

Paré, Luisa, ed. 1979a. *Ensayos sobre el problema cañero.* Mexico City: UNAM.

Paré, Luisa. 1979b. "El análisis económico de las clases sociales de Atencingo." 59–113 in Paré, 1979a.

Paré, Luisa, ed. 1987. *El estado, los cañeros y la industria azucarera 1940–1980.* Mexico: UNAM and UAM.

Pérez Arce, Francisco. 1979. "El marco jurídico y económico del problema cañero." 13–36 in Paré. 1979.

Posadas, Florencio and Benito García. 1986. "El movimiento de los obreros agrícolas en Sinaloa, 1977–1983." 161–183 in de Grammont, 1986.

Preibisch, Kerry Lynn. 1996. "Are Rural Women Mexico's Comparative Advantage?" M.A. Thesis. Latin American Studies Program, Simon Fraser University. Burnaby, British Columbia.

Prezeworsky, Adam. 1977. "Proletariat into a Class: The Process of Class Formation from Karl Kautsky's *The Class Struggle,* to Recent Controversies." *Politics and Society.* Vol 7, no. 4.

Pucciarelli, Alfredo R. 1985. "El Dominio Estatal de la Agricultura Campesina: Estudio sobre los Ejidatarios Minifundistas de la Comarca Lagunera." *Revista Mexicana de Sociología,* Año XLVII, núm. 3, Julio–Septiembre, 41–84.

Quintero M., Ariel. 1982. "La Coalición de Ejidos Colectivos de los Valles del Yaqui y Mayo." Paper presented at the Segundo Congreso Nacional sobre Problemas Agrarios. Chilpancingo, Guerrero, Mexico, June 7–11.

Randall, Laura. 1996. *Reforming Mexico's Agrarian Reform.* New York and London: M. E. Sharpe.

Redclift, M. R. 1981. "El Estado frente al campo." *Nexos.* Year IV, Vol. 4, no. 47, November.

Rello, Fernando. 1986a. *Las Clases Sociales en el Campo Mexicano: El Caso de La Laguna.* Manuscript, published in English in 1987 as: *State and Peasantry in Mexico: A Case Study of Rural Credit in La Laguna.* Geneve: United Nations Research Institute for Social Development.

Rello, Fernando. 1986b. *El Campo en la Encrucijada Nacional.* Foro 2000. Mexico: Secretaría de Educación Pública.

Restrepo, Iván, and Salomón Eckstein. 1975. *La agricultura colectiva en México: La Experiencia Lagunera.* Mexico City: Siglo XXI Editores.

Rey, Pierre Philip. 1976. *Las alianzas de clases.* Mexico City: Siglo XXI Editores.

Ronfeldt, David. 1973. *Atencingo: The Politics of Agrarian Struggles in a Mexican Ejido.* Stanford: Stanford University Press.

Rubin, Jeffrey W. 1997. *Decentering the Regime: Ethnicity, Radicalism, and Democracy in Juchitán, Mexico.* Durham and London: Duke University Press.

Rubio, Blanca. 1996. "Las organizaciones independientes en México: Semblanzas de las opciones campesinas ante el proyecto neoliberal." 113–163 in de Grammont 1996a.

Rudiño, Lourdes Edith. 1993. "66% de los Beneficiaries de Procampo Recibirá 12% de los Recursos" p. 38A *El Financiero,* 18 October.

Salazar, Gilda and Luisa Paré. 1986. "Una experiencia organizativa de cortadores de caña, El Dorado, Sinaloa." 185–202 in de Grammont, 1986.

Salinas de Gortari, Raúl, and José Luis Solís González. 1994. *Rural Reform in Mexico: The View from the Comarca Lagunera in 1993.* Transformation of Rural Mexico Series, Number 4. Trans. Aníbal Yáñez Chávez. La Jolla: Center for U.S.-Mexican Studies, University of California, San Diego.

SAM (Sistema Alimentario Mexicano). 1980. "Medidas operativas agropecuarias y pesqueras, estrategia de comercialización, transformación, distribución y consumo de los productos de la canasta básica recomendable." Mimographed edition.

Sanderson, Steven E. 1981. *Agrarian Populism and the Mexican State.* Berkeley: University of California Press.

Sanderson, Steven E. 1986. *The Transformation of Mexican Agriculture: International Structrure and the Politics of Rural Change.* Princeton: Princeton University Press.

SARH (Secretaría de Agricultura y Recursos Hidráulicos). N/d [1994]. *PROCAMPO: Vamos al Grano para Progresar.* Secretaría de Agricultura y Recursos Hidráulicos.

Sarmiento Silva, Sergio. 1996. "Movimiento indio, autonomía y agenda nacional." 355–395 in de Grammont 1996a.

Scott, James C. 1976. *The Moral Economy of the Peasantry: Rebellion and Subsistence in Southeast Asia.* New Haven and London: Yale University Press.

Scott, James C. 1977. "Hegemony and the Peasantry." *Politics and Society.* 7(3).

Scott, James C. 1990. *Domination and the Arts of Resistance: Hidden Transcripts.* New Haven and London: Yale University Press.

Semo, Ilán. 1996. *The Mexican Political Pretransition in Comparative Perspective.*" 107–126 in Otero 1996b.

Senior, Clearence. 1958. *Land Reform and Democracy.* Gainsville: University of Florida Press.

Siles-Alvarado, José S. 1968. *The Yaqui Valley of Sonora, Mexico: Its Agricultural Development, Resource Utilization and Economic Potential.* Ph.D. Dissertation, Cornell University. Ann Arbor, Michigan: University Microfilms.

Silverman, Sydel. 1979. "The Peasant Concept in Anthropology." *The Journal of Peasant Studies.* 7(1).

Singelmann, Peter and Gerardo Otero. 1995. "Campesinos, Sugar, and the Mexican State: From Social Guarantees to Neoliberalism." 7–22 in Singelmann 1995.

Singelmann, Peter, 1993. "The Sugar Industry in Postrevolutionary Mexico: State Intervention and Private Capital," *Latin America Research Review,* 26(1):61–88.

Singelmann, Peter, ed. 1995. *Mexican Cane Growers: Economic Restructuring and Political Options.* Transformation of Rural Mexico Series, no. 6. Ejido Reform Research Project. La Jolla, CA: Center for U.S.-Mexican Studies, University of California, San Diego.

Skocpol. Theda. 1979. *States & Social Revolutions: A Comparative Analysis of France, Russia, and China.* New York: Cambridge University Press.

Spicer, Edward H. 1969a. "Northwest Mexico: Introduction." In Vogt, 1969.

Spicer, Edward H. 1969b. "The Yaqui and the Mayo." In Vogt, 1969.

Spicer, Edward H. 1980. *The Yaquis: A Cultural History.* Tucson: University of Arizona Press.

Stavenhagen, Rodolfo, et al. 1968. *Neolatifundismo y explotación: De Emiliano Zapata a Anderson Clayton & Co.* Mexico City: Editorial Nuestro Tiempo.

Stinchcombe, Arthur L. 1961. "Agricultural Enterprise and Rural Class Relations." *American Journal of Sociology.* LXVII (1961–61):165–176.

Swidler, Ann. 1986. "Culture in Action: Symbols and Strategies." *American Sociological Review. 51(2).*

Szélenyi, Ivan. 1987. *Socialist Entrepreneurs: Transformations of Rural Social Structures under State Socialism.* Madison: University of Wisconsin Press.

Terán, Silvia. 1976. "Formas de conciencia social de los trabajadores del campo." *Cuadernos Agrarios.* Mexico City. No. 4, December.

Torres, Gabriel. 1997. *The Force of Irony: Power in the Everyday Life of Mexican Tomato Workers.* Oxford and New York: Berg.

Torres, Gabriel. 1997. *La fuerza de la ironía: Un estudio del poder en la vida cotidiana de los trabajadores tomateros del occidente de Mexico.* Guadalajara: El Colegio de Jalisco and CIESAS-México.

Touraine, Alain. 1997. *What Is Democracy?* Trans. David Macey. Boulder and Oxford: Westview Press.

Valdés Ugalde, Francisco. 1996. "The Private Sector and Political Regime Change in Mexico." 127–148 in Otero, 1996b.

Veltmeyer, Henry. 1997. "New Social Movements in Latin America: The Dynamics of Class and Identity." *The Journal of Peasant Studies.* 25(1):139–169.

Vogt, Evon Z, ed. 1966. *Los Zinacantecos: Un pueblo Tzotzil de los Altos de Chiapas.* Mexico City: Instituto Nacional Indigenista.

Vogt, Evon Z, ed. 1969. Volume 8 of Robert Wauchope (General editor), *Hanbook of Middle American Indians.* Austin: University of Texas Press.

Vogt, Evon Z. 1973. *Los Zinacantecos: Un grupo Maya en el siglo XX.* Mexico City: SEP-Setentas.

Warman, Arturo. 1975. "El neolatifundismo mexicano: Expansión y crisis de una forma de dominio." *Comercio Exterior.* Vol. 25, no. 12, December.

Warman, Arturo. 1976. *Y venimos a contradecir: Los campesinos de Morelos y el Estado nacional.* Mexico City: Ediciones de la Casa Chata.

Warman, Arturo. 1980. *Ensayos sobre el campesinado en México.* Mexico City: Nueva Imagen.

Warman, Arturo. 1983. "Invitación al pleito." *Nexos.* Mexico City. Year VI, vol 6, no. 71, November.

Weber, Max. 1978. *Economy and Society: An Outline of Interpretive Sociology.* Guenther Roth and Claus Wittich, eds. Trans. Ephraim Fischoff, et al. Berkeley: University of California Press.

Whetten, Nathan L. 1948. *Rural Mexico.* Chicago: University of Chicago Press.

Wilkie, Raymond. 1971. *San Miguel: A Mexican Collective Ejido.* Stanford: Stanford University Press.

Wolf, Eric. 1969. *Peasant Wars of the Twentieth Century.* New York: Harper & Row.

Womack, Jr., John. 1969. *Zapata and the Mexican Revolution.* New York: Vintage Books.

Wright, Erik Olin. 1978. *Class, Crisis, and the State.* London: New Left Books.

Wright, Erik Olin. 1979. *Class Structure and Income Determination.* New York: Academic Press.

Zamosc, León. 1979. "Notas teóricas sobre la subordinación de la producción mercantil campesina al capital." *Estudios Rurales Latinoamericanos.* Vol 2, no. 3, September–December.

About the Book and Author

Farewell to the Peasantry? questions class-reductionist assumptions in certain Marxist and populist approaches to political movements in twentieth-century rural Mexico. Focusing on agrarian social structures, political movements, and state intervention, it studies the political class trajectories of direct producers in three agricultural regions from the 1930s to the present. This study offers an analysis of varying intersections of class relations, political mobilization, and distinctive regional cultural traditions. Following a broader trend, this analysis seeks to transcend unidirectional and single-factor approaches to peasant mobilization and social transformation. The book offers an explanation of diverse political class destinations of agricultural workers in three regions from the 1930s to the present in terms of regional cultures, state intervention, and leadership types. Political class formation is seen as the process by which civil society is constructed and as a vital part in the transition toward a societal democracy.

This book also addresses Mexico's legendary agrarian reform in historical perspective. The author argues that land redistribution in Mexico was the way chosen to develop and entrench capitalism in Mexico while building a basis of support for the modern Mexican state. He provides an account of the global agrarian transitions and the social differentiation process in the Mexican countryside as well as the changes brought about in agrarian policies by the neoliberal reform that has swept Mexico since the mid-1980s. Neoliberalism has increased the insecurity of wage employment in most sectors of the economy, thus bringing about an ironic result in the agrarian social structure: On the one hand, it has created the conditions for an entrepreneurial peasantry to emerge, but on the other, while the middle peasantry shrinks, large masses of the rural population are becoming unemployed or resorting to subsistence production as a survival strategy. An impoverished peasantry thus lives on.

Gerardo Otero is associate professor of sociology and Latin American Studies in the Department of Sociology and Anthropology at Simon Fraser University in Vancouver, Canada (otero@sfu.ca). He obtained a *licenciatura* from the Instituto Tecnológico y de Estudios Superiores de Monterrey (1975), an M.A. at the University of Texas at Austin (1977), and a Ph.D. in sociology at the University of Wisconsin, Madison. His work has been published in several edited collections and scholarly journals including the *Canadian Review of Sociology and Anthropology, Revista Mexicana de Sociología, Rural Sociology* and *Sociological Forum.* He is the editor of *Neoliberalism Revisited: Economic Restructuring and Mexico's Political Future* (Westview 1996). He is currently doing research on the globalization of capitalism and the biotechnology revolution as it affects Latin American agriculture; he is also studying economic restructuring, employment, and competitive strategies in the sugar industries in NAFTA countries under neoliberalism.

Index